CAFE FLORA COOKBOOK

CAFE FLORA

COOKBOOK

Catherine Geier

with Carol Brown

To Mike,
Happy Cooking!
Catherine Geier

HP BOOKS

THE BERKLEY PUBLISHING GROUP
Published by the Penguin Group
Penguin Group (USA) Inc.
375 Hudson Street, New York, New York 10014, USA
Penguin Group (Canada), 90 Eglinton Avenue East, Suite 700, Toronto, Ontario M4P 2Y3, Canada
(a division of Pearson Penguin Canada Inc.)
Penguin Books Ltd., 80 Strand, London WC2R 0RL, England
Penguin Group Ireland, 25 St. Stephen's Green, Dublin 2, Ireland (a division of Penguin Books Ltd.)
Penguin Group (Australia), 250 Camberwell Road, Camberwell, Victoria 3124, Australia
(a division of Pearson Australia Group Pty. Ltd.)
Penguin Books India Pvt. Ltd., 11 Community Centre, Panchsheel Park, New Delhi—110 017, India
Penguin Group (NZ), Cnr. Airborne and Rosedale Roads, Albany, Auckland 1310, New Zealand
(a division of Pearson New Zealand Ltd.)
Penguin Books (South Africa) (Pty.) Ltd., 24 Sturdee Avenue, Rosebank, Johannesburg 2196,
South Africa

Penguin Books Ltd., Registered Offices: 80 Strand, London WC2R 0RL, England

This book is an original publication of The Berkley Publishing Group.

Copyright © 2005 by Comida, Inc. dba Cafe Flora.
Text design by Richard Oriolo

First edition: October 2005

Library of Congress Cataloging-in-Publication Data

Geier, Catherine
   Cafe Flora / by Catherine Geier; with a foreword by Scott Glascock.
      p.   cm.
   ISBN 1-55788-471-4
   1. Cookery, American.   2. Cafe Flora.   I. Title.

TX715.G3173 2005
641.5973—dc22
                                             2005043124

PRINTED IN THE UNITED STATES OF AMERICA

10   9   8   7   6   5   4   3   2   1

In loving memory of Scott Glascock.
May we always honor your spirit.

THE CAFE FLORA COOKBOOK would not have been possible without the help of many people. I owe thanks to:

The guests of Cafe Flora, first and foremost. Your curiosity about what you were eating, your many requests for the recipes, and our attempts to convert kitchen instructions into recipes for you led me to write this book.

Janine Doran, chef of Cafe Flora, for your many creative contributions to this book. I literally could not have done my job without you.

Jim Watkins and Karen Jorgensen Sando, former chefs of Cafe Flora, whose wonderfully imaginative menus laid a creative, solid foundation for me.

All the wonderful cooks at Cafe Flora, past and present, who had a hand in creating the dishes in this book for your inspiration, teamwork, and camaraderie. Special thanks to Amy Pinkis, Brian Dawbin, Dawnula Koukul, Fred Mulder, Jon Blanchard, Key Ransome, Kim Calvo Lance Okamoto, Leon Bloom, Lisa Lewis, Marie Holtz, Mike Miller, Pauline Wickey, Roxy Firincilli, Sarah Klein, and Sarah Wong.

Jeff Watanabe and James Sutherland at Cafe Flora for generally being cheerleaders for the book—digging for menus, photos, and articles, fielding calls about the book's publication date, and so on.

Jane Dystel, for your belief in the book, Miriam Goderich, for your guidance in writing a compelling proposal, and, of course, John Duff, for bringing our ideas to real life.

Robin Seigl, for your vision in choosing the best dishes to photograph and your tenacity in getting the perfect picture.

Angie Norwood Brown, for taking exquisite photographs that are fresh, lively, and seductive.

Beth Stroh-Stern, for going out in the middle of the night to pick out-of-season greens for the photographs.

Carol Brown, for your expertise and enthusiasm without which this project might have been abandoned. You found a way to present unwieldy recipes in a comprehensible manner, helped me find my voice, and kept me from going crazy more than a couple of times.

To all the home-cook testers whose meticulous testing and thoughtful feedback made each recipe more clear for our readers: Emily Lieberman, Jules Cohen, Carolyn Grönlund, Doralee Moynihan, Pam Mandel, Lisa Maki, Pam McClusky, Annie and Michael Rosen, Barry Briggs, Buck Close, Christine Happels, Daniel Shurman, Danielle Gibbs, David Foecke, Diane Murray, Doug and Jocelyn Plass, Ellen Ziegler, Frances Crouter, Gary Tucker, Geoff Hulten, Gerry Smith, Gracie Close, Heather Grube, Helen Phillips, Jane Glascock, Janie Somps, Jessica Hunicke, Judy Tobin, Julie Blakeslee, Kim Hunicke, Laura Phillips, Lauren Weber, Maggie Carr, Margaret Harris, Mary Glascock Anderson, Mary Holscher, Matthew Perez, Matthew Preusch, Meg Gage, Mike Baker, Noel Ragsdale, Paul Finley, Paul Huppert, Rachel Weber, Robin Siegl, Sarah Sterling, Scottie Rozenbaum, Shanti Soule, Stan Hiserman, Tim Harris, Trish Fields, Valerie Kelley, Vicki Halper, Wendy Goffe, and Zev Siegl.

Gracie Close, David Foecke, and Scott Glascock for opening Cafe Flora and for your trust and confidence in me. I'm not sure I would have continued my career as a cook had our paths not crossed.

Fred Kaplan, for introducing me to your Seattle food world.

My family and friends, who graciously cleaned up and washed the dishes after my multicourse recipe-testing extravaganzas.

The staff at Tierra Learning Center, for patiently listening to my grumbling and allowing me the time to complete this book.

And finally, my parents, who always put a good, nutritious meal on the table—I still don't know how you managed to feed all of us! My love for cooking started at home; thank you for encouraging my experiments in the kitchen.

CONTENTS

*All recipes marked with v are vegan.

SALADS

DINNERS AND SUPPERS

PIZZA

SANDWICHES

INGREDIENTS AND SOURCES

INDEX

∽ INTRODUCTION

A COUPLE OF YEARS AFTER we opened Cafe Flora, a delightful visitor to Seattle named David discovered the restaurant and chose throughout his week-long stay to have all of his lunchtime and evening meals with us.

On his way to the airport, David stopped in to tell us that he was a little embarrassed. He had eaten over a dozen meals at Cafe Flora and, while a committed carnivore, had not realized until the last minute the restaurant was vegetarian.

David's confession told us that we had succeeded. Meat-free dining had come of age!

Many, perhaps the majority, of the 100,000 or so guests who visit Cafe Flora each year do not consider themselves vegetarian. They come for meals because the food excites and satisfies them. They have learned that the old idea of a meal without meat, as a form of deprivation, is simply an anachronism.

We at Cafe Flora recognize that some of the most lively, tantalizing, and deeply satisfying foods from around the world are made without the use of meat products. We have learned to draw from diverse culinary traditions from different parts of the globe as we develop new dishes. These traditions, together with the availability of an abundance of locally grown produce and herbs, have been the inspiration for creating imaginative and dynamic menus. Cafe Flora's menus continue to evolve, with an emphasis on playfulness, seasonality, and variety of cooking traditions.

The *Cafe Flora Cookbook* is designed to give all of you who are cooking at home a broad selection of recipes that have been most popular and most accessible out of the thousands to come out of our kitchen during the restaurant's decade-plus history. It should be noted that many of the recipes included are vegan (entirely free of dairy products and eggs) or may easily be made so with one or two modifications.

A Short History of Cafe Flora

In the spring of 1990, three old friends and longtime residents of Seattle's Madison Valley met to consider purchasing an abandoned launderette and storefront church in the heart of the neighborhood, to be converted to a vegetarian restaurant.

Their shared motives were larger than the usual entrepreneurial bottom-line incentives. They hoped to create a great vegetarian place which would also help anchor the neighborhood and serve as a gathering place for building more of a sense of community. They wanted to construct the restaurant facility and design ongoing operations in ways that would be environmentally sensitive, and which would serve as a model business in attending to the health of the planet. They also wished to provide a humane and respectful workplace with decent benefits, a place where most of the employees—most of the time—could actually look forward to getting up and coming to work. They hoped to develop a business that could be successful enough to give generously back to the community. And finally, they wanted a restaurant that would challenge the clichés of vegetarian cooking and introduce imaginative nonmeat dishes, beautifully presented and genuinely satisfying.

After a feasibility study and a year-long planning and development process in which the launderette was gutted and rebuilt for its new purpose, Cafe Flora opened on schedule, October 1, 1991.

The selections of the architect and the construction firm were based on both the strength of their reputations and compatibility with the goals of environmentally positive, energy-efficient design and construction, and the owners' commitment to hiring minority- and women-owned businesses for all of the subcontracting work.

An environmental consulting firm, Ecotope, was engaged to help ensure maximum energy efficiency. J. Kenyon, the chef from Greens Restaurant in San Francisco, kindly assisted in designing the kitchen so that it would be appropriate for a vegetarian restaurant—that is, spacious and open, with large amounts of prep space and maximum opportunity for interaction and collaboration among the cooking staff. Vegetarian cooking tends to be labor intensive and requires much more prep work than a traditional kitchen where meat is prepared. The larger kitchen staff needs the space to stay connected and free to communicate with each other.

The owners had planned on a "soft" opening: no advertising, no PR, just quietly open the doors and see if anyone shows up. Staff and owners were stunned to find themselves inundated with guests. The restaurant had to nearly double its staff in the first two months of operation.

The author of this book, Cathy Geier, joined the restaurant in 1993 as a brunch cook, worked her way through various stations of the kitchen, became sous-chef, chef, and eventually executive chef. Our current chef, Janine Doran, has been with Cafe Flora since 1992. In fact, most of our lead managers have been with the restaurant for ten years and a few even longer.

The restaurant has received a great many culinary, community, and environmental awards, and has been honored as the subject of numerous articles in both local and national media.

Cafe Flora's Community

Restaurants nurture. That's the reason they exist—to nurture people with food, pleasure, visual beauty, good tastes, good smells, good feelings. They also can help to nurture community. We at Cafe Flora see the development of community as an essential aspect of what we do. We do this in a number of ways. We work to keep our prices in check so that we are accessible to diverse income levels. We maintain an elegant yet casual and warmly inviting dining room, which has proven to be a space where guests can comfortably hang out. We make an exceptional effort to give back to the community both as individual employees and through in-kind donations from the restaurant to a wide array of nonprofit schools, social agencies, environmental organizations, and community groups.

Cafe Flora was one of five Pacific Northwest organizations honored with the Good Works Award, which "recognizes extraordinary business efforts and partnerships that reflect unusual creativity and commitment to public service."

The Spirit and Philosophy of Cafe Flora

It would seem that, if we in the industrialized world were to reduce our meat consumption, many of the problems related to the raising and consumption of animals would cease, or at least greatly diminish. The raising of animals could more easily revert to organic, small scale, more humane methods. The detrimental impact of massive scale animal husbandry on our air, water, and land would be substantially reduced. The health consequences of a meat-based diet would also be alleviated.

Part of our job at Cafe Flora is to help make the shift to a dramatically less meat-centered diet a truly viable and desirable option for more people. We do not take the position that everyone should stop eating meat. To ask that of most Americans would, at this point, be unrealistic and even counterproductive. And to many, it would smack of self-righteousness and puritanism. We also understand there are many good reasons for doing without, or for cutting back on meat in one's diet, not least of which is the sheer joy to be found in well-prepared vegetarian dishes.

And it is our belief that there must be joy in food—in its preparation, presentation, and consumption—and that vegetarian dishes can be as playful, exciting, and deeply satisfying as any foods. Perhaps more so. You don't need meat on the plate to have a truly extraordinary meal. And if you choose to have meat from time to time, you should not be made to feel like a pariah.

There is a trend in the culinary world toward exoticism for its own sake. Cafe Flora is not about pretense. Food can be lovingly prepared and beautifully presented without making a designer statement. It is important to us that our dishes be healthy, without being "health food." So we strive to have plenty of choices on our menu that are on the light side or vegan.

Our home is the Pacific Northwest. Our foods reflect our climate, our geography, our farming communities. As much as possible our menus follow the seasons and maximize use of locally grown products. In the growing season, we buy from a number of small farmers, and we use organic produce as it becomes available.

Recipe Sources

The recipes in this book have been strongly influenced by the cooking styles of Asia, Europe, the Middle East, Mexico, and the American South and Southwest. If the origins were once meat based, they have been transformed into meat-free dishes, often with greater flair and flavor than the originals.

Also, we have chosen not to follow the "celebrity chef" system of recipe development at Cafe Flora. Our chefs are women and men who have a passion for food, *and* who know how to bring out the creativity of their kitchen teams. Some of our most inspired recipes have come from cooks working together on an idea. And at times our most successful creations have been the product of simple mistakes and happenstance.

Just as our chefs work with kitchen staff to promote creativity, we hope the *Cafe Flora Cookbook* encourages you to take risks and be adventurous in your cooking.

—Scott Glascock, cofounder of Cafe Flora

STARTERS AND SNACKS

APPETIZERS AT CAFE FLORA ARE all about sharing. From time to time we will have an appetizer that is fancy, vertical, and plated for one, but mostly we serve plates ample enough to be shared among two or three people. The theme may change—Asian, Mediterranean—but the elements of a platter stay the same: a rich savory spread, a tart or oniony side dish, something salty like olives or an olive tapenade, sometimes a cheese, and always bread or crackers.

At Cafe Flora we serve the components arranged together on a dinner-size plate. At a casual party where people are milling about snacking and drinking, you may find that the components work best in separate dishes, but grouped together so your guests know they go together. (You may also find this the best way to serve these "platters" at a small dinner party.) Place a stack of small plates, cocktail napkins, and knives and forks near the serving dishes so your guests can put together plates to suit their tastes.

You can also create your own platters. Throughout this chapter you'll find many recipes for dips and spreads to be mixed or matched, items to be wrapped in a lettuce leaf and dunked in a spicy chile sauce like our Coconut Tofu, and dishes like Roasted Beets to be served with Chive Yogurt Sauce on the side. And don't limit yourself to recipes here. Look for recipes in other chapters that you could use (or adapt).

You can also use these dishes as a springboard to a terrific light supper. Many of them are remarkably easy to make and are even better prepared in advance. So next time you want a get-together without the work of a full-fledged dinner party, make an assortment of dishes, serve them up in colorful bowls and platters, open a few bottles of wine, and sit back and relax, sharing food with your friends.

Linda's Marinated Goat Cheese

One of Cafe Flora's first dining room managers and our good friend, Linda Silberman, would bring this appetizer to dinner parties. It was always one of those dishes that guests seemed to hover around until it was all gone. Ultimately we adopted this dish on a larger scale as part of our repertoire of appetizers for catered events and fund-raisers.

Not only is it irresistibly delicious, but it's easy to put together, which is especially important when you're pressed for time and need to arrive at a party with a dish. Served with rustic bread or Crostini (see page 224), this simple hors d'oeuvre looks and tastes like you put much more time into it than you did. And if you're ever lucky enough to have some left over, just toss it cold (straight out of the refrigerator) with hot pasta for a delicious lunch or supper.

Serves 1–6

4 large fresh basil leaves, plus a sprig for garnish

4 Roma tomatoes, most of the seeds removed, diced

2 tablespoons capers, rinsed and drained, or 6 kalamata olives, pitted and roughly chopped

3 cloves garlic, minced

4 tablespoons extra-virgin olive oil

2 tablespoons balsamic vinegar

4-ounce log goat cheese

Salt and freshly ground pepper

CUT THE BASIL IN A CHIFFONADE. Stack the basil leaves on top of each other. Roll them up tightly, starting at the stem, and slice thinly across the rolled-up leaves. This will give you long thin strips of basil.

MIX THE MARINADE. In a bowl, combine all the ingredients except the goat cheese, salt, and pepper.

Put the log of goat cheese in the center of a shallow serving bowl, and pour the tomato mixture over it.

MARINATE THE GOAT CHEESE for about an hour. (If you're going to marinate the cheese longer than that, refrigerate it and then take it out half an hour or so before serving to return it to room temperature.)

SERVE THE GOAT CHEESE. Just before serving, taste it, add salt if you think it needs it, and grind pepper over all. Garnish with a sprig of basil. Serve with a knife to cut the goat cheese and a spoon to scoop up the flavorful tomato mixture.

> **TIP**
> We make this year-round at the restaurant, so much of the time we use Roma tomatoes. But if you're making this in the summer, definitely take advantage of the varieties that are in season.

Caprese Salad Skewers

I really don't know where I saw these appetizers for the first time, but it was love at first sight: a fresh bite-size appetizer that requires very little work, no cooking, and is as delicious as it is beautiful. What more could you ask for?

Makes 18 skewers

3 tablespoons olive oil

1 tablespoon balsamic vinegar

1 clove garlic, minced

Salt and freshly ground pepper

18 bocconcini (see Tip), or ½ pound fresh mozzarella, cut into cubes the size of cherry tomatoes

18 (6-inch) bamboo skewers (available at Asian markets)

18 cherry tomatoes

18 medium fresh basil leaves

MAKE THE DRESSING. In a small bowl, whisk together the olive oil, vinegar, garlic, and a pinch of salt and pepper. Toss the mozzarella balls in the dressing until coated.

SKEWER THE TOMATOES AND CHEESE. Slide 1 cherry tomato onto a skewer, about 2 inches up the skewer. Gently fold a basil leaf in half and slide it onto the skewer, and then add a mozzarella ball. Repeat to make a total of 18 skewers.

SERVE THE SKEWERS. Put the skewers on a platter, and drizzle with any leftover dressing. Sprinkle with salt and pepper to taste, and serve immediately, as the basil leaves will turn brown quickly.

> **TIP**
>
> Bocconcini vary in size, depending on who makes them; sometimes the smaller ones are called *ciliegine*. Whatever they're called, look for cherry tomato–size balls of fresh mozzarella.

Hot 'n' Spicy Artichoke Dip

At Cafe Flora we serve this appetizer baked in ramekins, enough for one or two people to share. Here the dip is baked in a one-quart dish, enough to serve at a party along with a basket of Crostini (see page 224), slices of crusty bread, and crackers (or any one of these if you don't have all three).

Makes 3½ cups

> **TIMING**
>
> Roast the red bell pepper first so it has time to cool before you add it to the mayonnaise. Then toast the bread crumbs before you mix up the dip.

1 teaspoon arame (seaweed [see page 238])
2 (14-ounce) cans artichoke hearts, drained
1 red bell pepper, roasted (see page 212) and finely diced

1 cup mayonnaise
1 tablespoon chopped garlic
1 tablespoon freshly squeezed lemon juice
1 teaspoon dried mustard
1 teaspoon Tabasco sauce
½ teaspoon salt
2 tablespoons chopped fresh basil
2 tablespoons chopped fresh parsley
½ cup grated Parmesan cheese
½ cup unseasoned bread crumbs, toasted (see page 129)

GET READY. Preheat the oven to 375 degrees, and grease a 1-quart baking dish.

PREPARE THE ARAME. Rinse the arame in a strainer under running water. Put it in a bowl and add cold water just to cover. Soak for 10 minutes. Drain well, coarsely chop, and set aside.

PREPARE THE ARTICHOKE HEARTS. Pour the artichoke hearts into a mesh strainer, rinse under running water, and drain thoroughly. Coarsely chop them.

MAKE THE ARTICHOKE DIP. In a medium bowl, mix the artichokes, arame, and red pepper.

In a small bowl, mix the mayonnaise, garlic, lemon juice, dried mustard, Tabasco sauce, and salt until completely blended.

Combine the mayonnaise mixture with the artichoke mixture. Fold in the basil, parsley, and cheese.

BAKE THE ARTICHOKE DIP. Spoon the mixture into the prepared baking dish, and top with toasted bread crumbs. Bake until the dip is bubbling around the edge of the dish, about 30 minutes.

SERVE THE ARTICHOKE DIP. Let it sit for 10 minutes before serving, and warn your guests that it is still very hot! This dish is best when it is hot, however, so if this is part of a buffet table, for example, keep it warm in a chafing dish.

Quesadillas with Tomatillo Salsa

To a traditional cheesy quesadilla, we add spicy roasted yams and a pumpkin-seed pesto. We serve it drizzled with crème fraîche and a sweet, tangy, and green tomatillo salsa.

We like the thick, white corn tortillas for this quesadilla. The thicker corn tortilla is sturdy enough for grilling—the way we cook them at the restaurant—and we like the taste of the slightly charred corn. Feel free to substitute flour tortillas, but you may have better luck cooking those in the oven or in a skillet. Keep in mind that this recipe uses six-inch tortillas, not the big burrito size.

Serves 4

TIMING

While the yams are roasting and cooling, make the Tomatillo Salsa.

1 cup raw green pumpkin seeds, hulled

Salt

1 teaspoon chili powder, or ground chipotle chile

½ teaspoon cumin seeds, toasted and ground (see page 52)

1 pound yams (see page 241), peeled and cut into ½-inch dice

¼ cup olive oil

4 scallions, white and green parts, chopped

½ cup chopped fresh cilantro

8 thick, white corn tortillas (or regular corn or small flour tortillas)

1 cup grated pepper jack cheese (4 ounces)

Vegetable oil for cooking the quesadillas

Crème fraîche (see page 230), or purchased crè fraîche

Tomatillo Salsa (recipe follows)

GET READY. Preheat the oven to 400 degrees. If you're going to grill the quesadillas over coals, get them going.

Toast the pumpkin seeds by tossing them in a dry sauté pan over high heat until they start to pop. Add salt to taste, and set aside to cool.

MIX THE SPICES. Mix the chili powder, cumin, and ½ teaspoon salt.

ROAST THE YAMS. Toss the yams with 1 tablespoon of the olive oil until fully coated, and then toss with the spice mixture. Put on a baking sheet, and roast until tender, for 20 to 25 minutes. Remove from the oven, and set aside.

MAKE THE PUMPKIN-SEED MIXTURE. Put the pumpkin seeds, scallions, and cilantro in a food processor. Pulse 3 or 4 times, and then scrape down the sides of the bowl.

With the machine running, drizzle in the remaining 3 tablespoons olive oil, and process until the mixture is the texture of coarse meal. Put the mixture in a bowl, and mix in the yams and a pinch of salt.

ASSEMBLE THE QUESADILLAS. Divide the yam-pumpkin-seed mixture among 4 tortillas, spreading it to the edge of each tortilla. Scatter one-quarter of the cheese evenly over each tortilla, and top with the remaining tortillas. Firmly press each quesadilla together.

COOK THE QUESADILLAS

- **Over coals.** Brush both sides of each quesadilla with oil. Place on a grill over ash-covered but glowing red coals. Cook on one side for about 3 minutes, flip over, and cook for 3 minutes more.

- **In a skillet.** Heat ½ teaspoon of vegetable oil in a skillet over medium-high heat. (A nonstick pan would work just as well, without the need for oil.) Put a quesadilla in the hot pan, and cook on one side for 2 minutes. Flip the quesadilla, and cook for 2 minutes more. Add more oil to the pan if you need it to cook each additional quesadilla.

SERVE THE QUESADILLAS. Cut each quesadilla in quarters, drizzle with crème fraîche, and top with Tomatillo Salsa.

.TIPS

- If you can't find crème fraîche at your local supermarket or you have the time to experiment, you can make your own following the instructions on page 230. Just note that it takes about 24 hours.
- If you find toasted pumpkin seeds (or pepitas), use those and skip the toasting instructions.

Tomatillo Salsa [v]

This will make way more salsa than you'll need for this dish. But go ahead and make it anyway because it will go well with your breakfast eggs or as a snack with tortilla chips. Try it with any of our Mexican-inspired dishes such as the Roasted Yam Enchilada (see page 111) or the Southwest Scramble (see page 202).

Makes about 2½ cups

8 to 10 tomatillos (about ¾ pound), husked and washed
1 tablespoon chopped garlic
3 tablespoons brown rice syrup (see page 238), or honey
3 scallions, white and green parts, very thinly sliced
3 tablespoons finely diced red onion
1 tablespoon chopped fresh cilantro
1 teaspoon minced jalapeño chile, seeds removed
½ teaspoon salt

Roughly chop the tomatillos, and put them in a food processor with the garlic and the brown rice syrup. Pulse 3 or 4 times, or until you have a chunky sauce. Put the tomatillo mixture in a bowl, and mix in the remaining ingredients.

Roasted Beets with Chive Yogurt Sauce

This dish is requested year after year by the planning committee of the Garden Party fund-raiser we hold each June for Bailey Boushay House, the extraordinary AIDS facility in our neighborhood. That always surprises us, since this light appetizer is part of an otherwise rich and hearty buffet. I find that generally people have a love-hate relationship with beets, but they're accustomed to the watery, flavorless canned beets that most of us grew up with. Beets taste best when roasted, and roasting them twice only intensifies their earthy flavor. The Chive Yogurt Sauce makes a sparkling contrast in color and flavor.

Serves 4 to 6

TIMING

While the beets are roasting, start draining the yogurt.

6 to 8 beets of equal size (2½ to 3 pounds), unpeeled, with ½ inch of the beet top left on
2 tablespoons balsamic vinegar
2 teaspoons extra-virgin olive oil
1 teaspoon salt
Chive Yogurt Sauce (recipe follows)
Optional: Snipped chives for garnish

ROAST THE BEETS. Preheat the oven to 350 degrees. Put the beets in a baking dish, pour in water to a depth of ½ inch, and cover. Roast until a thin-bladed knife or toothpick pierces the beet easily, about 1 hour. Remove the beets from the oven, and set aside.

CUT UP THE BEETS. When the beets are cool enough to handle, but still warm, remove the skins by rubbing the beets with a paper towel or your fingers (the skins will slip right off). Cut the beets in half and then into wedges, ½ to ¾ inch thick, so you have about 48 wedges. Put them in a bowl.

DRESS THE BEETS, AND ROAST THEM AGAIN. Drizzle the beets with the balsamic vinegar and olive oil, and sprinkle with the salt. Toss to coat.

Put the wedges in a single layer on a baking sheet with a rim, and roast again for 30 minutes. Remove the beets from the pan to the serving plate, taking care not to break them. Cool completely before serving.

SERVE THE BEET WEDGES on a platter with the yogurt sauce in a small bowl on the side. Sprinkle additional chives on the beets if you want. At a buffet, provide a small spoon for the yogurt because dipping the beets into the sauce will turn it pink. If you're dishing them up, serve the beets on small plates, spooning a little yogurt sauce over the top.

Draining Yogurt

If you're using nonfat yogurt, you may want to drain it first to enrich its flavor and texture. In that case, put the yogurt in a strainer lined with a paper coffee filter. Set the strainer over a deep container, and let the yogurt drain for an hour. When the yogurt is drained, you're ready to follow the recipe.

Draining enriches the flavor and body of yogurt, especially nonfat yogurt. All of our recipes calling for yogurt can be made with whole-milk, low-fat or nonfat yogurt from cow or goat milk, but the creaminess of these dishes will vary depending on the type of yogurt you have chosen. Also, the body, texture, and number of added ingredients can vary by yogurt brand.

When you drain yogurt, you're simply removing whey, which is essentially the same process that is used in making cheese.

NOTE: *Yogurt with gelatin added as a thickener will not drain.*

DRAIN YOGURT. Put plain yogurt in a strainer lined with a paper coffee filter or cheesecloth. Set the strainer over a container deep enough so the whey can drain without touching the strainer.

- Draining yogurt for a short time, about an hour, will remove about one-quarter of the volume. (For example, 2 cups of yogurt will yield about 1½ cups drained.)

- Draining yogurt overnight will reduce the volume by half and it will become as thick as cream cheese. (For example, 2 cups yogurt will yield about 1 cup drained). If you're draining yogurt for longer than an hour, put this whole contraption in your fridge.

When the yogurt has drained, scrape it out of the filter and use it or store in a covered container.

Chive Yogurt Sauce

Using whole-milk yogurt will give you a rich, creamy sauce, but you can use low-fat and nonfat yogurt with surprisingly luscious results, too. Try this on baked potatoes instead of sour cream.

Makes about ¾ cup

1 cup plain yogurt, drained for 30 minutes (see "Draining Yogurt")

2 tablespoons snipped fresh chives, or finely chopped dill

½ teaspoon salt

Put the drained yogurt in a bowl, and whisk in the chives and salt. Refrigerate until ready to serve.

Crudité with Dill Caper Tofu Aïoli [v]

For this platter, we mix raw and blanched vegetables to dip into a creamy, herby aïoli. (Blanching is the process of cooking vegetables briefly in boiling water and then plunging them in ice water to stop the cooking and keep the colors vibrant.) We toss the vegetables with a tiny bit of olive oil to make them glisten and mound them in a colorful tangle on a platter. We nestle a small bowl of the aïoli among the vegetables and, for the finishing touch, scatter chopped parsley and flower petals over all.

The vegetables we use change depending on what's in season, but we always aim for a bright balance of color and texture. In springtime until early summer, we use asparagus, bright orange baby carrots, radishes, sweet tiny potatoes, and snow or sugar snap peas. In deep summer, we might use sweet bell peppers in every color, cherry tomatoes, and green or pale yellow wax beans instead of the asparagus. Creamy white cauliflower is a good addition to this platter any time. We don't usually use beets because the deep red color bleeds onto other vegetables when they're tossed together. Whatever you choose, though, choose them for what's in season and with an eye for a variety of color.

Serves 8 to 10 as an appetizer

TIMING

Make the Dill Caper Tofu Aïoli before you begin to prepare the vegetables. You can also make this a day ahead.

Salt

¼ to ½ cup edible flower petals (see Cooking with Edible Flowers page 69 for suggestions)

About 3 pounds fresh vegetables (suggestions and cooking times follow)

1 tablespoon olive oil

Salt and freshly ground pepper

Dill Caper Tofu Aïoli (recipe follows)

1 tablespoon finely chopped fresh parsley

GET READY. Put 4 quarts water in a large pot. Add 1 tablespoon salt, and bring to a boil. Fill a large pot or bowl with 4 quarts of cold water and ice.

PREPARE THE FLOWER BLOSSOMS following the instructions on page 69.

BLANCH A VEGETABLE. Drop the first vegetable into the pot, and cook until tender but still crisp, using as a guide the time suggested for each vegetable in the instructions that follow. Just before the cooking time is up, carefully pull one out of the water and bite into it to test its doneness. Cook longer if need be, checking doneness every 30 seconds or so.

When the vegetables are done, quickly scoop them out of the hot water (a big mesh strainer or small colander works well for this), and plunge them into the ice water. When they're cold, scoop them out, drain them, and pat them dry, or lay them out on a clean dish towel or paper towels to dry.

REPEAT THIS PROCESS for all the remaining vegetables you plan to blanch. (You may need to add more ice to the bowl to keep the water cold.)

TOSS THE VEGETABLES WITH OIL. Put all the blanched vegetables in a large mixing bowl. Drizzle with the olive oil and toss gently to coat. Sprinkle with a pinch or two of salt and pepper to taste, and toss again.

ARRANGE THE VEGETABLES. If you're going to put the aïoli bowl on the platter, place it in the middle or to one side, and mound the vegetables around it. Scatter the parsley and flower petals over all.

Preparing and Cooking the Vegetables

Here are some approximate quantities with preparation instructions for each vegetable.

Asparagus 1 bunch thinner asparagus spears, usually about 1 pound. (It's not that thinner asparagus is better; it's just more likely a bunch will have enough spears to serve 8 to 10 people.)

Cut or snap off the tough ends, and blanch until tender but still crisp, 30 seconds to 1 minute, depending on the thickness of the spears.

Baby carrots 1 bunch baby carrots (about 12 ounces), 4 to 5 inches long, with stems and fronds still intact.

Cut off most of the fronds but leave a little bit (about ¼ inch) of the stems attached. Wash or scrub the carrots to remove any dirt. We don't bother peeling them unless the dirt is really imbedded in the crevices or they're not organic. If you do peel them, do it with a light touch; you don't want to peel away the whole carrot. Blanch baby carrots until they're tender and firm, but not crunchy, 30 seconds to 1 minute.

Radishes 1 bunch radishes (about 8 ounces), with their leafy, green tops attached. We especially love the magenta and white French Breakfast radish or the long slender White Icicle radish, but any variety will do.

Trim the tops, leaving a bit of the stem attached to serve as a handle for picking up and dipping the radish. Slice radishes down the center, through the stem, and store in ice water until ready to serve. Then dry them just before you toss them with the other vegetables.

Potatoes About ½ pound small red, yellow-skinned, or fingerling potatoes.

Leave the skin on the potatoes and simmer gently. Rapidly boiling water will cause the skin and the potato to part ways while cooking. Cook until just tender when pierced with a thin-bladed knife. Cool, and then cut each potato in half, halving fingerlings and oval-shaped potatoes lengthwise.

Snow or sugar snap peas About 4 ounces.

Remove the string that runs along the straight edge of the pod. Serve them raw, or blanch them no longer than 15 seconds so they keep their crispness. Blanching enhances their flavor, too.

Bell peppers 1 large or 2 small to medium bell peppers, orange, red, or yellow, depending on the color of the other vegetables you're serving.

Split the pepper in half through the stem, remove the seeds and pithy stuff, and slice into ½-inch strips.

Cherry tomatoes ½ pint basket (1 cup) round, grape, or pear-shaped cherry tomatoes in a variety of colors. Sometimes you can find pint baskets that include a mix of colors and shapes.

Cauliflower About 1 pound, a small head or half a larger head.

Break apart and cut the cauliflower into equal-size florets. Blanch just long enough to get the raw taste out of them, about 30 seconds.

Green or yellow wax beans About 1 pound. If you can get a mix of green and yellow beans, even better. In summer, you may also find purple beans, although once blanched, the purple bean is disappointingly dark green with just a hint of purple.

Top and tail the beans, and blanch until tender yet still crisp, about 1 minute.

Dill Caper Tofu Aïoli [v]

Makes about 2 cups

1¼ cups silken tofu (about 12 ounces)
¼ cup freshly squeezed lemon juice
1 teaspoon Dijon mustard
1 teaspoon tamari (see page 240)
1 clove garlic, chopped
3 tablespoons olive oil
2 tablespoons capers, rinsed and roughly chopped
2 tablespoons finely chopped fresh dill
Salt and freshly ground pepper

MAKE THE AÏOLI. Drain the tofu if it's packed in water. Put it in a blender along with the lemon juice, mustard, tamari, and garlic, and blend until smooth. With the machine running, drizzle in the olive oil until it is fully incorporated.

ADD THE REMAINING INGREDIENTS. Remove the mixture from the blender, and mix in the capers and dill by hand. Add salt and pepper to taste. Spoon the aïoli into a small serving bowl, cover, and refrigerate until ready to use.

Arancini with Zesty Fennel Marinara

These cheesy, deep-fried risotto nuggets are a favorite at our annual Garden Party fund-raiser for Bailey Boushay House, the extraordinary AIDS facility in our neighborhood. The balls are called *arancini* because they resemble "little oranges," from the Italian word for orange, *arancio*. We use a combination of freshly chopped herbs to season the risotto, but you could use any one of the herbs alone (or substitute peppery arugula).

Serves 10 to 12, about 40 balls

GET A HEAD START

Make the Zesty Fennel Marinara sauce and the Herbed Risotto a day or two ahead of time and store in the fridge tightly covered. (The risotto must be cold before you can roll it into bite-size arancini balls.)

TIMING

If you want to make this in one day, the Herbed Risotto takes about 30 minutes to make and then it must chill until it's firm, about an hour. While it's cooling, you can cook the Zesty Fennel Marinara sauce, and then deep-fry the arancini.

In this dish

- **Herbed Risotto**
- **Zesty Fennel Marinara**
- **Arancini**

Herbed Risotto

When making risotto, the stock has to be hot to keep the temperature as constant as possible. So make sure to heat it before you start the risotto, and keep it at a low simmer as you add it. Also, you'll get the best results if you use Arborio or other Italian rice. The kernels of Italian rice are sheathed in a soft starch known as *amylopectin*. It is through the gradual addition of liquid and the evaporation and absorption that takes place as it's added, that the starch gradually dissolves into a creamy binding that holds the grains together.

Makes 5 cups

2 tablespoons olive oil
1 onion, diced
1½ cups Arborio or other Italian rice, unwashed
½ cup dry white wine, room temperature
3 cups hot Vegetable Stock (see page 39), or purchased vegetable stock
½ cup chopped fresh herbs (parsley, basil, oregano, thyme), or 1 cup chopped arugula
1 cup shredded smoked mozzarella (4 ounces)
½ cup grated Romano, Parmesan, or Asiago cheese
Salt and freshly ground pepper

SAUTÉ THE ONION AND RICE. Heat the olive oil in a large, heavy saucepan over medium heat. Add the onion and sauté until it's soft and translucent, about 10 minutes. Add the rice, and stir quickly until the grains are thoroughly coated.

ADD THE LIQUID, STIRRING CONSTANTLY. Add the wine, stirring constantly until most of it has evaporated and been absorbed.

Add the hot stock, ½ cup at a time, stirring until the rice absorbs it. Follow this process until the grains of rice are al dente (the center is tender but not soft, firm, but not chalky). Begin tasting the rice after about 18 minutes, although the cooking process will most likely take 20 to 30 minutes.

FINISH THE RISOTTO WITH CHEESE, AND CHILL UNTIL FIRM. Stir in the herbs and cheeses, and add salt and pepper to taste. Transfer the risotto to a wide bowl or pan to cool. Cover with plastic wrap, and refrigerate until well chilled and firm.

Zesty Fennel Marinara [v]

This marinara would make a good sauce for spaghetti or linguine, too.

Makes about 5 cups

1 fennel bulb (about 1 pound)
1 tablespoon olive oil
1 onion, thinly sliced
6 cloves garlic, minced
½ teaspoon dried thyme
½ teaspoon dried oregano
½ teaspoon red pepper flakes
1 cup dry red wine
1 (28—ounce) can diced tomatoes in juice
Salt and freshly ground pepper

SAUTÉ THE FENNEL AND ONION. Remove the top and tough stem end of the fennel bulb. Cut the bulb in half and slice it thinly.

Warm the olive oil in a large, heavy-bottomed saucepan over medium heat. Add the fennel and onion, and sauté, stirring often, until the fennel is tender and the onion translucent, about 10 minutes.

ADD MOST OF THE REMAINING INGREDIENTS, AND SIMMER. Add the garlic, thyme, oregano, and red pepper flakes, and sauté for 2 minutes.

Raise the heat to high, and stir in the wine and tomatoes with juice. Bring to a boil, reduce the heat to low, and simmer, uncovered, for 30 minutes.

PURÉE THE SAUCE. While it is still hot, put the sauce in a blender or food processor, and purée. Add salt and pepper to taste.

Arancini

Makes about 40 balls

1 cup unbleached all-purpose flour
1 tablespoon onion powder
½ teaspoon salt
¼ teaspoon freshly ground pepper
2 eggs, lightly beaten
1½ cups cornmeal
Herbed Risotto (recipe above)
Vegetable oil for frying
Zesty Fennel Marinara (recipe above)

MAKE BALLS OF RISOTTO. Mix the flour, onion powder, salt, and pepper in a shallow bowl. Put the eggs and cornmeal each in separate shallow bowls.

Using about 2 tablespoons risotto at a time, form tiny balls. Roll the balls in the seasoned flour until they are well coated, shaking off any excess flour. Dip the balls in the eggs, and then roll in the cornmeal.

Put the coated risotto balls on a baking pan lined with parchment paper, and refrigerate until you're ready to fry them.

FRY THE RISOTTO BALLS. Put the oil in a heavy pot to a depth of 2 inches. (Make sure the pot is at least 4 inches tall to reduce spattering.) Heat the oil until a fryer thermometer reads 370 degrees. (If you don't have a thermometer, see page 199 for alternative instructions.)

Cook a few risotto balls at a time until they are golden brown, about 2 minutes, and drain them on paper towels. Repeat until all the risotto balls are fried, skimming the oil between batches to remove bits of cornmeal before they burn. You can hold the arancini in a warm (200-degree) oven for up to an hour before serving.

SERVE THE ARANCINI. Serve hot Zesty Fennel Marinara on the side as a dipping sauce, or, for individual servings, ladle some sauce onto a plate, and place a couple of arancini balls on top.

TIP

For suggestions about how to save oil for later use, read "Saving Oil," on page 199.

Blue Corncakes with Smoked Mushroom Mousse and Hot Pepper Jam

Here we top light and lacy blue cornmeal cakes with a rich, smoky mousse and a drizzle of sweet and spicy jam for a dish that's been described as "a wonderful, magical surprise for the palate." The dish has eye appeal, too: blue cornmeal cooks up into lavender blue pancakes, and the jam is bright red with flecks of green jalapeño chile.

Serves 4 to 6

GET A HEAD START

Your best bet is to make the Smoked Mushroom Mousse ahead. After you smoke and sauté the mushrooms, they must cool completely, and then the mousse must chill for at least 30 minutes in the refrigerator. You can make this the day before and store it in the fridge.

The Hot Pepper Jam doesn't take long to make and it keeps for weeks in the fridge.

In this dish

- Smoked Mushroom Mousse
- Hot Pepper Jam
- Blue Corn Pancakes

Smoked Mushroom Mousse

The Smoked Mushroom Mousse is wonderfully versatile. Spread it on toasted bagels and top with sliced tomato and red onion, or use it as a smoky complement to an avocado, lettuce, and tomato sandwich. For an elegant canapé, cut cooked baby red potatoes in half, gently scoop out a little of each potato with a melon baller, and fill them with the mousse and a sprinkling of snipped chives.

Makes about 2 cups

½ pound crimini mushrooms, smoked (see page 79)
Olive oil cooking spray
2 tablespoons dry sherry
1 teaspoon salt
½ teaspoon freshly ground pepper
1 (7-ounce) container mascarpone cheese
¼ cup sour cream
¼ cup heavy whipping cream
¼ cup finely chopped fresh chives

MINCE THE MUSHROOMS. Pulse the mushrooms in a food processor until thoroughly minced but not a completely smooth paste.

SAUTÉ AND COOL THE MUSHROOMS. Spray a sauté pan with the cooking spray, and heat over high heat until it is very hot. Add the mushrooms, and sauté, stirring several times, until most of the liquid evaporates.

When the pan is almost dry, add the sherry, and stir to remove any bits from the bottom of the pan. Cook until evaporated, about 1 minute. Stir in the salt and pepper, and cool completely.

MAKE THE MASCARPONE MIXTURE. Using an electric mixer, combine the mascarpone with the sour cream and heavy cream at low speed. When they are fully combined, raise the speed to medium-high, and whip for no longer than 30 seconds. Fold in the chives.

FOLD THE COOLED MUSHROOMS INTO THE MASCARPONE. Cool in the refrigerator for at least 30 minutes before serving.

> **TIP**
> Mascarpone is a cheese that isn't widely used in the United States, so check the date before you buy it.

Hot Pepper Jam [v]

This jam was inspired by the homemade red pepper jelly given as a gift or served with cream cheese and crackers at holiday parties I attended as a kid in the South. This recipe makes more than you need for any one recipe in this book, but it's handy to have around for snacks; it's also terrific on cornbread. It will last for two weeks in your refrigerator.

Makes about 1½ cups

1 small red bell pepper, seeds removed and finely chopped
1 jalapeño chile, seeds removed and minced
⅔ cup red wine vinegar
1 cup sugar
1 teaspoon pectin powder (used in making jam)

COOK THE PEPPERS IN VINEGAR. In a medium saucepan, bring the bell pepper, jalapeño chile, and vinegar to a boil, and simmer for 5 minutes.

COOK THE PEPPERS WITH THE SUGAR AND PECTIN. In a mixing bowl, whisk the sugar and pectin powder together. Slowly pour this sugar mixture into the pepper sauce, stirring constantly. Bring to a boil again, and remove from the heat. The mixture jells as it cools.

Blue Corncakes

Makes 16 corncakes

1 cup blue cornmeal, or regular stone-ground cornmeal
1 cup unbleached all-purpose flour
2 teaspoons baking powder
½ teaspoon baking soda
1 tablespoon sugar
1 teaspoon salt
2 large eggs
1½ cups buttermilk, or milk
2 tablespoons unsalted butter, melted and cooled
Vegetable oil for the griddle

MIX UP THE PANCAKES. In a bowl, whisk together the cornmeal, flour, baking powder, baking soda, sugar, and salt. In a separate bowl, mix the eggs, buttermilk, and butter. Then sift the dry ingredients into the wet ingredients. Stir just until all the dry ingredients are incorporated, being careful not to overmix.

COOK THE PANCAKES. Heat a lightly greased griddle or nonstick skillet over medium heat. When it is hot, pour 3 tablespoons of batter onto it. Cook until bubbles form, about 1 minute. Flip the pancake, and cook for 45 seconds. (You may need to grease the griddle between pancakes.)

Keep the pancakes warm in a 200-degree oven, covered with a damp towel while you finish cooking the rest of them.

> **TIP**
> If you can't find blue cornmeal in your local natural-food or specialty-food store, Bob's Red Mill sells it (www.bobsredmill.com).

Serve the Blue Corn Pancakes

Blue Corn Pancakes (recipe above)

Smoked Mushroom Mousse (recipe above)

Hot Pepper Jam (recipe above)

Chopped chives for garnish

Place 2 or 3 pancakes overlapping in a circle on each warm plate. Put a big dollop, about 3 tablespoons, of the Smoked Mushroom Mousse in the middle of the pancakes. Drop a smaller dollop, about 1 tablespoon, of the Hot Pepper Jam just to the side of the mousse. Sprinkle with the chives.

Edamame Dip [v]

One day we were playing around with ingredients found in Japanese cooking and stumbled on this variation of hummus, with edamame, green soybeans, standing in for chickpeas. Serve this dip with crunchy rice crackers, sturdy potato chips, or raw vegetables such as sticks of jicama, baby carrots, and snow peas.

Makes about 2 cups

2 cups fresh or frozen edamame (green soybeans) (see below)

5 fresh green shiso leaves (Japanese basil), chopped

3 tablespoons light (shiro) miso (see page 239)

1 clove garlic

1 star anise (see page 240), ground (see page 52)

2 tablespoons rice vinegar

¼ cup vegetable oil

3 tablespoons cold water

GET READY. Fill a large pot or bowl with 4 quarts of cold water and ice.

About the Ingredients

EDAMAME You can find these green soybeans in two forms at Asian markets, Trader Joe's, or natural-food grocers:

Frozen shelled. **One pound has three cups.**

Fresh in the shell. **You'd probably need about 1½ pounds to give you two cups shelled beans.**

SHISO Also called *perilla* or *Japanese basil*, this herb in the basil-mint family is used in Japanese cooking. Its pretty, jagged-edged leaf comes to a sharp point, and its very delicate and distinctive flavor hints at mild basil.

There are two types of shiso, green and red. We use green shiso here to keep the clear green color of the dip. (Red shiso, often dried, is used to color and flavor the Japanese pickled plums, umeboshi, as well as pickled sushi ginger.) You'll find fresh shiso at large Asian markets with extensive produce departments, or try Amazon.com, which has a huge gourmet food department. (For details about how to find shiso on Amazon, see page 243.)

COOK THE EDAMAME. In boiling water for 5 minutes. Dump into a sieve, drain, and then plunge sieve and all into the ice water. When the edamame are cold, drain them well. Shell if necessary.

MIX THE DIP. Put the cooled edamame in the bowl of a food processor with all the ingredients except the oil and water. Turn the machine on and process until smooth, scraping down the bowl as needed.

ADD THE OIL AND WATER. While the machine is running, drizzle in the oil. When it is fully incorporated, add the water. Process until smooth.

Thai Corncakes with Cucumber Sambal [v]

Not only are these corncakes a refreshingly different appetizer, but they make a great side dish, too. For a summer barbecue, serve them with a mixed tofu and vegetable grill basted with Cafe Flora Fu Sauce (see page 206): skewers of tofu, sweet onion, red or yellow bell pepper, and crimini mushroom. Add a salad of seasonal lettuces and greens, slices of ripe nectarine, and toasted cashews tossed with the Ginger Miso Dressing (see page 64).

Serves 8 to 10, about 20 corncakes

TIMING

The corncake batter must chill for an hour. While it chills, make the Cucumber Sambal so it can get cold while you fry the corncakes.

2 cups corn kernels, fresh or frozen

2 stalks celery, roughly chopped

¼ cup rice flour

½ teaspoon baking powder

1 tablespoon purchased red curry paste, or Cafe Flora Red Curry Paste (see page 93)

½ teaspoon sea salt

1 tablespoon Egg Replacer (see page 239), thoroughly mixed with 4 tablespoons of water, or other egg substitute or 2 eggs

Vegetable oil for frying

MIX THE INGREDIENTS. In a food processor, pulse 1 cup of the corn with the celery a couple of times to chop finely. In a medium bowl, mix the chopped corn and celery with the rest of the whole corn kernels and all the remaining ingredients except the vegetable oil. Refrigerate for at least an hour.

PANFRY THE CORNCAKES. Heat ¼-inch oil in a heavy-bottomed skillet over medium heat. When the oil is hot, drop a tablespoonful of batter for each corncake into the hot oil. Do not crowd the corncakes.

Cook for about 2 minutes on one side, flip the corncakes over, and cook until golden brown, an additional 2 minutes. Remove from the pan, and drain on paper towels. Serve immediately.

Cucumber Sambal [v]

Sambal seems to be a catchall term for condiments popular in Indonesian, Malaysian, and Indian cooking. They can be made from a variety of ingredients and are usually served as an accompaniment to curries or rice dishes. Here, our sambal acts as tart relish to cool the palate after the spicy corn fritters. The leftovers would be good as a relish with our Curried Lentil and Quinoa Burger (see page 175) or tucked inside a Falafel Sandwich (see page 168).

Makes about 2 cups

1 slender English or hothouse cucumber
1 tablespoon chopped fresh cilantro
1 tablespoon chopped fresh mint
1 tablespoon chopped fresh basil
¼ cup rice vinegar
2 tablespoons sugar
1 teaspoon red pepper flakes

CUT THE CUCUMBER in half lengthwise, scoop out the seeds, and cut into ½-inch pieces. Put them in a food processor, and pulse a few times to chop finely. In a small bowl, combine the cucumber with the cilantro, mint, and basil.

MAKE THE SAUCE. In a small saucepan combine the vinegar, sugar, and red pepper flakes. Bring to a boil, and then remove from the heat.

MARINATE THE CUCUMBERS. Pour the vinegar mixture over the cucumber, and stir to combine. Set aside for about 30 minutes before serving to let the flavors develop.

Coconut Tofu with Sweet Chile Dipping Sauce [v]

It delights us when a dish involves our guests' participation. This appetizer, inspired by a dish at one of Seattle's many wonderful Vietnamese restaurants, is one. Serve this as a platter from which everyone helps themselves. To eat, set a golden fried tofu block on a lettuce leaf, lay on sprigs of cilantro and Thai basil, and then wrap it up. Dip it in our spicy sweet sauce, and pop it into your mouth. You can also have Coconut Tofu for dinner by serving it alongside the Soba Salad (see page 75). Just toss the soba noodles in the spicy peanut sauce and forget about the vegetables.

Serves 4 to 6

GET A HEAD START

This appetizer requires a bit of advance planning.

- Pressing the tofu takes an hour, and then marinating the tofu takes another 8 to 12 hours. (The longer you marinate the tofu, the more flavorful it will be. It can even sit in the marinade for a day or two, as long as it's in the fridge.)

- If you don't have time to press the tofu, you can use extrafirm tofu instead, but the finished tofu cubes aren't quite as good. With the pressed tofu, they're lighter and crunchier on the outside, and more tender inside.

Pressing Tofu

Pressing tofu removes excess water, giving it a firmer texture that holds together better while cooking. At Cafe Flora we buy firm tofu and always press it for any recipe where we'll grill or sauté the tofu. If you're short on time, you can substitute extrafirm tofu for pressed tofu, although there will be a little more water in the extrafirm tofu than in the pressed.

WEIGHT THE TOFU. Put the block of tofu on a flat plate, cover with plastic wrap, and put a plate or cutting board on top of it. Weight it further with some cans or more plates, up to three pounds. (Don't use more weight than this, or you'll squash the tofu.)

REFRIGERATE THIS WHOLE SETUP until the tofu releases the excess water, about an hour. Discard the water that's been released, and the tofu is ready to use.

- You can coat the pressed tofu cubes up to three days ahead, and store the coconut-coated tofu in a covered container in the refrigerator.

- You can make the Sweet Chile Dipping Sauce in just 10 minutes before you fry the tofu, but it keeps refrigerated for 2 weeks, so you can make it well in advance.

1 medium onion, roughly chopped

1 teaspoon black peppercorns

2 (4-inch) pieces of ginger, unpeeled, roughly chopped

¼ cup arame (seaweed [see page 238])

¼ cup tamari (see page 240) or soy sauce

¼ cup rice vinegar

2 tablespoons red miso (Japanese bean paste [see page 239])

1 quart water

1 (14- to 16-ounce) block firm tofu, pressed (see above) or use extrafirm tofu

1½ cups finely ground unsweetened dried coconut

½ cup all-purpose wheat flour, or rice flour

½ cup coconut milk (not light coconut milk)

3 to 4 cups vegetable or peanut oil for frying

6 large lettuce leaves, torn in half

12 sprigs cilantro

12 sprigs Thai basil, or regular basil

Sweet Chile Dipping Sauce (see page 235), or purchased sweet chile sauce

MAKE THE TOFU MARINADE. In a saucepan, mix the onion, peppercorns, ginger, arame, tamari, vinegar, and miso with the water, and bring to a boil. Lower the heat, and simmer, covered, for 20 minutes. Remove from the heat and cool in the pan. Strain the cooled marinade into a deep, narrow container with a tight lid.

MARINATE THE TOFU. Cut the tofu into 12 to 16 (1½- to 2-inch) cubes, and put them in the marinade. (The container you choose should allow the marinade to completely cover the tofu blocks.) Refrigerate, and marinate for 8 to 12 hours. (The longer you leave the tofu in the marinade, the more flavorful it will be.)

COAT THE TOFU. Put the coconut, flour, and coconut milk in three separate shallow bowls.

Remove a couple of blocks of the tofu from the marinade with a slotted spoon or strainer, letting the excess liquid drain off. Roll them in the flour to coat, and dip them into the coconut milk. Then roll in the coconut, pressing the coconut onto the tofu to coat it completely.

Repeat this process until you've coated all the tofu.

DEEP-FRY THE TOFU. Put the oil in a wok or heavy pot, deep enough to cover the tofu blocks. Heat the oil, and when it reaches 350 to 360 degrees, gently drop some tofu cubes into the hot oil, leaving enough room to turn them. (If you don't have a thermometer, see page 199 for alternative instructions.) Be careful not to add too many at one time, or the temperature of the oil will drop.

Turn the cubes over a couple of times while frying. When they are golden brown, remove with a slotted spoon, and drain on paper towels.

SERVE THE TOFU. Serve the tofu blocks on a platter with lettuce leaves, cilantro, and basil sprigs, and several shallow bowls of Sweet Chile Dipping Sauce, one for every couple of people.

To eat, put a tofu block in a lettuce leaf with a sprig of cilantro and basil, wrap it up like a burrito, and dip in the sweet chile sauce.

TIPS

- You can find many of the ingredients in this recipe at a well-stocked pan-Asian market: ginger, arame, tamari, red miso, coconut, rice flour (if you decide to use it), Thai basil, and cilantro. (I suggest pan-Asian because these ingredients cut across many cultures, from Japan to Thailand.)

- Unsweetened coconut comes in either large flakes or finely ground. If you cannot find the finely ground variety, available in most health-food stores, just give the large flake coconut a spin in your food processor until it is finely ground. You cannot substitute sweetened coconut.

- You can use the marinade again; just strain and refrigerate it for a week or freeze it up to a month.

- For suggestions about how to save oil for later use, read "Saving Oil," on page 199.

Fig-and-Cabrales-Stuffed Phyllo Cups

This starter is perfect for later summer and early fall when figs are less expensive. We combine tender roasted figs with crumbly, buttery Cabrales, a blue cheese of Spain, for these flavorful appetizers. If Cabrales is unavailable, substitute Gorgonzola or a fine domestic blue cheese such as Oregon Blue, Maytag, or Point Reyes.

Makes 24 cups

½ pint fresh figs (8 to 10 figs), ripe but not at all soft or mushy

2 tablespoons balsamic vinegar

1 tablespoon olive oil

Salt and freshly ground pepper

1 tablespoon minced shallot

1 teaspoon fresh thyme, or ½ teaspoon dried thyme

½ cup crumbled Cabrales, or other blue cheese

24 Phyllo Cups (recipe follows)

PREPARE THE FIGS. Preheat the oven to 350 degrees. Trim the stems from the figs, and cut them into quarters. Toss the fig quarters with the balsamic vinegar, 1 teaspoon of the olive oil, and sprinkle with salt and pepper.

BAKE THE FIGS. Drain the figs, reserving the liquid, and spread them on a rimmed baking sheet large enough to accommodate all the figs in a single layer without crowding. Bake them for 10 minutes. (You're not trying to cook the figs, but rather trying to dry them a bit, so they absorb the balsamic vinegar.)

SAUTÉ THE SHALLOT AND FIGS. Heat the remaining 2 teaspoons olive oil in a skillet over medium heat. Add the shallot and sauté until soft, about 2 minutes. Add the figs, the reserved liquid from the baked figs, the thyme, and a pinch of salt and pepper to the pan. Cook until the liquid evaporates, about 5 minutes, trying not to break up the fig quarters too much. Cool the fig mixture.

MIX IN THE BLUE CHEESE, AND FILL THE CUPS. In a bowl, gently mix the cooled figs with the crumbled blue cheese. Put about 1 tablespoon of the fig and cheese mixture into each phyllo cup and serve at once.

TIP

If you make the fig and Cabrales mixture in advance, when you pull it out of the fridge, bring it to room temp before filling the phyllo cups.

Phyllo Cups [v]

Little phyllo cups with flavorful fillings make perfect one-bite appetizers, and these are as easy to make as they are delicious. Three sheets of phyllo make a delicate cup that is sturdy enough for the fillings we suggest. However, if you choose a really moist filling such as a salsa, increase the number of phyllo sheets to four. Don't fill these cups until *just* before you serve them so they stay crispy.

Makes 24 small cups

GET A HEAD START

You can make the phyllo cups up to three days ahead: gently stack the cooled phyllo cups in an airtight container.

3 sheets phyllo dough
2 tablespoons olive oil, or melted butter

GET READY. Preheat the oven to 350 degrees. Unroll the phyllo dough, covering it with a damp towel to keep it from drying out. Lay out one sheet on your work surface, and brush it gently with some of the oil. Repeat with two more sheets, layering them one on top of the other.

MAKE THE PHYLLO CUPS. Cut the phyllo sheets into 24 equal squares (approximately 2½ × 2½ inches).

Using a miniature muffin pan as a mold, scrunch each square into the muffin cups, pressing the dough against the sides. The top edges will be uneven, but that's OK. It just adds to the charm of these cups.

BAKE THE PHYLLO CUPS for 4 to 6 minutes, or until light golden brown. Cool them in the muffin pan, and then gently remove them from the pan to a baking sheet until you're ready to fill them.

Chanterelle Mushrooms in Phyllo Cups

If you love chanterelles, this appetizer is a great way to serve them without breaking the bank. If you're one of those who say, "Chanterelles don't taste like anything. What's the big deal?" My answer is that you need to coax out the flavor of chanterelles.

Cooking them with butter adds nutty flavor, but because you're cooking at a high temperature, butter may burn. Using a combination of butter and olive oil allows you to cook at a higher temperature and still get the flavor of butter in your sauté. In a sizzling hot pan, sear the chanterelles until they're a nice caramel color. Then deglaze the pan with a dry sherry, season liberally with fresh herbs (thyme, sage, and parsley are good choices), and add salt and pepper to taste. The reward? Succulent mushrooms bursting with chanterelle flavor.

Chanterelles come to market in the late summer and fall. But try this in spring with morels—it's divine! In fact, all mushrooms taste great prepared this way, even the humble domestic button mushroom.

Makes 24 cups

½ pound chanterelle mushrooms

1 tablespoon butter

1 tablespoon olive oil

1 teaspoon fresh thyme

2 tablespoons dry sherry

Salt and freshly ground pepper

24 Phyllo Cups (see page 24)

CLEAN AND TRIM THE CHANTERELLES by brushing off any excess dirt with a towel or pastry brush. If the mushrooms are especially dirty, quickly rinse them under running water, and let dry for several hours on paper towels. Trim the stem ends, and cut the chanterelles into pieces about 1 inch long.

SAUTÉ THE CHANTERELLES. Heat the butter and olive oil in a skillet over medium-high heat. When the butter is foamy and the pan sizzling hot, add the mushrooms. Toss and stir the mushrooms constantly, trying to sear the entire surface of each piece. Sauté until the chanterelles take on a nice caramel color, and any liquid the mushrooms have released has evaporated, 6 to 8 minutes.

ADD THE THYME AND SHERRY. Lower the heat to medium, add the thyme and sherry, stirring to remove any bits from the bottom of the pan. Cook until the liquid has evaporated, about 1 minute. Add salt and pepper to taste, and let sit at room temperature a bit before filling the cups.

JUST BEFORE SERVING, FILL EACH PHYLLO CUP with about 1 tablespoon of the chanterelles, and serve at once.

> **TIP**
>
> Instead of mixing oil and butter, you could make and use clarified butter (see page 201). In that case, double the butter and omit the oil.

Provençal Appetizer Platter

For an extraordinarily yummy variation, substitute Linda's Marinated Goat Cheese (page 7) for the Herbed Goat Cheese and Cherry Tomato Salad. It contains similar ingredients in a different, but equally delicious, form.

Serves 10 to 12 as a starter or snack

> **GET A HEAD START**
>
> You can make everything in this platter a day ahead except the Cherry Tomato Salad, which should be made no longer than an hour before you plan to serve it.

Kalamata Tapenade (see page 227)

Roasted Eggplant, Walnut, and Basil Pâté (recipe follows)

Herbed Goat Cheese (recipe follows)

Cherry Tomato Salad (recipe follows)

Crostini (see page 224), 2 to 3 slices per person

Serve the Kalamata Tapenade and the Roasted Eggplant, Walnut, and Basil Pâté in separate dishes. Put the Herbed Goat Cheese in a wide shallow bowl surrounded by the Cherry Tomato Salad. Serve the Crostini in a basket on the side. If you're in a hurry, substitute slices of rustic bread, crackers, and flatbreads for the homemade Crostini.

Roasted Eggplant, Walnut, and Basil Pâté [v]

Being a lazy cook, I leave the skins on roasted eggplant; I also happen to like the flecks of color from the skin in this recipe. However, if you prefer to peel the eggplant, the result will be just as tasty.

Makes about 2 cups

1 large eggplant (about 1½ pounds), unpeeled, cut in ½-inch cubes

2 tablespoons olive oil

2 tablespoons balsamic vinegar

1 tablespoon Basil Pesto (see page 233), or prepared pesto

½ cup walnut pieces, toasted (see page 150) and chopped

Salt and freshly ground pepper

PREPARE THE EGGPLANT. Preheat the oven to 400 degrees. Put the eggplant cubes in a large bowl and drizzle with the olive oil and balsamic vinegar. Toss the eggplant until it is evenly coated.

ROAST THE EGGPLANT. Spread the eggplant cubes on a rimmed baking sheet large enough to accommodate them in a single layer without crowding. (If you crowd them, you will steam rather than roast them.) Roast until the eggplant is soft, for about 30 minutes. Remove it from the oven, and cool.

PROCESS THE EGGPLANT AND WALNUTS. When the eggplant is cool enough to handle, put it in a food processor. Add the Basil Pesto, and process until the eggplant is smooth. Add the walnut pieces, and pulse several times. Process just long enough to fully incorporate the walnuts with the eggplant while preserving the texture of the walnuts and without creating a paste. Add salt and pepper to taste, and serve at room temperature.

Herbed Goat Cheese

You can use different combinations of fresh herbs, but I always use parsley and in a slightly higher proportion than the other herbs. Its bright green color and neutral herbiness goes well with just about everything. (The obvious omission is basil, which tends to turn black when finely chopped.) The lemon zest adds a tart freshness, and the black pepper a little warmth.

Serves 6 to 8

1 tablespoon finely chopped fresh parsley

1 teaspoon fresh thyme leaves

1 teaspoon finely chopped fresh rosemary, sage, or chives

½ teaspoon finely chopped lemon zest

Salt and freshly ground pepper

1 (4-ounce) log goat cheese

MIX THE HERBS AND LEMON ZEST with a couple of pinches of salt and pepper in a small bowl.

ROLL THE GOAT CHEESE IN THE HERBS. Spread the mixed herbs on a cutting board or other flat surface in a thin layer about the width of the goat cheese log. Roll the whole goat cheese log back and forth over the herbs once or twice, pressing lightly as you roll. Serve at room temperature.

> **TIP**
>
> You can also shape the herbed goat cheese into little balls. Start with a cold goat cheese log right out of the refrigerator. It's easier to work with when it's firm and cold. Divide the cheese into eight pieces, and roll them in your hands to form balls. Then roll each ball in the herbs (as you did with the whole log).

Cherry Tomato Salad [v]

We created this little salad for a sweet, tart, and light counterpart to the big, rich flavors of the other parts of this platter. Garlic is used heavily in those other components as well, so here we use the mild onion taste of shallot to flavor the salad. Make this salad about an hour before you intend to serve it so the flavors intensify, but no longer than that because it doesn't hold very well.

Makes 2 cups

1 pint basket cherry tomatoes
1 tablespoon minced shallot
1 tablespoon fresh thyme leaves, roughly chopped
2 tablespoons olive oil
1 teaspoon white wine vinegar
Salt and freshly ground pepper

Cut the cherry tomatoes in half and put in a mixing bowl. Add all the remaining ingredients, and toss several times, adding salt and pepper to taste. Serve the salad at room temperature, stirring once or twice before serving.

Tuscan Appetizer Platter

A "grazing" supper is a great way to eat with a small group of friends. Everything should be able to be served at room temperature so the meal is as relaxed for the cook as for the guests.

This platter can be the centerpiece of just such a supper with the addition of a few dishes. A platter of roasted asparagus would be perfect in spring, or sliced heirloom tomatoes in summer. In fall or winter, marinate portobello mushroom caps in a mixture of olive oil, balsamic vinegar, garlic, salt, and freshly ground pepper. Then broil or grill them, and serve thinly sliced.

To any of these, add a big Caesar Salad (see page 71), or organic mixed greens tossed with our Herbed Balsamic Vinaigrette (see page 87). To round out this delicious and satisfying meal, make sure you have something crispy such as Crostini (see page 224) or crackers to eat with the bean purée, and bread to sop up the delicious goat cheese marinade.

Serves 8 to 10 as a starter or snack

GET A HEAD START

You probably won't want to come home from work and start this appetizer plate (unless you want a very late dinner!). But you can make the White Bean and Roasted Garlic Purée and grill the eggplant the day before. Marinate the goat cheese slices the day you plan to serve the platter, a couple of hours max ahead of the meal.

White Bean and Roasted Garlic Purée (recipe follows)
Olive oil
Marinated Goat Cheese (recipe follows)
Grilled Eggplant (recipe follows)
3 red bell peppers, roasted (see page 212) and cut in 1-inch strips

2 cups mixed olives, such as kalamata, cerignola, picholine, or oil-cured olives

Sliced rustic bread and Crostini (see page 224) or crackers, 2 or 3 pieces per person

Drizzle the White Bean and Roasted Garlic Purée with olive oil and serve it and the Marinated Goat Cheese in separate dishes. On a large plate or in a shallow bowl, arrange the Grilled Eggplant, roasted bell pepper strips, and olives. Serve the bread and Crostini in baskets on the side.

White Bean and Roasted Garlic Purée [V]

You can adapt this purée as a salad. Instead of puréeing the beans, simply fold the roasted garlic, rosemary, thyme, and lemon juice into the whole cooked beans, adding salt and pepper to taste.

Makes 2½ cups

1 cup dried navy, great northern, or cannellini beans, soaked for 3 to 8 hours

2 bay leaves

1 sprig rosemary, leaves chopped, reserving the stem

1 sprig thyme, leaves chopped, reserving the stem

1 head garlic, unpeeled, plus 3 cloves, peeled

½ cup olive oil, plus some for roasting the garlic

2 tablespoons freshly squeezed lemon juice

Salt and freshly ground pepper

GET READY. Preheat the oven to 350 degrees.

COOK THE WHITE BEANS. Drain the soaked beans, put them in large pot, and cover with 3 cups fresh water. Add the bay leaves, the stems of the rosemary and thyme, and 3 cloves garlic.

Bring the pot to a boil, lower the heat, and simmer, covered, until the beans are tender, 1 to 1½ hours. (They should squoosh easily between your fingers.)

If they're not done after an hour, check every 10 minutes or so until they're done.

Remove the herb stems and the bay leaves, and drain the beans, reserving the cooking liquid.

ROAST THE GARLIC. While the beans are cooking, rub the garlic bulb with some olive oil, wrap it in foil, and put it in a small baking dish. Roast in the oven until soft, about 30 minutes. When it's cool enough to handle, cut off the top of the bulb and squeeze out the roasted garlic pulp.

PURÉE THE BEANS AND ROASTED GARLIC. Put the beans in a food processor with the roasted garlic, rosemary and thyme leaves, lemon juice, and ½ cup olive oil. Process until smooth, adding some of the cooking liquid (or water) if the mixture is too thick. Season with salt and pepper to taste, and serve at room temperature.

> **TIP**
>
> The cooking time we give is approximate because it varies wildly for soaked dried beans, from 30 minutes to a couple of hours, depending on the age of the beans, how dry they are, the soaking time, and the beans' size.

Marinated Goat Cheese

Makes 10 to 12 slices

1 (8-ounce) log goat cheese, cold

2 tablespoons minced garlic

½ cup extra-virgin olive oil

Coarse sea salt, or kosher salt

Freshly ground pepper

Cut the goat cheese into 10 to 12 rounds. (You can also roll these slices into little balls if you want.) Put the goat cheese slices in a wide shallow bowl.

Scatter the garlic over the goat cheese, and pour the olive oil over all. Sprinkle generously with salt and a few grindings of pepper.

Marinate for at least an hour, occasionally basting the goat cheese with oil. Serve it within 2 hours.

Grilled Eggplant [v]

These grilled eggplant slices offer a smoky counterpart to the savory bean purée, rich goat cheese, and briny olives on this platter.

We always have a grill going at Cafe Flora, so we can grill anything we like at a moment's notice. If you don't have a barbecue going at home, an indoor gas grill or one of those great cast-iron grill pans works well, as will broiling the eggplant in the oven.

Look for eggplants on the slender side, three to four inches in diameter at their widest point. Bigger eggplants have a lot more seeds and, once sliced, don't hold together as well. Although we don't mind the skin on grilled eggplants when they are young, some people find the cooked skin a little too chewy next to the tender flesh. If you're one of those people, feel free to peel the eggplant before you grill it.

Makes about 24 slices

¼ **cup balsamic vinegar**
¼ **cup olive oil**
1 **tablespoon minced garlic**
1 **big sprig rosemary, finely chopped**
3 **slender eggplants (about 2 pounds)**
Salt and freshly ground pepper

GET READY. If grilling on a barbecue, brush the grill with a bit of oil, and start the coals. If you're using the oven, preheat the broiler.

MAKE THE DRESSING. Whisk together the balsamic vinegar, olive oil, garlic, and rosemary.

TRIM AND MARINATE THE EGGPLANTS. Remove both ends of the eggplants, and peel if you want. Slice into rounds about ½ inch thick, and brush both sides of the slices with the dressing.

GRILL THE EGGPLANT. When the fire is medium-hot, lay the slices on the grill, reserving any leftover dressing. Sprinkle them generously with salt and pepper. Cook until there are dark grill marks on each side and the eggplant is tender to the touch, 6 to 8 minutes per side. Keep a spray bottle of water handy to douse any flare-ups.

SERVE THE EGGPLANT. Arrange the eggplant slices hot off the grill on a serving platter. Serve at room temperature.

Lebanese Platter

Most of the dishes on the Lebanese Platter are probably familiar favorites. In addition to being great party fare, they're also the start of a great dinner of meze, or small plates. Round out the meal with the Curried Grain Salad (see page 83) or a rice pilaf. You could also mix up a salad of baby spinach, bell peppers, cucumber, and cherry tomatoes, and toss it with Lemon Garlic Vinaigrette (see page 134).

Serves 10 to 12 as a starter or snack

GET A HEAD START

You can make the Laban, the Spicy Hummus, and the Baba Ghanoush a day or more ahead. Make the Marinated Red Onions a couple of hours in advance of when you plan to serve it. If you're using dried chickpeas for the hummus, start them soaking at least 3 hours ahead (or the night before).

Spicy Hummus (recipe follows)

Marinated Red Onion (recipe follows)

Laban (recipe follows)

Baba Ghanoush (recipe follows)

Kalamata olives

Pita bread, one per person, warmed

Serve the hummus, marinated onion, laban, baba ghanoush, and olives in separate shallow serving bowls or in mounds arranged on a large platter. Cut the warm pita bread into triangles and serve in a basket.

Spicy Hummus [v]

There are many hummus recipes out there, but most are variations of the same ingredients. I like to be able to taste the pleasant nuttiness of the chickpeas and tahini, which often seems to be overpowered by too much garlic. (Yes, there is such a thing as too much garlic!) In this recipe, one tablespoon of chopped garlic is just enough to balance the other flavors. As always, taste for seasonings before serving. And if you think it might need a bit more salt, it probably does!

Makes 2 cups

1 cup dried chickpeas (garbanzos), soaked for 3 to 8 hours, or 1 (14-ounce) can (about 2 cups cooked)

Juice of 1 lemon

¼ cup sesame tahini

1 tablespoon chopped garlic

¼ teaspoon cumin, toasted and ground (see page 52)

⅛ teaspoon cayenne pepper

3 tablespoons extra-virgin olive oil, plus some for garnish

¼ teaspoon paprika, for garnish

Salt

COOK THE CHICKPEAS. If you are using dried chickpeas, drain them and, put in a pot with enough fresh water to cover by 2 inches. Cook the chickpeas, uncovered, until they are tender, about an hour. Drain them, and chill.

If you're using canned chickpeas, rinse them under cold water, and drain well.

PURÉE THE CHICKPEAS AND TAHINI. Put the chickpeas in the bowl of a food processor, and pulse until well chopped. Add the lemon juice, tahini, garlic, cumin, and cayenne, and process until smooth. With the machine running, drizzle the 3 tablespoons of olive oil into the food processor and process until the mixture is soft and creamy, adding water if you want a looser consistency. Add salt to taste.

SERVE THE HUMMUS. Put it in a wide shallow bowl or mound on a plate, drizzle it with additional olive oil, and sprinkle with paprika.

Marinated Red Onion [v]

Thinly sliced red onion marinated in lemon juice softens the onion's "bite," and turns it a beautiful shade of bright pink. These tart onions make a fine balance for the richness of the Spicy Hummus and laban.

Makes 1 cup

1 red onion

1 teaspoon salt

Juice of 2 lemons

Slice the onion as thinly as possible. Put the slices in a bowl, add the salt and lemon juice, and mix well. Cover the bowl tightly, and refrigerate for at least 2 hours, or up to overnight, tossing the onion occasionally. Drain the onion before you serve it.

Laban (Yogurt Cheese)

Because the other dishes in this platter are so flavorful, we keep the laban simple and lightly seasoned. However, you can always add a clove of chopped garlic, minced fresh mint or cilantro, chopped cucumber, or cayenne if you want more flavor.

Makes ¾ cup

2 cups plain yogurt
¼ teaspoon salt
1 teaspoon extra-virgin olive oil
Freshly ground pepper

DRAIN THE YOGURT TO MAKE THE LABAN. Line a strainer with a paper coffee filter, cheesecloth, or any thin clean cloth, and put the yogurt in it. Put the strainer over a deep bowl, and cover with plastic wrap. Let it drain 8 hours (or overnight) in the refrigerator. It will become very thick and reduce to 1 cup.

SERVE THE LABAN. Put the laban in a small bowl, stir in the salt, drizzle with the olive oil, and grind black pepper over all.

TIP

Draining yogurt removes water and, depending on how long you drain it, can make the yogurt about as thick as cream cheese. (It's a great way to turn even low-fat yogurt into a lush cheese.) For more information, see "Draining Yogurt," on page 11.

Baba Ghanoush [v]

It is in charring and blistering the skin of the eggplant that you create the distinctive smoky flavor of baba ghanoush. Mixing the dip by hand gives it a pleasingly chunky texture.

Makes about 2 cups

1 large firm eggplant, about 1½ pounds
3 tablespoons tahini

3 tablespoons freshly squeezed lemon juice
2 cloves garlic, minced
1 teaspoon salt
¼ cup chopped fresh Italian parsley
1 tablespoon olive oil

GET READY. If you're going to grill the eggplant over coals, get them going. If you're using a gas flame, preheat the oven to 400 degrees; if you're using a broiler, turn it on.

CHAR THE EGGPLANT. There are three methods, after which you set the eggplant aside to cool:

- **On a grill.** Cut the eggplant in half and grill the eggplant halves until all the surfaces are blistered and charred, and the eggplant deflates and becomes tender.

- **Over a gas flame on the stove.** Turn the gas flame on medium-high. Using tongs, hold the whole eggplant over the flame, and turn it every 20 or 30 seconds until all the skin is blistered and charred. (This may create smoke, so turn on your exhaust fan or open a window.)

  To finish the cooking, put the charred eggplant in a baking dish, and roast in the 400 degree oven until it is tender and deflated, for about 30 minutes.

- **Under the broiler.** Turn on the broiler, and put the whole eggplant on the broiler pan under the broiler. (You may have to lower the oven rack to fit the eggplant under the broiler.) Turn the eggplant over every couple of minutes until the entire eggplant is blistered and charred.

  Lower the oven temperature to 400 degrees. Put the charred eggplant in a baking dish and roast until it is tender and deflated, for about 30 minutes.

MIX THE TAHINI DRESSING. In a small bowl, mix the tahini, lemon juice, garlic, and salt and blend well.

REMOVE THE EGGPLANT SKIN. When the eggplant is cool enough to handle, remove the stem cap and scrape off most of the skin (a small amount remaining is OK). Roughly chop the soft flesh, trying not to mash it up too much.

MIX THE EGGPLANT WITH THE TAHINI DRESSING. Put the eggplant in a bowl and mix in the tahini dressing. Fold in the parsley. Taste and add more salt if needed. Drizzle with olive oil and serve.

Lentil Pecan Pâté Platter [v]

This is a vegan spin on the classic French accompaniments to a pâté, with the Lentil Pecan Pâté standing in for a liver pâté. However, it's one that will satisfy even your most carnivorous guests.

Serves 10 to 12 as a starter or snack

GET A HEAD START

The Lentil Pecan Pâté takes more than an hour to make, and then it must be chilled before you can serve it. But make this a day or two ahead to give the flavors time to develop. You can also make the Red Onion Confit several days ahead.

Lentil Pecan Pâté (recipe follows)

Red Onion Confit (recipe follows)

Stone-ground mustard

Cornichons (French sour gherkin pickles), assorted olives, and caper berries (see "About Caper Berries")

Sliced rustic bread, and Crostini (see page 224) or crackers, 2 or 3 pieces per person

To serve, mound the chilled pâté on a platter, and pile the Red Onion Confit right next to it. Put the mustard in a ceramic pot or small bowl with a tiny serving spoon. Serve the cornichons, olives, and caper berries each in a separate small bowl. Pass the bread in a basket.

About Caper Berries

Caper berries are the mature fruit of the caper bush. (Capers are actually the bush's flower bud.) They look like very plump, large olives with a stem attached, and are eaten as one would eat an olive. Like capers, they should be drained and rinsed before eating. Look for them among the olives and condiments in any well-stocked deli.

Lentil Pecan Pâté [v]

Our Lentil Pecan Pâté is wildly popular and our guests request this recipe often. Its flavor is amazingly similar to that of liver pâté, thanks to the use of meaty, rich, light miso, the mellow sweetness of mirin (a golden rice wine), and the flavor-balancing effect of umeboshi, very tart and salty pickled Japanese plums.

Makes 2 cups

1 cup red lentils

2 cups water

1 bay leaf

1 tablespoon olive oil

1 medium onion, diced

1 tablespoon chopped garlic

½ teaspoon dried thyme

½ teaspoon dried sage

2 tablespoons mirin (rice wine [see page 239])

1 teaspoon umeboshi (sour plum) paste (see "About the Ingredients")

1 tablespoon light miso (Japanese bean paste [see page 239])

½ cup pecan pieces, toasted (see page 150)

½ teaspoon salt

½ teaspoon freshly ground pepper

COOK AND COOL THE LENTILS. Rinse the lentils. Put them in a pot with the water and bay leaf. Bring to a boil over medium heat, lower the heat, and simmer, covered, until the lentils are very soft and most of the water has been absorbed, 15 to 20 minutes, adding more water if necessary. Remove the bay leaf, and set aside to cool.

SAUTÉ THE ONION. While the lentils are cooking, heat the olive oil in a pan over medium heat. Add the onion, and cook until it has reduced in volume and begun to soften, about 5 minutes, stirring once or twice.

Turn down the heat to low, and cook the onion for 15 to 20 minutes, stirring occasionally. If the onion starts to stick, add 1 or 2 tablespoons water (or cooking sherry, if you have it), and stir to remove any bits of onion from the bottom of the pan. When done, the onion should be various shades of brown, soft, and sweet.

ADD THE GARLIC AND HERBS. To the onion, add the garlic, thyme, and sage, and cook for 1 minute. Remove from the heat, and set aside to cool.

PURÉE THE LENTILS AND ONIONS. Put the lentils and onion mixture in a food processor. Add all the remaining ingredients, and process until the mixture is a smooth paste. Transfer to a bowl, cover, and chill before you serve it.

About the Ingredients

RED LENTILS **If you do not find these in your grocery store, look for them in an Indian or Middle Eastern market.**

UMEBOSHI PASTE **is a purée of umeboshi, Japanese pickled plums; the fruit (ume) is pickled before it's ripe and then brined with red shiso, which gives umeboshi its characteristic pink color. Like ume vinegar, umeboshi paste is welcome in dishes for its unique tart, fruity, and salty flavor.**

It's packaged in small tubs or tubes and you'll find it refrigerated in Asian markets near the pickled ginger and other condiments. Umeboshi is a staple in macrobiotic cooking, so you'll often find it with other staples of macrobiotic cooking at natural-food stores.

If you can't find umeboshi paste or it costs more than you want to spend, substitute sherry vinegar. The result will still be delicious; it will just be missing the tangy saltiness that umeboshi paste gives.

Red Onion Confit [v]

This thick sweet confit is handy to have around for snacks and sandwiches. Dollop it on Crostini (see page 224) spread with softened goat cheese or atop a slice of warm Brie for an easy, elegant appetizer. Or try it on our Mushroom Pecan Pâté Sandwich (see page 172).

Makes about 2 cups

1 tablespoon olive oil

2 large red onions, cut in half and thinly sliced

1 tablespoon chopped garlic

¼ cup balsamic vinegar

½ cup red wine or port

2 tablespoons light or dark brown sugar

½ teaspoon salt

¼ teaspoon freshly ground pepper

SAUTÉ THE ONIONS. In a large heavy saucepan, heat the olive oil over medium heat. Add the onions and cook, stirring occasionally, until the onions are soft and translucent, about 10 minutes.

COOK THE ONIONS WITH THE REMAINING INGREDIENTS. Add the remaining ingredients, reduce the heat to low, and cook, stirring often, until the liquid has been reduced to a thick syrup coating the onions, about 15 minutes. Set aside to cool. Serve warm or at room temperature.

Curried Lentil Pâté Platter [v]

The Lentil Pecan Pâté (see page 32) was so popular, we decided to make a variation with an Indian theme. (Plus we wanted to think of a way to use pappadams because we love them so much.)

Serves 10 to 12 as a starter or snack

GET A HEAD START

You can make the Apricot Chutney several days in advance. The lentils and onions must cool before you can mix them together to form the pâté. The other parts of this platter are best made the day you plan to serve them, although they do require some lead time.

Curried Lentil Pâté (recipe follows)

Apricot Chutney (recipe follows)

Coconut Raita (see page 225)

Marinated Red Onion (see page 000) or Cucumber Sambal (see page 21)

2 or 3 pappadams or 1 pita bread per person, toasted, or crackers

Serve the spreads, dips, and relishes in bowls clustered together on a tray or table alongside a basket of pappadams, pita wedges, or crackers. Suggest to your guests that they spread the pappadams or crackers with pâté. Top with a dollop of one or all of the following—Apricot Chutney, Coconut Raita, and a few strands of pickled red onion. Of course they can also eat these dishes however they like.

About Pappadams

Pappadams (available at Indian grocers) are a very delicate crackerlike bread from India: instructions for heating them up are usually right on the package. They're brittle, though, so scoop up the pâté carefully.

If you can't find pappadams, you can make crispy pita triangles. Brush pita bread with oil or melted butter, sprinkle with nigella, black onion seed (see page 109), and warm it in the oven. Cut into triangles to serve. Or for something even simpler, there's a huge variety of crackers to choose from.

Curried Lentil Pâté [v]

Makes 2 cups

1 cup red lentils

2 cups water

1 bay leaf

1 tablespoon olive oil

1 medium red onion, diced

1 tablespoon chopped garlic

2 tablespoons mirin (rice wine [see page 239])

1 tablespoon curry powder

1 tablespoon light miso (Japanese bean paste [see page 239])

½ cup unsalted pistachio nuts, toasted (see page 150)

½ teaspoon salt

COOK AND COOL THE LENTILS. Rinse the lentils. Put them in a saucepan with the water and bay leaf. Bring to a boil over medium heat, lower the heat, and simmer, covered. Cook until the lentils are very soft and most of the water has been absorbed, 15 to 20 minutes, adding more water if necessary. Remove the bay leaf, and set aside to cool.

SAUTÉ THE ONION. While the lentils are cooking, heat the olive oil in a pan over medium heat. Add the onion, and cook until it has reduced in volume and begun to soften, about 5 minutes, stirring once or twice.

Turn down the heat to low, and cook the onion for 15 to 20 minutes, stirring occasionally. If the onion starts to stick, add 1 to 2 tablespoons water (or cooking sherry, if you have it), and stir to remove any bits of onion from the bottom of the pan. When done, the onion should be various shades of brown, soft, and sweet.

ADD THE GARLIC AND SPICES. Add the garlic and cook for 1 minute. Add the mirin and curry powder, and stir to mix well. Remove from the heat, and set aside to cool.

PURÉE THE LENTILS AND ONIONS. Put the lentils and onion mixture in a food processor. Add the remaining ingredients, and process until the mixture is a smooth paste. Transfer to a bowl, cover, and chill before you serve it.

Apricot Chutney [v]

Makes 1 cup

1 teaspoon olive oil

2 tablespoons chopped shallots

2 cloves garlic, minced

1 teaspoon grated, peeled, fresh ginger

1 cup dried apricots, chopped

½ jalapeño chile, seeded and minced

3 tablespoons cider vinegar

2 tablespoons freshly squeezed lime juice

1 teaspoon grated lime zest

2 tablespoons raisins or dried cranberries

½ teaspoon salt

¼ teaspoon cumin seeds, toasted and ground (see page 52)

¼ teaspoon fennel seeds, toasted and ground (see page 52)

¾ cup water

SAUTÉ THE SHALLOTS, GARLIC, AND GINGER. Heat the olive oil in a heavy-bottomed saucepan over medium heat. Add the shallots and sauté, stirring occasionally, until translucent and beginning to brown, about 3 minutes. Add the garlic and ginger, and cook for 1 more minute.

SIMMER THE SAUCE. Add the remaining ingredients, lower the heat, and simmer, partially covered. Stir occasionally to prevent sticking, and cook until the apricots have completely softened and most of the liquid has been absorbed, about 20 minutes. Remove from the stove, and set aside to cool.

SOUPS

"RING IT IN, CREEPS!" BELLOWS Lisa, our sous-chef and chief soup maker. (This is how we track employee meals, ringing whatever we eat into the cash register.) She has just made five gallons each of three different kinds of soup, and we'll be lucky if we don't sell out every drop of those soups in one day. She would like these soups to be served to our guests, not devoured by staff. But sometimes we can't help ourselves. We want, we NEED, a cup of Lisa's soup. We are convinced that a cup of soup is the only thing that will get us through the day, although we said that about the third espresso we had an hour ago. Sometimes the soup is completely new, sometimes it's an old favorite, but whatever soups happen to be in the warmer that day—we always have two, one vegan, one not—they're sure to please, and to fill you up, because many of our soups (like the ones in this chapter) are substantial enough for supper rather than as a first course.

This was probably the hardest chapter to write because, with a few exceptions, we don't have any soup recipes. We have a soup log which lists ingredients and has a blank box for the soup creator's interpretive drawing, but little else. (Lisa is an artist so every soup description comes with a little sketch, sometimes a cartoon of one of the ingredients or a drawing of how she feels that day.) The good part for the home cook is that the steps for making almost all of our soups are basically the same. Cook the onions in some oil, add some garlic and any dried herbs or spices. Then add the vegetables, beans or grains, add water or stock, bring the pot to a boil, and then simmer. Sometimes, instead of going crazy with the saltshaker, we heighten the soup's flavor by adding fresh herbs or a splash of vinegar at the end, when the soup pot is off the heat. To thicken soups, we usually purée a portion of the soup and add it back to the pot. Nothing fancy here.

For every soup in this book, I use one pot—my trusty Le Creuset four-quart Dutch oven. Its enamel-coated cast iron and heavy bottom are important for making soup. In the soup-making process, you turn the heat up and down several times, so you need a pot that can react well to these temperature changes and distribute the heat evenly. A soup pot with a thinner bottom will have hot spots and may end up scorching all your hard work as the soup simmers.

I'm sure it's no big surprise to most people that the "scratch" soups in restaurants are the necessary result of an overabundance of a particular ingredient. For example, we feature roasted beets in salads throughout the year, and sometimes we roast a few too many. That became the inspiration for Roasted Beet and Lentil Soup. A guest and staff favorite, Dutch Potato Soup, was inspired by a chunk of smoked Gouda cheese that was left over when we took a certain sandwich off our lunch menu. Having one or two ingredients that you need to use up is a bonus when making soups. These few ingredients, some of which would never occur to you to use in a soup, become your starting point and inspiration. The beautiful thing is that the ingredients for soups are usually not that expensive, so it's a cheap way to be creative in the kitchen. And if you make something that doesn't taste right, just feed it to the dog!

Vegetable Stock [v]

We don't really have a recipe for vegetable stock. We just throw stuff in a "stock bucket," and when it's full, we make stock. What do we toss into the bucket? We save any bits and scraps that aren't used in a dish: the tops of leeks, scallions, and celery, the stems from parsley, herbs, and mushrooms, the trimmed ends and peel from carrots, potatoes, and turnips, and so on. We steer clear of strongly flavored vegetables such as broccoli, cauliflower, cabbage, and cilantro or vegetables like beets that would give a distinctive color to what should be a flavorful, but still neutral, broth. And of course we never use any vegetables that are shriveled or spoiled in any way.

You can take the same approach, but use your freezer as a stock bucket. When you're ready to make stock, also root around in your fridge for odds and ends of fresh vegetables and herbs that aren't quite enough to build a meal around, and throw those in too.

Here are some other suggestions about making the stock:

- If you're using organic vegetables, you don't need to peel them.

- If you can't find fresh herbs, just omit them. But if you have stems and scraps of fresh herbs (mushroom stems as well), go ahead and use those. (It's a great way to use up every last bit of something that was expensive.)

- If you want a light-colored stock, leave out the tomato paste and miso.

- Don't add salt because you have more control of the saltiness by adding it to the finished soup.

- Make a gallon of stock at a time and split up what you don't use in plastic containers or freezer bags, and freeze them; the stock will keep a couple of months.

And for those days when you just don't have the time to make stock from scratch and you don't have any homemade broth stored in your freezer, go ahead and use boxed or canned vegetable broth. Choose the low-sodium variety if at all possible, because it gives you more control of the soup's saltiness. The quality of commercial broth these days is really quite good and there are many brands to choose from. Two brands stand out: Pacific and Imagine Foods. These are sold at larger supermarkets, natural-food stores, and specialty stores such as Trader Joe's.

Makes about 16 cups (1 gallon)

3 medium carrots

1 yellow onion

4 ribs celery

1 leek

2 medium potatoes

½ pound fresh button or crimini mushrooms (and stems)

6 cloves garlic, slightly smashed

6 sprigs fresh parsley

6 sprigs fresh thyme

2 sprigs fresh oregano

2 bay leaves

10 black peppercorns

Optional: 2 tablespoons tomato paste

Optional: 1 tablespoon red miso (see page 239)

PREPARE THE VEGETABLES. Roughly chop the carrots, onion, and celery. Cut the leek in half lengthwise, wash it, and roughly chop the whole thing. Quarter the potatoes and the mushrooms.

COOK THE STOCK. Dump all the ingredients except the tomato paste and miso in a large pot. Cover with 4½ quarts of water. Bring to a boil, lower the heat, and simmer uncovered for 1 hour.

ADD THE TOMATO PASTE AND MISO. If you're adding them, mix them in a little broth that you've ladled from the pot. Then add that to the stock, and stir until they have dissolved.

STRAIN THE STOCK. Strain the stock, pressing gently to remove the liquid from the vegetables. Discard the vegetables.

Smoked Jalapeño Black-Eyed Pea Soup [v]

Black-eyed peas are soaked and cooked separately for this soup; otherwise you would have to cook the entire pot of soup for close to two hours, which would be detrimental to the flavor. After the peas are cooked, drain them, but save one cup of the rich cooking liquid, which, along with the okra, will thicken the soup. Fresh basil, added at the very end, brightens the flavors; fresh chopped tomatoes would be a good addition as well.

Serve this with Tangy Swiss Chard (see page 134) and your favorite cornbread.

Makes 7 cups

TIMING

Smoke the jalapeño chile before you start the soup.

1 cup dried black-eyed peas, soaked for 2 hours or up to 8 hours, or 2 (15-ounce) cans (about 2½ cups cooked)

1 tablespoon olive oil

1 medium yellow onion, diced

Salt

4 cloves garlic, minced

2 medium carrots, peeled and diced

2 ribs celery, diced

1 teaspoon dried oregano

1 teaspoon dried thyme

2 smoked jalapeño chiles (see page 79), ribs and seeds removed, finely chopped

1 cup frozen sliced okra, thawed but not cooked

4 cups Vegetable Stock (see page 39), or purchased vegetable stock

1 teaspoon rice vinegar

1 tablespoon chopped fresh basil, or 1 teaspoon dried basil

Freshly ground pepper

COOK THE BLACK-EYED PEAS. If you are using dried peas, drain them, and cover with about 1 inch of fresh water in a pot. Bring to a boil, lower the heat, and simmer, uncovered, until tender, 45 minutes to 1 hour. Check the pot during cooking to see if it needs more water. Drain, reserving 1 cup of the cooking liquid. Set aside to cool.

If you're using canned black-eyed peas, rinse them under cold water, and drain well.

SAUTÉ THE ONION AND GARLIC. In a heavy-bottomed soup pot, heat the olive oil over medium heat. Sauté the onion with ½ teaspoon salt until the onion is soft and translucent, about 10 minutes. Add the garlic, and cook 1 minute.

ADD MOST OF THE REMAINING INGREDIENTS, AND SIMMER. Add the carrots, celery, oregano, thyme, and smoked chiles, and cook for 3 minutes more.

Add the black-eyed peas, the reserved cup of their cooking liquid, okra, and the stock. If you're using canned black-eyed peas, add them to the pot with their liquid and 1 cup of water (or additional stock, if you have it). Bring the pot to a boil, lower the heat, and simmer, uncovered, for 20 minutes.

SERVE THE SOUP. Take the pot off the heat, and add the vinegar and basil. Taste the soup for salt and pepper, and serve.

Brandied Apple with Stilton Soup

We often make puréed fruit soups, especially pear and apple soups in the winter. Finished with some cream and a flavorful cheese, they're quite rich and best suited for small portions as a first course. In fact, it would be a delicious prelude to the Lentil Pecan Pâté Platter (see page 32), which with a good bread would make a gratifying supper. This soup would also make an interesting final course instead of dessert.

You can use most any variety of apples (or pears) to make this soup, but a crisp, tart apple like Granny Smith or Braeburn works best. And you don't need to use your best brandy in this soup!

Makes 6 cups

2 tablespoons butter

1 medium yellow onion, thinly sliced

1 leek, white and very pale green part only, cut in half lengthwise and thinly sliced

1 shallot, thinly sliced

Salt

4 apples, peeled, cored, and sliced

¼ cup brandy

4 cups Vegetable Stock (see page 39) omitting the tomato paste and red miso, or purchased vegetable stock

1 bay leaf

4 sprigs fresh thyme or 1 teaspoon dried thyme

1 cup heavy cream

¼ cup Stilton or Gorgonzola cheese, plus some for garnish

Ground white pepper

SAUTÉ THE ONION AND APPLES. In a heavy-bottomed soup pot over medium heat, melt the butter. Add the onion, leek, shallot, ½ teaspoon salt, and the dried thyme if you're using it. Sauté until the onion is soft and translucent, about 10 minutes, stirring several times.

Increase the heat to medium-high, and add the apples. Heat the apples, stirring once or twice, for 1 minute.

ADD THE BRANDY, STOCK, AND FRESH HERBS. Add the brandy, scraping any browned bits from the bottom of the pan, and cook until most of the brandy has evaporated. Add the stock, bay leaf, and fresh thyme sprigs if you're using them. Return to a boil, lower the heat, and simmer, covered, for 20 minutes.

PURÉE THE SOUP. Remove the thyme sprigs and bay leaf, and purée the soup in batches in a blender, being careful to fill the blender jar no more than halfway. Return the soup to the pot, add the cream and the cheese, and heat gently. DO NOT BOIL, or you will curdle the soup. Season to taste with salt and white pepper.

SERVE THE SOUP. Pass a bowl with crumbled Stilton cheese for your guests to sprinkle on top of the soup.

> **TIP**
>
> To reheat, bring the soup just to a simmer in a heavy-bottomed pot over low heat, stirring constantly. (Creamed soups will stick to the bottom of the pan and burn if you don't stir while you heat them up.)

Dutch Potato Soup

One of the all-time most requested soups by guests and staff alike, Dutch Potato Soup has undergone several alterations since its creation by one of our former cooks, Pauline Wickey. The original soup recipe contained smoked Gouda—hence the Dutch in the soup's name—and caraway seeds, but over the years we have used different smoked cheeses, added beer, and sometimes even left out the caraway. The beer is a natural complement to cheese in a soup, but it's the nutty, aniselike flavor of caraway that makes this soup unique. For a complete meal, serve with the Red Jewel Salad (see page 78).

Makes about 8 cups

2 tablespoons olive oil

1 medium yellow onion, thinly sliced

Salt

4 cloves garlic, minced

1½ pounds potatoes (white or yellow thin-skinned varieties like Yukon Gold or White Rose), unpeeled and sliced

4 cups Vegetable Stock (see page 39), or purchased vegetable stock or broth

1 teaspoon caraway seeds, toasted and then ground (see page 52)

¾ cup beer, like a lager or pilsner

1 cup heavy cream

1½ cups grated smoked Gouda cheese (about 6 ounces)

Freshly ground pepper

SAUTÉ THE ONION AND GARLIC. Heat the oil in a heavy-bottomed soup pot over medium heat. Add the onion and ½ teaspoon salt, and sauté until the onion is soft and translucent, about 10 minutes, stirring several times. Add the garlic, and cook 1 minute more.

COOK THE POTATOES. Add the potatoes and stock. Bring the pot to a boil, cover, and cook the potatoes until tender, about 10 minutes.

PURÉE THE SOUP in batches in a blender, being careful to fill the blender jar no more than halfway.

ADD THE REMAINING INGREDIENTS. Return the purée to the pot, and add the ground caraway seeds and beer. Bring to a boil, and then stir in the cream.

Return the soup to simmer and stir in the cheese, a half cup at a time until it's melted. Simmer for 2 minutes, stirring constantly, to melt the cheese. DO NOT BOIL, or you will curdle the soup. Season to taste with salt and pepper, and serve at once.

> **TIP**
>
> To reheat, bring the soup just to a simmer in a heavy-bottomed pot over low heat, stirring constantly. (Creamed soups will stick to the bottom of the pan and burn if you don't stir while you heat them up.)

Carrot Tomato Soup with Quirky Pasta [v]

When our chef, Janine Doran, found some pasta shaped like autumn leaves, we decided to make this mildly seasoned, creamy golden soup filled with fallen leaves for our kid's menu. Of course you can use any kind of pasta that delights your little ones—alphabets, stars, wagon wheels. Just make sure to cook the pasta first—it's a great way to use leftover pasta—and add it to the soup right before you serve it. This is such a simple soup that it would make a good introductory cooking lesson for a child.

For a complete meal for kids of any age, serve a cheese quesadilla or a grilled cheese sandwich alongside.

Makes about 5 cups

1 teaspoon vegetable oil

½ onion, diced

1 cup chopped carrot (about 1 large carrot)

Salt

¼ teaspoon dried thyme

1 cup fresh or canned tomatoes with juice, diced

3 cups Vegetable Stock (see page 39), or purchased vegetable stock or broth

¼ cup fresh parsley sprigs

¼ teaspoon onion powder

⅛ teaspoon ground cinnamon

½ cup pasta (about 1 cup cooked)

SAUTÉ THE FRESH VEGETABLES AND THYME. Heat the oil in a saucepan over medium heat. Add the onion, carrot, and a pinch of salt. Sauté until the onion is soft and translucent, about 10 minutes. Add the thyme, and sauté for 1 more minute.

COOK THE SOUP. Add the tomatoes, 2 cups of the vegetable stock, parsley, onion powder, and cinnamon. Bring to a boil, reduce the heat to low, and simmer, uncovered, for 20 minutes.

COOK THE PASTA. While the soup simmers, cook the pasta following the directions on the package.

PURÉE THE SOUP. Pour the soup into a blender, and purée until smooth.

FINISH THE SOUP. Return the soup to the pot, stir in the remaining cup of stock, and add salt to taste. Return the soup to a simmer over low heat, add the cooked pasta, and serve immediately.

Roasted Garlic Dijon Lentil Soup [v]

Here we add a paste of roasted garlic and Dijon mustard to the pot, which adds a sharp, clean tang to an otherwise earthy soup. We use French green (Le Puy) lentils for this recipe since they hold their shape and don't get mushy when cooked. For a complete supper, start with Linda's Marinated Goat Cheese (see page 7) and serve a spinach salad with the soup.

Makes 7 cups

12 cloves garlic, unpeeled

2 tablespoons olive oil

1 tablespoon Dijon mustard

1 yellow onion, diced

Salt

2 medium carrots, peeled and diced

1 potato, peeled and diced

1 teaspoon dried thyme

5 cups Vegetable Stock (see page 39), or purchased vegetable stock or broth

½ cup French green (Le Puy) lentils, rinsed

Freshly ground pepper

ROAST THE GARLIC. Preheat the oven to 350 degrees. Toss the garlic cloves with the olive oil, and put in a small baking dish. Cover with foil, and roast in the oven until soft, about 30 minutes. Drain the oil from the roasted garlic into a heavy-bottomed soup pot.

MAKE THE ROASTED-GARLIC AND DIJON PASTE. When the garlic is cool enough to handle, squeeze out the pulp into a small bowl. Add the Dijon mustard, and mix well. Set aside.

SAUTÉ THE ONIONS AND OTHER VEGETABLES. Heat the roasted-garlic oil over medium heat. Add the onion and ½ teaspoon salt, and sauté until the onion is soft and translucent, about 10 minutes, stirring several times. Add the carrots, potato, and thyme, and sauté for 3 minutes more.

SIMMER THE SOUP. Add the vegetable stock and lentils, and bring the pot to a boil. Lower the heat, and simmer until the lentils are tender, 25 to 30 minutes.

STIR IN THE ROASTED-GARLIC PASTE, and simmer for 10 minutes. Add a pinch or two of ground pepper, add salt to taste, and serve.

> **TIP**
>
> This soup will thicken as it sits, so you may need to add water or vegetable stock to get the consistency you want.

Mushroom Madeira Stew [v]

This chunky soup was inspired by the flavor of the Madeira Sauce we serve with Portobello Wellington (see page 135). Madeira is a fortified wine that, like sherry, goes well with mushrooms. If you have neither Madeira nor sherry on hand, you could substitute red wine, but the finished soup will be more fruity and tannic. Nutritional yeast adds a rich, meaty flavor to the pot, and thickening with a roux pulls the whole soup together with a delicious gravy.

In Cajun and Creole cooking a dark roux is the basis of many dishes. It's added to gumbos, sauces, and other regional specialties to thicken them while adding a deep, roasted flavor. A dark roux is made by slowly cooking a mixture of flour and some form of fat, usually butter. Here we use olive oil (to keep the soup vegan), stirring constantly over low heat so it does not burn, until the mixture is a deep, nut brown.

Balance this luscious stew with our refreshing and beautiful Persimmon Curry Spinach Salad (see page 58).

Makes about 8 cups

3 tablespoons olive oil

2 tablespoons unbleached all-purpose flour

1 medium yellow onion, diced

Salt

4 cloves garlic, chopped

1 tablespoon chopped fresh thyme, or 1 teaspoon dried thyme

3 tablespoons chopped fresh parsley

2 tablespoons nutritional yeast

1 tablespoon tomato paste

½ pound mushrooms, thickly sliced (about 2½ cups)

6 cups Vegetable Stock (see page 39), or purchased vegetable stock or broth, warmed

2 large potatoes, cut into ½-inch dice (about 2 cups)

2 large carrots, cut into ¼-inch thick slices (about 1½ cups)

1 bay leaf

½ cup dry to medium-dry Madeira

1½ cups frozen green peas

½ teaspoon freshly ground pepper

MAKE THE ROUX. Heat 2 tablespoons of the olive oil in a small skillet over medium heat. Add the flour, and cook, stirring constantly, until it gives off a toasty aroma and is golden brown. Remove from the heat, and set aside.

SAUTÉ THE ONION, GARLIC, HERBS, AND MUSHROOMS. Heat the remaining 1 tablespoon oil in a heavy-bottomed soup pot over medium heat. Add the onion and ½ teaspoon salt, and sauté until the onion is soft and translucent, about 10 minutes, stirring several times. Add the garlic, and cook 1 minute more.

Add the mushrooms, and cook until they begin to release their juices, about 5 minutes. Add the thyme, parsley, nutritional yeast, and tomato paste, and cook 2 minutes.

STIR IN THE ROUX AND STOCK. Stir in the roux and add the stock, 1 cup at a time, blending completely with the roux after each addition.

ADD THE VEGETABLES AND SIMMER. Add the potatoes, carrots, and bay leaf, and bring the pot to a boil. Cover the pot, reduce the heat to low, and simmer for 20 minutes.

ADD THE REMAINING INGREDIENTS. Add the Madeira and the peas to the pot, and return the soup to a boil. Lower the heat and simmer for no more than 5 minutes. Remove the bay leaf, add the pepper, add salt to taste, and serve.

> **TIP**
>
> **Use crimini, portobello, or shiitake mushrooms, or a combination of all three.**

Ocean Chowder

Another fabulous creation by our soup master, Lisa Lewis, this chowder is a vegetarian twist on a New England classic, with arame (seaweed) providing the taste of the sea. Balance this cream soup with the tart flavors of the Avocado Grapefruit Salad with Ginger Miso Dressing (see page 63).

Makes 9 cups

¼ cup arame (seaweed) (about ½ ounce)

2 tablespoons unsalted butter

2 medium yellow onions, cut in ½-inch dice

Salt

1 tablespoon minced garlic

2 ribs celery, cut in ¼-inch dice

1 large carrot, cut in ¼-inch dice

2 pounds Yukon Gold potatoes, cut in ½-inch dice

2 bay leaves

4 cups Vegetable Stock (see page 39), or purchased vegetable stock or broth

2 cups heavy cream

2 tablespoons chopped, fresh Italian parsley

1 tablespoon chopped fresh thyme

Freshly ground pepper

PREPARE THE ARAME. Rinse the arame in a strainer under running water. Put it in a bowl and add cold water just to cover. Soak for 10 minutes. Drain well, and chop very coarsely. (Chopping the arame strands too finely will make the soup too black in color.) Set aside.

SAUTÉ THE ONIONS AND GARLIC. Melt the butter in a large, heavy-bottomed pot over medium heat. Add the onion and ½ teaspoon salt, and sauté until the onion is soft and translucent, about 10 minutes, stirring several times. Add the garlic, and cook 1 minute more.

ADD THE REMAINING VEGETABLES, BAY LEAVES, AND STOCK. Add the celery and carrot, and sauté for 5 minutes. Add the arame, potatoes, bay leaves, and stock, and bring to a boil.

Reduce the heat to low, and simmer until the potatoes and carrots are firm but tender, about 20 minutes.

ADD THE CREAM, FRESH HERBS, AND SERVE. Stir in the cream, parsley, and thyme, and gently simmer for 10 minutes. DO NOT BOIL, or you will curdle the soup. Remove the bay leaf, add salt and pepper to taste, and serve.

> **TIP**
>
> **To reheat, bring the soup just to a simmer in a heavy-bottomed pot over low heat, stirring constantly. (Creamed soups will stick to the bottom of the pan and burn if you don't stir while you heat them up.)**

Pear Parsnip Soup with Gorgonzola Croutons

This soup is ideal for pears that have reached that final stage of ripeness where they look less than perfect, have a few gouges in them, and turn into mush if carried in your lunch bag. (In fact, the riper the pears, the better the soup is.) This soup is rich and sweet, so we serve it in small amounts, usually as a first course. Further embellishment with a crunchy Gorgonzola crouton makes this a perfect start to a celebration dinner.

Makes about 6 cups

TIMING

To shorten your time in the kitchen, make the Gorgonzola Croutons while the parsnips cook.

1 tablespoon olive oil

1 yellow onion, thinly sliced

Salt

½ teaspoon dried thyme

4 ripe pears, unpeeled, cored, and cut into chunks

2 parsnips (about 1 pound), peeled and sliced ½ inch thick

1 bay leaf

4 cups Vegetable Stock (see page 39), or purchased vegetable stock or broth

½ cup heavy whipping cream

White pepper

6 Gorgonzola Croutons (recipe follows)

SAUTÉ THE ONION. Heat the oil in a heavy-bottomed soup pot over medium heat. Add the sliced onion and ½ teaspoon salt, and sauté until the onion is soft and translucent, about 10 minutes.

ADD MOST OF THE REMAINING INGREDIENTS AND SIMMER. Add the thyme, and cook 1 minute. Add the pears, parsnips, bay leaf, and vegetable stock, and bring to a boil. Lower the heat, and simmer, covered, until the parsnips are very tender, about 30 minutes.

PURÉE THE SOUP. Remove the bay leaf and purée the soup in batches in a blender, being careful to fill the blender jar no more than halfway.

SERVE THE SOUP. Return the puréed soup to the pot, add the cream, and heat through. DO NOT BOIL, or you will curdle the soup. When hot, season with salt and white pepper to taste.

Ladle the soup into 6 bowls, float a Gorgonzola Crouton on top of each serving, and serve immediately.

> **TIP**
>
> To reheat, bring the soup just to a simmer in a heavy-bottomed pot over low heat, stirring constantly. (Puréed soups will stick to the bottom of the pan and burn if you don't stir while you heat them up.)

Gorgonzola Croutons

Makes 6 croutons

6 (½-inch) slices of a rustic baguette

2 tablespoons olive oil

½ cup Gorgonzola cheese (2 ounces)

TOAST THE BAGUETTE SLICES. Preheat the oven to 375 degrees. Brush the baguette slices with olive oil on both sides. Bake on a baking sheet for 8 to 10 minutes until golden brown and very crisp.

MELT THE CHEESE ON THE TOAST. Remove slices from the oven, and set the oven to broil. Crumble the cheese over the croutons, and return to the oven. Broil until the cheese begins to melt, about 2 minutes.

Roasted Beet and Lentil Soup [v]

Roasting beets, rather than boiling, intensifies their earthy character and produces a very flavorful juice. We like the color (and name) of black Beluga lentils, along with the fact they don't turn into mush when cooked. If you can't get them, French green (Le Puy) lentils make a good substitute. Ume (plum) vinegar adds a salty and acidic, yet fruity touch.

For a complete meal, serve this soup with the Mushroom Pecan Pâté (see page 137) or the Cafe Flora French Dip sandwich (see page 170).

Makes 6 cups

TIMING

It takes about an hour to roast the beets and they must cool to the point that you can remove the skins and cut them up for the soup.

1½ pounds beets, unpeeled, with ½ inch of the beet top left on

½ cup lentils (such as black Beluga or French green (Le Puy) lentils)

1 bay leaf

1 tablespoon olive oil

1 medium yellow onion, diced

1 leek, white and very pale green parts only, cut in half lengthwise, washed, and thinly sliced

Salt

4 cloves garlic, minced

About 4 cups Vegetable Stock (see page 39), or purchased vegetable stock

1 tablespoon chopped, fresh dill

1 tablespoon ume (plum) vinegar (see "About Ume Vinegar," page 48), or raspberry vinegar

Freshly ground pepper

Optional: Sour cream or crème fraîche for garnish

ROAST THE BEETS. Preheat the oven to 350 degrees. Put the beets in a small lidded baking dish with 1 cup water, and cover. Roast until a knife inserted into a beet offers no resistance, about 1 hour. Set aside to cool.

COOK THE LENTILS. Rinse the lentils, and put them in a small pot with 2 cups cold water and the bay leaf. Bring to a boil, and then lower the heat. Simmer, covered, until tender, 20 to 25 minutes, adding more water if necessary. Drain, remove the bay leaf, and set aside.

CUT THE BEETS INTO STICKS. Remove the beets from the pan, reserving the deep red cooking liquid. Rub off the skins using a paper towel. Cut the beets into sticks about ¼ inch wide and 1 inch long, and set aside.

SAUTÉ THE ONION AND GARLIC. Heat the oil in a heavy-bottomed soup pot over medium heat. Add the onion, leek, and ½ teaspoon salt, and sauté until the onion is soft and translucent, about 10 minutes, stirring several times. Add the garlic, and cook for 1 minute more.

ADD MOST OF THE REMAINING INGREDIENTS. Measure the beet-cooking liquid; it should be about 1 cup. If it isn't, add stock or water to make up the difference, and add it to the pot along with the stock, beets, lentils, and dill. Bring the pot to a boil, lower the heat, and simmer, uncovered, for 20 minutes.

SERVE THE SOUP. Take the pot off the heat and add the ume vinegar. Add salt and pepper to taste. If you're using it, serve each bowl of soup with a dollop of sour cream or a swirl of crème fraîche.

About Ume Vinegar

Ume vinegar, a staple in macrobiotic cooking, is a salty, fruity by-product of making umeboshi, Japanese pickled plums. Ume vinegar adds a unique tangy zing to dishes, and we sometimes finish soups and sauces with a splash of ume vinegar instead of adding more salt. Look for it near the vinegars in Asian grocers or near other macrobiotic or traditional Japanese foods in natural-food stores.

Peanut, Yam, and Chipotle Soup [v]

In America it seems we only eat peanuts in candy bars, in peanut-butter sandwiches, or at baseball games. But around the world, peanuts are widely used in savory dishes, perhaps because they're high in protein, which makes them an ideal ingredient in vegetarian cooking. This recipe is an adaptation of various African peanut (or groundnut) soup recipes we've tasted over the years. Most peanut soup recipes seem to call for cayenne (perhaps another African legacy), but we like the smoky heat of the chipotle pepper. This soup would make a delicious supper served with Hoppin' John Fritters (see page 207) and Fried Green Tomatoes (see page 166).

Makes about 7 cups

1 tablespoon vegetable oil

1 medium yellow onion, diced

Salt

1 tablespoon minced, peeled, fresh ginger

4 cloves garlic, minced

1 teaspoon coriander seeds, toasted and ground (see page 52)

1 large yam (about 1 pound [see page 241]), peeled and cubed (about 2½ cups)

4 cups Vegetable Stock (see page 39), or purchased vegetable stock or broth

3 tablespoons natural peanut butter

1 teaspoon Chipotle Chile Purée (see page 225)

1 (14-ounce) can diced tomatoes in purée

Peanuts, toasted (see page 150) and chopped

SAUTÉ THE ONION AND SPICES. Heat the oil in a heavy-bottomed soup pot over medium heat. Add the onion and ½ teaspoon salt, and sauté until the onion is soft and translucent, about 10 minutes, stirring several times. Add the ginger, garlic, and coriander seed, and cook for 1 minute.

ADD THE YAM AND STOCK. Add the yam and stock, and bring the pot to a boil. Reduce the heat to low, and cook, covered, until the yam is very tender, about 10 minutes.

PURÉE SOME OF THE SOUP. Remove 2 cups of the yam and broth from the pot, purée in a blender, and return to the soup pot.

ADD THE REMAINING INGREDIENTS, SIMMER, AND SERVE. Stir in the peanut butter, chile purée, and tomatoes. Bring the pot to a boil, lower the heat, and simmer for 10 minutes. Add salt to taste. Ladle into bowls, sprinkle with chopped peanuts, and serve.

> **TIP**
>
> To reheat, bring the soup just to a simmer in a heavy-bottomed pot over low heat, stirring constantly. (Puréed soups will stick to the bottom of the pan and burn if you don't stir while you heat them up.)

Sesame Vegetable Soup with Miso [v]

This soup is a combination of two soups—Chinese hot and sour and Japanese miso. It starts with *dashi*, a Japanese soup stock made with konbu (seaweed), dried bonito flakes, and water. We omit the bonito for a vegetarian version. The rice wine vinegar is a finishing touch that heightens the flavors. The rich, warm flavors of this soup make it a perfect winter supper. Round out your meal with Soba Salad with Spicy Peanut Sauce and Vegetables (see page 75) on the side.

Makes 8 cups

½ ounce dried shiitake mushrooms

1 (6-inch) piece konbu (kelp [see Tips])

1 tablespoon sesame oil

3 tablespoons raw sesame seeds

1 leek, white and very pale green parts only, cut in half lengthwise, washed, and thinly sliced

2 tablespoons minced, peeled, fresh ginger

2 medium carrots, thinly sliced at a very sharp angle

2 ribs celery, thinly sliced at a very sharp angle

3 tablespoons tamari (see page 240)

3 tablespoons red miso (see page 239)

8 ounces tofu, silken or firm, cut into small cubes

2 scallions, white and green parts, thinly sliced at a very sharp angle

1 teaspoon rice vinegar

MAKE THE DASHI. Put the mushrooms and konbu in a pot with 7 cups water. Heat it over medium-high heat, and just as it is about to boil, remove the konbu. (Konbu gives off a strong smell when it's boiled.) Bring the stock to a full boil, lower the heat, and simmer for 10 minutes.

Remove the mushrooms from the pot, cut off and discard the stems, and thinly slice the caps. Set the sliced mushroom caps aside. Cover the dashi, and keep it warm over low heat.

SAUTÉ THE SESAME SEEDS AND VEGETABLES. Heat the sesame oil in a heavy-bottomed soup pot over medium heat. Add the sesame seeds, and cook, stirring frequently, until fragrant, about 2 minutes. Add the leek and ginger, and sauté for 5 minutes. Add the carrots and celery, and cook for 2 minutes.

ADD THE TAMARI AND THE WARM DASHI and bring the pot to a boil. Lower the heat, and simmer, covered, for 20 minutes.

FINISH THE SOUP, AND SERVE. Stir in the miso, and add the tofu, sliced mushroom caps, and scallions. Simmer for 5 minutes more to fully heat the last ingredients. Take the soup off the heat, and stir in the vinegar. Serve immediately.

TIPS

- Freeze the mushroom stems until you're ready to make a mushroom stock, like our Mushroom Essence (see page 172).

- Konbu (seaweed) is a form of kelp used in Japanese cooking. Dark brown or gray green, it comes dried in folded sheets or strips usually packaged in cellophane.

Smoky Split Pea Soup [v]

This soup was inspired by traditional split pea soup recipes, but we substitute smoked mushrooms for the smoked ham. Unlike the classic soup with meat, however, our version needs only a small amount of smoked mushrooms. Accompany this soup with the Yam and Cheese Sandwich (see page 181) or the Fried Green Tomato Sandwich (see page 166) for a comforting supper or lunch.

Makes about 9 cups

1 tablespoon olive oil

4 ounces domestic or crimini mushrooms, smoked (see page 79) and roughly chopped

1 yellow onion, diced

Salt

4 cloves garlic, chopped

2 medium carrots, cut into ¼-inch dice (about 1 cup)

1 medium potato, cut into ¼-inch dice (about 1 cup)

1 cup dried split peas, rinsed

6 cups Vegetable Stock (see page 39), or purchased vegetable stock or broth

Freshly ground pepper

SAUTÉ THE MUSHROOMS, ONION, AND GARLIC. Heat the oil in a heavy-bottomed soup pot over medium heat. Add the smoked mushrooms, and cook for 1 minute. Add the onion and ½ teaspoon salt, and sauté until the onion is soft and translucent, about 10 minutes, stirring several times. Add the garlic, and cook 1 minute more.

ADD THE REMAINING INGREDIENTS, AND SIMMER. Add the carrots, potato, split peas, and stock. Bring the pot to a boil. Lower the heat, and simmer, covered, until the split peas are soft, about 45 minutes. Add salt and pepper to taste.

TIPS

- If you don't have the time or inclination to smoke mushrooms, you can substitute four ounces of commercially prepared smoked tofu. Cut it into tiny dice, and add it during the last ten minutes of cooking. It's generally available in the refrigerator case at natural-food stores.

- This soup will thicken as it sits, so add water or vegetable stock to get the consistency you want.

Summer Vegetable Soup with Polenta [v]

This is a basic vegetable soup recipe, but the addition of polenta gives it a little more oomph. This recipe also makes a big batch, which is hard not to do when you use a variety of vegetables, but you can eat half and freeze the rest.

You may be tempted to add more polenta, as I did the first time I made this soup. Resist the temptation, or you'll end up with a stew of vegetables floating in a very soft polenta, not a soup. Sprinkle a bit of Romano, Asiago, or Parmesan on top before serving. Turn this into a perfect summer supper with the addition of a crisp salad, like our Caesar Salad (see page 71), and a loaf of crusty bread.

Makes about 12 cups

1 tablespoon olive oil

1 large yellow onion, diced

Salt

5 cloves garlic, chopped

2 teaspoons dried oregano

¼ cup white wine

1 rib celery, diced

1 large carrot, peeled and diced

5 cups Vegetable Stock (see page 39), or purchased vegetable stock or broth

1 small yellow squash, diced (about 1 cup)

1 small zucchini, diced (about 1 cup)

4 cups chopped fresh tomatoes, or 2 (14.5-ounce) cans diced tomatoes in juice

½ cup polenta (or grits), not instant

1 tablespoon balsamic vinegar

6 large basil leaves, chopped

8 sprigs Italian parsley, chopped

A few pinches of pepper

Optional: Freshly grated Parmesan, Asiago, or Romano cheese

START THE SOUP. Heat the oil in a heavy-bottomed soup pot over medium heat. Add the onion and ½ teaspoon salt, and sauté until the onion is soft and translucent, about 10 minutes, stirring several times. Add the garlic and oregano, and cook 1 minute more. Then add the wine, and cook until it has just about evaporated.

ADD THE VEGETABLES AND STOCK. Add the celery, carrot, and stock. Bring to a boil, lower the heat, and simmer, covered, for 10 minutes. Add the squash, zucchini, and the tomatoes and their juice.

ADD THE POLENTA, AND SIMMER THE SOUP. Return the pot to a boil, and sprinkle in the polenta, stirring constantly to avoid lumping. Lower the heat, and simmer, uncovered, for 20 minutes. The polenta will plump up and thicken the soup.

SERVE THE SOUP. Take the pot off the heat, add the balsamic vinegar, basil, parsley, a few pinches of pepper, and salt to taste. Ladle into bowls, and sprinkle each with 1 tablespoon freshly grated cheese if you're using it, or pass the cheese and grater so people can help themselves.

TIP

We chose yellow squash and green zucchini to keep the soup as colorful as possible, but if one or the other of these is not available, feel free to substitute all yellow or green summer squash.

Curried Butternut Squash Soup [v]

This creamy, soothing soup is one of the first things we make when butternut squash hits the markets in mid-September. The curry in this soup gives it a little kick even with the mellowing effect of the coconut milk. I like that, but for less heat and more subtle curry flavor, reduce the curry powder by half. For those, like me, who like to crank up the heat, taste it before serving, and add a pinch of cayenne pepper or a splash of hot sauce.

Like many homemade soups, this is much better several hours after cooking when all the flavors have had time to meld and develop. For a perfect autumn lunch, make this soup the night before, and serve it with our Pear Sandwich with Pecan Parsley Pesto (see page 163).

Makes 9 cups

1 medium butternut squash (about 2½ to 3 pounds)

1 tablespoon vegetable oil

1 large yellow onion, diced

Salt

4 cloves garlic, minced

2 tablespoons minced, peeled, fresh ginger

2 tablespoons curry powder

1 teaspoon cumin seeds, toasted

½ teaspoon coriander seeds, toasted

1 bay leaf

2 (14-ounce) cans coconut milk

1 tablespoon fresh lime juice

Optional: Pinch of cayenne pepper or hot sauce

GET READY. Peel the butternut squash and cut it in half. Remove the seeds, and cut into 1- to 2-inch chunks.

Toasting and Grinding Spices

If you use a certain spice often, go ahead and toast and grind up a small batch, a few tablespoons perhaps. Store it in a small jar with your other spices. And obviously you can choose not to toast and grind the spices for a dish, particularly when you're in a hurry, but the flavors of the dish may be less vibrant as a result.

Many cookbooks and cooking programs don't instruct you to toast whole spices and grind them just before you use them. (I've teased my mother relentlessly about having the same spices that she had around when I was a kid!) But I admit to being a fanatic about this. Lightly toasting and grinding spices just before using them greatly enhances their flavor and aroma by releasing the natural oils which otherwise deteriorate over time. The spices that benefit from toasting are most often seeds and include anise and star anise, cloves, coriander, cumin, fennel, fenugreek, and mustard.

Another way to make sure that you're using the freshest spices is to buy spices and dried herbs in small amounts every few months. Not only are they fresher and cheaper, but the freshness is built in because you buy only what you can use in a few months. Many natural-food stores, co-ops, and grocers that sell bulk foods may sell spices in bulk as well.

TOAST THE SPICES. Put a dry skillet over medium heat. When the pan is hot, add the spice, shaking the pan back and forth to roll the seeds around so they toast evenly and don't burn. Toast until fragrant, 1 or 2 minutes. Remove the spice from the pan, and cool it slightly before you grind it.

GRIND THE SPICES. Thoroughly clean your coffee grinder, and grind the spice until it's the consistency of cornmeal (although uneven bits are fine). When you're done, clean the grinder meticulously. (Grinding spices is a great use for an old coffee grinder or one that you picked up second hand.)

SAUTÉ THE ONIONS AND GARLIC. Heat the oil in a heavy-bottomed soup pot over medium heat. Add the onion and ½ teaspoon salt, and sauté until the onion is soft and translucent, about 10 minutes, stirring several times. Add the garlic and ginger, and cook 2 minutes more.

ADD THE SPICES, SQUASH, AND WATER. Add the curry powder, cumin, and coriander, and sauté for 15 seconds, stirring constantly. Add 4 cups of water, the butternut squash, and bay leaf, and bring to a boil. Lower the heat and cook, covered, at a low boil until the squash is soft, about 20 minutes.

PURÉE THE SOUP. Remove the bay leaf and purée the soup in batches in a blender, being careful to fill the blender jar no more than halfway.

FINISH THE SOUP. Return the puréed soup to the pot, add the coconut milk, and bring just to a boil. Take the soup off the heat, add the lime juice, and salt to taste. Add cayenne or hot sauce if you want, and serve.

Yam Corn Chowder

We have served hundreds of gallons of this soup throughout the years, with little variations here and there. This particular version uses a poblano chile, but you could add a chipotle pepper or chopped red bell peppers. Since we make this year-round, we often use frozen corn kernels, but if you have fresh corn, use that instead. Be creative, but remember that the slightly sweet yams and the cream or milk make this soup rich, so make sure you always have something acidic to balance these two elements. Here we use a vinegar-based hot sauce, but a splash of vinegar will also do.

A beautiful complement to this soup in both flavor and color would be the Red Jewel Salad (see page 67) or the Fried Green Tomato Sandwich (see page 166).

Makes 7 cups

1 tablespoon olive oil

1 yellow onion, diced

Salt

4 cloves garlic, minced

2 ribs celery, diced

2 teaspoons dried oregano

1 teaspoon cumin seeds, toasted and ground (see page 52)

1 large yam (about 1 pound [see page 241]), peeled and cut into ¼- to ½-inch dice (about 2 cups)

1 bay leaf

1 poblano chile, roasted (see page 212) and chopped

1 (10-ounce) package frozen corn (about 2 cups), thawed but not cooked

4 cups Vegetable Stock (see page 39), or purchased vegetable stock

1 cup half-and-half, or milk

1 teaspoon Tabasco sauce

Freshly ground pepper

SAUTÉ THE ONION AND GARLIC. Heat the oil in a heavy-bottomed soup pot over medium heat. Add the onion and ½ teaspoon salt, and sauté until the onion is soft and translucent, about 10 minutes, stirring several times. Add the garlic, and cook for 1 minute more.

ADD MOST OF THE REMAINING INGREDIENTS AND SIMMER. Add the celery, oregano, and cumin, and sauté for 2 minutes. Add the diced yam, bay leaf, chile, corn, and vegetable stock. Bring to a boil, lower the heat, and simmer, covered, for 10 minutes.

PURÉE SOME OF THE SOUP. Remove 2 cups of the soup from the pot, purée it in a blender, and return it to the soup pot.

ADD THE CREAM AND TABASCO SAUCE. Add the half-and-half, and simmer gently for 5 minutes. DO NOT BOIL, or you will curdle the soup. Add the Tabasco sauce, and season with salt and pepper.

> **TIP**
>
> To reheat, bring the soup just to a simmer in a heavy-bottomed pot over low heat, stirring constantly. (Creamed soups will stick to the bottom of the pan and burn if you don't stir while you heat them up.)

.

SALADS

AT CAFE FLORA, SALADS HOLD a prominent place, and our guests expect an intriguing, well-conceived variety. We always have five or six salads on our lunch and dinner menus. Some are mainstays—the garlicky Caesar, the rich and satisfying Warm Spinach Salad with Smoked Mushrooms, and the Asian-influenced Soba Salad dressed in Spicy Peanut Sauce, with steamed vegetables and Pickled Red Cabbage. But each week we create one or two special salads featuring seasonal fruits and vegetables, a new cheese we've discovered, or an interesting vinaigrette someone dreamed up.

We're inspired by the new and heirloom varieties of vegetables and fruits our local growers bring us each season. Full Circle Farm in the Snoqualmie Valley near Carnation, Washington, gets our creative juices flowing with lipstick-shaped French Breakfast radishes and others in a surprising assortment of colors (white, pink, red, and even black); purple torpedo onions; round lemon cucumbers; cherry and pear-shaped baby tomatoes in sunset colors; red, golden, and candy-cane beets; and bouquets of arugula, watercress, and edible flowers (calendula, bachelor button, viola, and nasturtium).

Throughout most of the year, our mix of salad greens comes from Susan Schmoll and Beth Stroh-Stern, whose company, Garden Gatherings, is also located in Carnation. Before they came to us, we had been serving an organic salad mix grown in California—good, but no more exciting than what you'd find in many grocery stores. Now we use their colorful, vibrant mix of lettuces, herbs, and unusual greens, even "weeds," that make eating a salad at Cafe Flora an adventure and an education. Our guests often ask for help identifying this or that—burnet, mizuna, mâche, tatsoi, amaranth, and chickweed nestled in with arugula, baby red and green romaine, red and green oak leaf, and speckled leaf lettuce.

Every fall, Susan and Beth invite the Cafe Flora staff to the Garden Gatherings fields to pick our own pumpkins and hard winter squashes (sweet dumpling, delicata, acorn, butternut, Cinderella, and kabocha). Full Circle Farm invites us for its own Fall Harvest Festival, one of the few times we see with our own eyes where the food we cook comes from. I love to walk through the rows of red kale, parsnips, chard, and squashes, too. Or I wander through the greenhouse with row upon row of rose geranium, lemon verbena, and the last of the local lettuces. Menu ideas race through my head. (Really, the best way to write a seasonal menu would be to go out there once a week and just walk around.)

A great salad starts with seasonal locally grown ingredients. Then, think about different textures. For example, one of our favorite salads for staff meals is substantial and filling with tender garbanzos, halved juicy cherry tomatoes, strips of bell pepper, crunchy julienned carrots, slices of red onion, and toasted sunflower seeds tossed with our Lemon Garlic Vinaigrette and crisp sweet romaine.

For added crunch, toss toasted nuts, croutons, crisp cabbage, or radish in with the greens, or serve a crusty crostini alongside. Walnuts and pecans are a natural paired with apple and pear salads; cashews, slivered or sliced almonds, and pistachios are especially good in salads with Asian, Indian, or Middle Eastern flavors. We always toast the nuts for extra crispness and to release their flavor, adding them just before serving so they don't get soggy.

Another element of a tempting salad is a variety of color. Although you probably wouldn't add cherry tomatoes or pomegranate seeds to a Caesar salad, many predominantly green salads are more appealing when you mix in strips of yellow, red, orange, or purple bell pepper, a mix of cherry tomatoes, beets, or radishes—whatever's in season. Or you could go slightly more exotic with blood oranges, kumquats, or persimmons, or mix a bit of brilliant yellow curry into the vinaigrette.

Persimmon Curry Spinach Salad [v]

This is a beautiful salad—both for the eyes and palate—for the dead of winter. Spinach is generally available year-round, as are dried fruits and nuts, which add flavor and texture. Persimmon season is generally October to February, but if you make this salad at other times of the year, apple slices, mango chunks, or orange segments would make good substitutes.

Serves 6

8 cups loosely packed spinach, stemmed

½ cup mixed dried fruit, such as cranberries, apricots (chopped to raisin size), and golden raisins

¼ to ½ cup Dijon Curry Vinaigrette (see page 87)

½ cup almond slices, toasted (see page 150)

2 scallions, white and green parts, thinly sliced

1 firm Fuyu (not Hachiya) persimmon, peeled and thinly sliced (see "About Persimmons")

TOSS THE SALAD. Put the spinach and dried fruit in a large mixing bowl. Toss with ¼ cup Dijon Curry Vinaigrette, adding more if needed to coat the leaves fully.

SERVE THE SALAD. Divide the dressed spinach equally among 6 chilled salad plates, making sure that each plate gets its share of dried fruit. Sprinkle each salad with the sliced almonds, scallions, and a few slices of the persimmon.

About Persimmons

Hachiya and Fuyu are the two most common types of persimmons found in the United States. Hachiya have a slightly elongated, pointed base, while Fuyu are usually smaller and tomato shaped. Hachiya can be eaten only when they are fully ripe and soft; eating one even slightly underripe is a mouth-puckering experience! Fuyu persimmons, on the other hand, are ripe (and delicious) when they are still firm, as well as when they're very soft.

Figs, Raspberries, and Almonds on Butter Lettuce with Tarragon and Goat Cheese

Make this salad in early fall when figs are in season or in summer during raspberry season. That way paying for at least one of the fruits won't break the bank.

We create this salad to resemble a blossoming flower by taking the heads of lettuce apart to wash them. Then we reassemble the leaves into a small, loose head of lettuce on each plate. Try to find smaller, compact heads of butter lettuce, about seven or eight inches across, because it's easier to form their smaller leaves into a flower.

Serves 4

2 heads butter or Bibb lettuce (about 1 pound)

3 tablespoons fresh tarragon leaves

2 tablespoons white wine vinegar

1 tablespoon finely minced shallot

1 teaspoon Dijon mustard

¼ teaspoon salt

⅛ teaspoon freshly ground pepper

6 tablespoons olive oil

8 fresh figs, quartered

½ pint basket (1 cup) raspberries

1 (4-ounce) log goat cheese, chilled

¼ cup sliced almonds, toasted (see page 150)

SEPARATE THE LETTUCE LEAVES. Gently remove the lettuce core and separate the leaves, being careful to keep them whole. Gently wash and dry them well.

MAKE THE DRESSING. Finely chop 1 tablespoon of the tarragon leaves, reserving some whole leaves for garnish. In a small bowl, combine the chopped tarragon, vinegar, shallot, mustard, salt, and pepper. Whisk in the olive oil until well combined.

DRESS THE LETTUCE. In a large bowl, drizzle all but 1 tablespoon of the vinaigrette over the lettuce leaves. Using your hands, very gently toss the lettuce with dressing until the leaves are well coated.

ARRANGE THE LETTUCE LEAVES on 4 chilled salad plates to resemble a blossoming flower by placing 2 or 3 large leaves on each plate and then adding progressively smaller leaves inside the larger ones.

ADD THE FIGS AND RASPBERRIES. Put the figs in the salad mixing bowl, and drizzle with the reserved 1 tablespoon of tarragon vinaigrette. Toss gently to coat them well. Then tuck the figs among the leaves so they are distributed evenly on each plate. Scatter the raspberries among the leaves.

FINISH THE SALAD. Crumble one-fourth of the goat cheese over each salad, and scatter each with the almonds and remaining tarragon leaves.

TIPS

- If you can only find butter lettuce packaged in those plastic clamshell containers, I would choose another lettuce, or combination of lettuces, that look and taste more alive.

- The fresh tarragon is an important part of this dish, but if you can't find it, you could use one teaspoon dried tarragon in the vinaigrette, and omit the tarragon garnish at the end. Or you could substitute tarragon vinegar for the white wine vinegar.

Strawberry Salad with Walnut Vinaigrette [v]

Try this salad when local strawberries are abundant and you've run out of ideas for how to eat them before they're out of season. (Although the use of strawberries is so economical you can also make this salad when local berries are out of season; just make sure the strawberries are flavorful!) You can use any type of salad greens. The organic spring mixes that are commonly available are fine, but peppery arugula and watercress contrast nicely with the sweetness of the berries.

Serves 6

2 tablespoons champagne wine vinegar or white wine vinegar

½ cup walnut oil

Salt and freshly ground pepper

10 cups loosely packed mixed salad greens, including trimmed watercress and arugula

2 cups strawberries, hulled and quartered

¼ cup sliced almonds, toasted (see page 150)

Optional: 2 ounces crumbled goat cheese

MAKE THE VINAIGRETTE. Whisk together the vinegar and oil, adding salt and pepper to taste.

DRESS THE GREENS. Put the salad greens in a large mixing bowl, and drizzle in one-half the vinaigrette a little at a time, tossing as you go. Taste a leaf, and add more dressing if you want, reserving at least 2 tablespoons for the berries. Divide the salad greens among 6 chilled salad plates.

DRESS THE STRAWBERRIES. Put the strawberries in the bowl used to toss the greens, and drizzle with 2 tablespoons of the vinaigrette. Add salt and pepper to taste, and toss again.

SERVE THE SALAD. Tuck the dressed strawberries among the leaves on each plate to distribute them evenly. Scatter each salad with almonds, and top with goat cheese if you're using it. Serve at once.

Warm Pear Salad with Orange Vinaigrette and Spiced Walnuts

In this salad, we warm ripe pear slices in a fragrant orange vinaigrette. We balance the rich sweetness of the warm pears by tossing them with a hearty mix of salad greens that will hold up without wilting and top it all with spicy nuts and Gorgonzola cheese.

Because we heat the pears briefly in the dressing, we choose pears that are tender and ripe but not mushy. For their lively red skin, look for Red Anjou or Bartlett pears. For the salad greens, we use organic seasonal greens mixed with heartier greens such as curly endive, watercress, chard, escarole, or kale. I like to serve this salad in a deep platter so I can see the pear slices peeking out among the greens (rather than buried in a deep bowl).

Serves 4

2 ripe Anjou or Bartlett pears at room temperature, ripe but not mushy, unpeeled

1 shallot, minced

1 tablespoon grated orange zest

2 tablespoons freshly squeezed orange juice

2 tablespoons white wine vinegar

¼ teaspoon salt

¼ teaspoon freshly ground pepper

4 tablespoons olive oil

8 cups loosely packed, hearty salad greens such as curly endive, watercress, chard, escarole, or kale, or a mix

1 cup Spiced Walnuts (recipe follows)

½ cup crumbled Gorgonzola cheese

SLICE THE PEARS. Halve the pears and remove the cores and stems. Cut the pear halves lengthwise in ¼-inch thick slices, and set aside.

MAKE THE ORANGE VINAIGRETTE. Combine the shallot, orange zest, juice, vinegar, salt, and pepper in a small bowl. Whisk in the olive oil until combined.

WARM THE DRESSING WITH THE PEARS. In a medium saucepan, warm the vinaigrette over medium heat until hot. Add the pear slices, and gently turn the pears until they're completely coated and warm, about 2 minutes.

DRESS THE GREENS. Put the salad greens in a large bowl. Pour the pears and the vinaigrette over the salad greens, add half of the spiced nuts, and toss gently, trying not to break up the pear slices.

SERVE THE GREENS. Pile the salad greens onto a deep platter, making sure pear slices are evenly distributed among the greens. Scatter the top of the salad with the spiced walnuts and the cheese. Serve immediately.

Spiced Walnuts [v]

Spicy, sugar-glazed nuts are good on a lot of salads, and you can use this same recipe for pecans. The spice mix you use does not have to be exact but it definitely has to have cayenne. If you have trouble remembering what goes in the spice mix, use this tip a chef once gave me: "Think of Christmas. Christmas begins with a *c*, so just use all the spices on the rack that begin with a *c*." (I just assume he didn't mean cream of tartar.)

Makes about 1 cup

GET A HEAD START

These spicy walnuts are best made a few days ahead so the flavors can really permeate the nuts.

1 cup walnut halves

1 tablespoon olive oil

¼ teaspoon *each* ground cardamom, cinnamon, cloves, coriander, and cumin

⅛ teaspoon cayenne pepper

½ teaspoon salt

2 tablespoons powdered sugar

GET READY. Preheat the oven to 350 degrees. Grease a baking sheet. Put the walnuts in a mixing bowl. Drizzle with the olive oil, tossing to coat the nuts thoroughly.

MIX THE WALNUTS WITH THE SPICES. Mix the spices and salt, and sprinkle the mixture over the walnuts, tossing again to coat fully. Toss again with the powdered sugar.

ROAST THE WALNUT MIX. Spread the walnut mixture on the greased baking sheet. Bake for 10 to 12 minutes, until crisp and brown, stirring the nuts halfway through the roasting time so they toast evenly. Cool completely before serving.

Fresh Pear, Stilton, and Walnut Salad with Scallion Cream Dressing

Most varieties of pear will work for this salad. Just make sure the pear is perfectly ripe (or allow time for it to ripen). There is nothing yummier than buttery slices of pear with a silky dressing, pungent blue cheese, and crunchy nuts. Although we have given restaurant-style instructions for serving this salad, you might find it a bit fussy. If so, just gently toss the ingredients together in your salad bowl, and dig in.

Serves 4

1 head butter (Bibb) lettuce

1 tablespoon champagne vinegar

3 tablespoons olive oil

3 tablespoons heavy cream

1 scallion, white and pale green parts, thinly sliced

Salt and freshly ground pepper

1 large ripe but firm pear, unpeeled

½ cup crumbled Stilton or other blue cheese

½ cup walnuts, toasted (see page 150)

SEPARATE THE LETTUCE LEAVES. Gently remove the lettuce core and separate the leaves, trying to keep them whole. Gently wash and thoroughly dry them.

MAKE THE DRESSING. Whisk together the vinegar and oil until thoroughly blended. Add the cream and scallion, and season with salt and pepper to taste.

DRESS THE LETTUCE AND ARRANGE THE LEAVES. In a large bowl, use your hands to toss the lettuce leaves gently with the dressing until well coated.

Arrange the lettuce leaves on 4 chilled salad plates to resemble a blossoming flower by placing a large leaf on each plate and then adding progressively smaller leaves inside the larger leaves.

SLICE THE PEAR AND DRESS THE SLICES. Halve the pear and scoop out the stem and core. Slice each pear half lengthwise into about 10 slices.

Put the pear slices in the bowl you used to dress the lettuce, and gently toss to coat with the residual dressing.

FINISH THE SALAD. Tuck the pear slices among the leaves, so they're distributed evenly on each plate and don't weigh down the lettuce. Scatter the Stilton and walnuts over each salad.

Hazelnut-Crusted Goat Cheese Salad with Roasted Pear and Herbed Sherry Vinaigrette

The centerpiece of this salad is a warm, nut-encrusted goat cheese croquette. For a taste of salad heaven, take a bit on your fork along with a bite of roasted pear and perfectly dressed salad greens.

We use sherry vinegar in the dressing for its slightly honeyed and nutty taste. Its sweetness is a delicious alternative to more acidic red or white wine vinegars, and it's more subtle than balsamic. I encourage you to keep a bottle of good sherry vinegar on hand and try it on all types of salads.

Serves 4

TIMING

To make this jewel of a salad, you have to work fast. Dress and plate the greens and roasted pear while the goat cheese warms in the oven; when it's ready, serve immediately.

2 medium, firm yet ripe pears, such as Bosc, unpeeled

1 (4-ounce) log goat cheese, chilled

2 ounces hazelnuts, toasted (see page 150), peeled, and finely chopped (about ½ cup)

8 cups loosely packed hearty salad greens

ROAST THE PEARS. Preheat the oven to 400 degrees. Halve the pears, and remove the stems and cores. Put the pears on a lightly oiled baking sheet, cut sides down. Roast until tender, 15 to 20 minutes. (A thin-bladed knife should easily pierce the pear.) When they're done, remove from the oven to cool. (Leave the oven on for baking the goat cheese.)

SHAPE THE GOAT CHEESE PATTIES. Slice the goat cheese into 4 equal portions. Let the slices sit at room temperature to soften a bit, 5 to 10 minutes. (Very cold goat cheese will just crumble when you try to shape it.) Roll the softened slices into balls.

COAT THE GOAT CHEESE WITH CHOPPED NUTS. Put the chopped hazelnuts into a small bowl. Roll the goat cheese balls in them, one at a time, pressing in the nuts to coat each ball fully. Flatten each ball into a patty, 1½ inches in diameter and 1 inch thick. Chill the goat cheese in the refrigerator until firm, about 10 minutes. (This makes it easier to handle for baking.)

DRESS THE GREENS. Put the salad greens in a large bowl. Drizzle with the vinaigrette, and toss to coat the leaves evenly. Taste a leaf and add more salt or pepper if needed.

ARRANGE THE GREENS AND PEARS. Divide the greens among 4 chilled salad plates, piling the greens high in the center. Cut each cooled pear half into ¼-inch slices, and spread the slices into a fan shape. Lean each cooled pear fan against a pile of dressed greens.

BAKE THE GOAT CHEESE, AND SERVE THE SALAD. Put the chilled goat cheese patties on a lightly greased baking sheet, and bake in the 400 degree oven until very soft to the touch, 5 to 7 minutes. Remove them gently from the pan with a spatula, and place a patty at the base of each pear fan. Serve immediately.

Herbed Sherry Vinaigrette

Makes about 6 tablespoons

1 teaspoon finely minced shallot

1 teaspoon Dijon mustard

1 tablespoon sherry vinegar

2 teaspoons finely chopped fresh thyme

¼ teaspoon salt

⅛ teaspoon freshly ground pepper

3 tablespoons olive oil

Mix all the ingredients except the oil in a small bowl. Drizzle in the olive oil, whisking constantly.

Avocado Grapefruit Salad with Ginger Miso Dressing [v]

This salad was inspired by a trip I made with Janine Doran, our current chef, on a cold and rainy February evening to one of Seattle's oldest Japanese restaurants, Maneki. The salad we had there was crisp and lively, but rich and satisfying with its avocado and miso dressing. Janine changed it around a bit, adding meaty shiitake and bright, tart pomegranate seeds, but the result is still the same—mood-lifting goodness for a dreary winter day. You could also make this salad without the shiitake, and serve it as a refreshing complement to a rich main course.

Serves 4

TIMING

Sauté the shiitake first because they must cool before you put them in the salad. Then make the dressing so it's ready to go when you put the salad together.

In this dish

- Avocado Grapefruit Salad
- Ginger Miso Dressing
- Garlicky Sweet Shiitake Mushrooms

Avocado Grapefruit Salad

1 red or pink grapefruit

1 avocado, ripe but firm

1 (4- to 5-inch) piece (about 4 ounces) daikon (Asian radish), peeled and cut into matchsticks

8 cups loosely packed mixed salad greens

6 tablespoons Ginger Miso Dressing (recipe follows)

Garlicky Sweet Shiitake Mushrooms (recipe follows)

½ cup pomegranate seeds (about ½ pomegranate)

SEGMENT THE GRAPEFRUIT. Using a small serrated knife, peel the grapefruit, removing the outside thick white membrane. Using a seesaw motion, cut the membranes away from each grapefruit segment. Drain the juice (or better yet, drink it). Set the grapefruit segments aside in a small bowl.

CUT THE AVOCADO in half lengthwise and remove the pit. Remove the skin from the avocado and cut each half of avocado lengthwise into ¼-inch slices.

TOSS THE SALAD. Put the daikon, grapefruit sections, and salad greens into a large bowl. Drizzle with ¼ cup of the dressing and toss gently to coat the greens evenly, trying not to break up the grapefruit sections. Add more dressing if you want.

SERVE THE SALAD. Divide the greens among 4 chilled salad plates, piling them on the center of each plate. Top each salad with a quarter of the shiitake mushrooms. Spread the slices of one-fourth of an avocado into a fan shape. Rest each avocado fan against a pile of dressed greens, and drizzle each with ½ tablespoon dressing. Scatter pomegranate seeds over each salad.

TIPS

- Pomegranates are in season in fall through late winter and of course grapefruit are at their best in the winter.

- Daikon is a white radish that looks like a thick carrot and is used primarily in Asian food. When eaten raw, it is a little hotter than small red-skinned radishes. Daikon radishes are usually very large, and so are often sold portioned in 6- to 8-inch lengths. Look for them among the produce in Asian markets and larger grocery stores.

Ginger Miso Dressing [v]

This rich, gingery dressing also makes a great sauce drizzled over grilled tofu, brown rice, and steamed veggies.

Makes about 1 cup

2 tablespoons light miso (Japanese bean paste [see page 239])
¼ cup rice vinegar
2 tablespoons minced, peeled, fresh ginger
1 clove garlic
½ cup vegetable oil

Combine the miso, vinegar, ginger, and garlic in a blender jar. With the blender running, drizzle in the vegetable oil. Add ¼ cup water to thin the mixture, and blend until smooth.

Garlicky Sweet Shiitake Mushrooms [v]

Makes about 1 cup

6 ounces fresh shiitake mushrooms
2 tablespoons vegetable oil
1 tablespoon minced garlic
2 tablespoons dry sherry
2 tablespoons sweet soy sauce (see page 240), or 2 tablespoons soy sauce or tamari mixed with 1 teaspoon brown sugar

PREPARE THE MUSHROOMS. Remove the stems, and slice the caps in ½-inch-wide pieces.

SAUTÉ THE MUSHROOMS. Heat the vegetable oil in a large nonstick pan over medium heat. When it is hot, add the mushrooms and garlic. Cook, stirring and tossing constantly, until the mushrooms are tender and the gills begin to brown, 5 to 8 minutes.

FINISH THE SAUTÉ. Add the sherry to the pan, and cook, stirring constantly, until the sherry evaporates, about 2 minutes. Add the sweet soy sauce, stirring and tossing the mushrooms until they are completely coated. Remove from the heat and cool to room temperature before serving on the salad.

TIP

Freeze the mushroom stems until you're ready to make a mushroom stock, like our Mushroom Essence (see page 172).

Blood Orange, Asian Pear, and Kumquat Salad with Five-Spice Lotus Root Chips [v]

This is a good salad for winter when citrus is cheap and abundant. Asian pear adds contrasting flavor and texture. The lotus-root chips are fun with their interesting shape, but toasted almond slices or walnuts would be good, too.

Asian pears are harvested July through October but are often available, like most pears, through the winter. They do not really change in color or texture from the time they are picked or during storage. Just make sure they're as firm as a crisp apple, with no hint of softness to the touch.

Serves 6

TIMING

Cut the lotus-root chips, fry them, and toss with the spices before you start the salad.

2 blood oranges

2 tablespoons rice vinegar

1½ tablespoons minced ginger

6 tablespoons canola or vegetable oil

Salt and freshly ground pepper

10 cups loosely packed mixed salad greens,

including stemmed watercress and arugula

1 Asian pear, peeled and thinly sliced

6 kumquats, unpeeled and thinly sliced

Five-Spice Lotus Root Chips (recipe follows)

SEGMENT THE ORANGES. Using a small serrated knife, peel the oranges, removing the outside thick white membrane. Using a seesaw motion, cut the membranes away from the orange segments; put the segments in a small bowl with their juice, reserving 2 tablespoons of juice for the dressing.

MAKE THE DRESSING. Whisk together the blood orange juice, rice vinegar, ginger, and oil. Add salt and pepper to taste.

TOSS THE SALAD, AND SERVE IT. Combine the salad greens in a large bowl, and toss with the dressing.

Divide the salad greens among 6 chilled plates. Top the greens with equal amounts of orange segments, Asian pear, and kumquat, and then scatter with lotus-root chips.

Five-Spice Lotus Root Chips [V]

Lotus is a water lily whose roots, leaves, and seeds are used in Asian foods (and so you'll find it at most Asian grocers). Lotus root looks like a salami or a log of liverwurst, and when you slice it crosswise, it has holes that look a little like the spokes of a wheel. Although lotus root can be used in a variety of ways, both raw and cooked, we like to showcase its interesting shape by turning it into crunchy and flavorful chips.

Makes about 40 chips (a bunch)

1 (6-inch) piece lotus root, peeled
1 teaspoon Chinese five-spice powder (see Tips)
2 teaspoons sugar
2 teaspoons salt
½ teaspoon freshly ground pepper
Vegetable oil for frying

PREPARE THE LOTUS ROOT. Slice the lotus root using a very sharp knife or mandoline. Try to get the slices very thin and about the same thickness. Put them in cold water to keep them from discoloring. When you're ready to fry, pat the slices dry with paper towels.

MIX THE SPICES TOGETHER. Combine the five-spice powder, sugar, salt, and pepper in a small bowl and set aside.

DEEP-FRY THE LOTUS-ROOT SLICES. Over high heat, heat oil in a wide heavy pot to a depth of 3 inches. Make sure the pot is at least 4 inches tall to reduce spattering. When the oil is hot (350 to 360 degrees), drop some lotus-root slices into the hot oil, being careful not to crowd the pan. (If you don't have a thermometer, see page 199 for alternative instructions.) Be careful not to add too many at one time or the temperature of the oil will drop.

Cook until golden brown, 2 or 3 minutes total. Drain on paper towels.

About the Fruit

BLOOD ORANGES are sweet and tart with a red blush to their skin and bright red or red-streaked flesh. We love their vivid deep color in this salad, but you can substitute any orange. Look for blood oranges between December and March.

KUMQUATS are tiny, egg-shaped citrus fruit with a sweet, bright orange skin and tart flesh. They're about the size of a cherry and in season from November until March. In this salad, they're sliced thinly, but you can also eat them out of hand. Just pop one in your mouth for a tangy-sweet miniexplosion.

ASIAN PEARS look like large, very round apples and are sometimes called apple-pears or pear-apples, but they are true pears. They're different from more common European varieties, like Barlett, Anjou, or Bosc, in that they remain crisp and juicy after picking and do not soften as they ripen. They're usually eaten raw and unpeeled. The color of Asian pears varies: some are the color of a russet potato; others have an almost translucent, yellow-green skin which gets yellower when ripe.

Harvest times vary depending on the type, but most are harvested from midsummer to midautumn. Asian pears store well under refrigeration, so you'll find them in the produce department well into the winter.

TOSS THE lotus-root chips with spices in a large bowl until evenly coated.

- Five-spice powder is a mixture of ground spices often used in Chinese cooking. It usually includes equal parts of ground cinnamon, clove, fennel, star anise, and Szechuan peppercorns. Look for it in small, cellophane packages or jars at Asian markets and larger grocery stores in the spice section.

- For suggestions about how to save oil for later use, read "Saving Oil," on page 199.

Red Jewel Salad [v]

This festive salad was served as part of a prix fixe menu celebrating the winter solstice. The jewels in this salad are the seeds of a pomegranate, orange segments, and slices of roasted beets. The tart, juicy seeds of pomegranates, in season from September to January, are dazzling against the green of any salad, and a kick for the palate. A simple dressing of good-quality sherry vinegar and extra-virgin olive oil is all that's needed with such colorful and flavorful ingredients.

Serves 4

½ pound beets (about 2 medium), unpeeled, with ½ inch of the beet top left on

1 tablespoon sherry vinegar

4 tablespoons extra-virgin olive oil

Salt and freshly ground pepper

2 oranges

10 cups loosely packed mixed salad greens

½ cup pomegranate seeds (about ½ medium pomegranate)

1 scallion, green and white parts, cut very thinly at a sharp angle, or 12 chives, cut in 1-inch sticks

Optional: 2 ounces goat cheese, chilled, or blue cheese

GET READY. Preheat the oven to 400 degrees. Wash the excess dirt from the beets.

ROAST THE BEETS. Put the beets in a lidded baking dish with ½ inch of water, and cover. Roast until tender, so a sharp knife easily pierces the beets, about 1 hour.

MAKE THE DRESSING. While the beets are cooking, whisk together the sherry vinegar and oil in a small bowl until thoroughly combined. Add salt and pepper to taste.

SEGMENT THE ORANGES. Using a small serrated knife, peel the oranges, removing the outside thick white membrane. Using a seesaw motion, cut the membranes away from the orange segments, and put the segments in a small bowl. (Go ahead—drink the juice! You don't need it for the salad.)

PEEL AND CUT THE BEETS. When the beets are cool enough to handle, rub them with a paper towel or your fingers to slip off the skins. Cut the beets into ½-inch-wide sticks or wedges, and set aside.

DRESS THE GREENS. In a large bowl, toss the greens with 2 tablespoons of the dressing until they are well coated. Add another tablespoon of the dressing if you want. Taste a leaf and add salt to the greens, if needed, and then toss again. Divide the greens among 4 chilled salad plates.

DRESS THE BEETS AND ORANGES. Put the beets and orange segments in the bowl the greens were in, add 1 tablespoon of the dressing, and toss gently to coat. Add salt and pepper to taste.

ARRANGE THE SALAD. Tuck the dressed beets and orange segments among the greens on each plate to distribute them evenly (so they don't weigh down the greens). Scatter each salad with the pomegranate seeds and scallion. Crumble the cheese, if you're using it, over everything, and serve.

Assorted Lettuces with Flower Blossoms and Mixed Cherry Tomatoes with Tapenade Toasts [v]

Between the months of May and November, we are extremely lucky to get fabulous salad greens from two local growers, Susan Schmoll and Beth Stroh-Stern of Garden Gatherings (see page 56). I remember when they first came in to talk to us about giving their salad mix a try. I think we ended up buying their entire crop that year! The best part about their mix of lettuces, bitter greens, herbs, and plain ol' "weeds" is the riot of color and the wide variety of different leaves that end up on each plate. You can find salad mixes in most grocery stores these days (or in a local farmer's market), which you can augment with flowers or greens from your own garden.

Serves 4

TIMING

Make the tapenade and the crostini for the toasts, and the herbed vinaigrette before you put the salad together.

Assorted Lettuces with Flower Blossoms and Mixed Cherry Tomatoes

12 to 15 edible organic flower blossoms like violas (Johnny-jump-ups), nasturtium, bachelor buttons, or pansies
8 cups loosely packed mixed salad greens
½ pint yellow cherry-size pear tomatoes, or mixed yellow, orange, and red cherry tomatoes, halved
Herb Vinaigrette (recipe follows)
Tapenade Toasts (recipe follows)

WASH AND DRY THE FLOWERS. Rinse the blossoms in cool water and dry them by spinning once or twice (but no more) in a salad spinner. Spread out on paper towels to absorb any remaining moisture.

TOSS THE SALAD WITH THE VINAIGRETTE. In a large bowl, toss the salad greens and tomato halves with ¼ cup of the Herb Vinaigrette. Taste a leaf and add more vinaigrette if you want.

SERVE THE SALAD. Divide the dressed salad greens and tomatoes among 4 chilled salad plates. Sprinkle each salad with flower blossoms or petals. Rest 2 Tapenade Toasts on the rim of each plate.

About Edible Flowers

Not all flowers are edible. Among the most common edible flowers are peppery nasturtiums, calendula, chive and dill blossoms, pansies, violets, violas, roses, lavender, chrysanthemums, daisies, bachelor buttons, geraniums, lilacs, borage and marigolds. If you're using flowers from your garden and are uncertain which ones you can eat, consult a reference book or your local agricultural extension agent.

Steer clear of flowers that have been sprayed with pesticides. This usually rules out flowers sold at most florists and garden centers, as well as those found by the side of the road. Using flowers from your garden is safest, but you may be able to buy them at a farmer's market, where you can inquire about the use of pesticides. Look for them, too, at a large grocery store or specialty-food market among the fresh herbs.

When we use edible flower blossoms at Cafe Flora, we often pull the blossoms apart, separating the petals. This makes scattering the flowers evenly over the whole salad a bit easier, and it stretches a limited supply of flowers a little further. Dry washed flowers thoroughly before pulling the blossoms apart or the petals will stick together.

WASH THE FLOWER BLOSSOMS by rinsing them in cool water.

DRY THE FLOWERS in a salad spinner by spinning them once or twice (but no more). Spread out on paper towels to absorb any remaining moisture.

Herb Vinaigrette [v]

This also makes a flavorful dressing for a cold pasta or potato salad. If you grow chervil in your garden, or can find it at a summer farmer's market, try it instead of tarragon.

Makes about ¾ cup

1 tablespoon minced shallot, about 1 small shallot

1 tablespoon chopped fresh tarragon

1 tablespoon chopped fresh chives

1 teaspoon Dijon mustard

3 tablespoons white wine vinegar or tarragon vinegar if you can't find fresh tarragon

½ cup light olive oil or vegetable oil

Salt and freshly ground pepper

Put all the ingredients except the oil, salt, and pepper in a blender or food processor, and blend until well combined. With the motor running, drizzle in the oil. Add salt and pepper to taste.

Tapenade Toasts [v]

Kalamata Tapenade spread on crispy crostini would spruce up any simple salad. These toasts are also a great snack topped with strips of roasted red pepper or a crumbling of goat cheese or feta.

Makes 8 toasts, 2 for each salad

About ½ cup Kalamata Tapenade (see page 227)

8 Crostini (see page 224)

Just before serving the salad, thinly spread the tapenade on each crostini.

Black-Eyed Pea Salad with Grilled Corn, Arugula, and Roasted Red Pepper Vinaigrette [v]

Arugula, corn, basil, and tomatoes are a classic summer salad combination. Adding black-eyed peas, a tangy red pepper vinaigrette, and some crumbled cotija cheese makes it a substantial entrée. (Cotija is a Mexican cheese with a salty, tangy flavor and a dry, crumbly texture; feta would be a good substitute.) Serve this with the Southwestern Yam and Bean Burger (see page 178), and you'd probably have enough for eight as a side salad.

Serves 4

TIMING

If you're using dried black-eyed peas, start them soaking at least 2 hours ahead. (It's also OK to start them the night before.) Roast the red pepper and make the vinaigrette before you start work on the salad.

2 ears corn

½ cup dried black-eyed peas, soaked for 2 hours or up to 8 hours, or 1 (15-ounce) can (about 1¼ cups cooked)

Olive oil for corn

Salt and freshly ground pepper

8 leaves fresh basil

8 cups lightly packed arugula leaves

½ cup Roasted Red Pepper Vinaigrette (recipe follows)

1 cup cherry or grape tomatoes, halved

4 ounces cotija or feta cheese, about ½ cup crumbled

GET READY. Start the coals for grilling the corn. Shuck the corn, being careful to remove all the silk.

COOK THE BLACK-EYED PEAS. If you're using dried peas, drain them, and cover with about an inch of fresh water in a pot. Bring to a boil, lower the heat, and simmer uncovered until tender, 45 minutes to 1 hour. Check the pot during cooking to see if it needs more water. Drain and set aside to cool.

If you're using canned black-eyed peas, rinse them under cold water, and drain well.

GRILL THE CORN. While the black-eyed peas cook, brush each ear with olive oil, and sprinkle with salt and pepper. Put right on the grill and cook, turning several times, until some of the kernels are black. When the corn is cool enough to handle, scrape the kernels from the cob.

CUT THE BASIL IN A CHIFFONADE. Stack the basil leaves on top of each other. Roll them up tightly starting at the stem, and slice thinly across the rolled-up leaves. This will give you long thin strips of basil.

DRESS THE GREENS. In a large mixing bowl, toss the arugula with ¼ cup of the Roasted Red Pepper Vinaigrette, adding more if needed to coat the leaves fully. Add salt to taste. Divide the arugula among 4 chilled salad plates.

DRESS THE REMAINING VEGETABLES. Mix the black-eyed peas, corn, tomatoes, and basil in the bowl the arugula was in. Add the remaining ¼ cup Roasted Red Pepper Vinaigrette, and toss to combine, adding more dressing if you want.

SERVE THE SALAD. Divide the black-eyed pea mixture among the 4 plates, mounding it in the center of the arugula. Sprinkle each salad with crumbled cotija.

TIP

If you don't feel like firing up the grill, this salad is good with fresh raw corn, too. Just make sure it's in season and truly fresh.

Roasted Red Pepper Vinaigrette

This deep red vinaigrette would also be good dribbled over steamed asparagus, our Artichoke Croquettes (see page 121), or Ocean Cakes (see page 117).

Makes about 1 cup

1 small red bell pepper, roasted (see page 212) and roughly chopped

1 clove garlic, roughly chopped

3 tablespoons red wine vinegar

6 tablespoons canola oil

Salt and freshly ground pepper

Combine the red pepper, garlic, and vinegar in a blender. Blend the ingredients and then, with the motor running, drizzle the oil in a steady stream until the mixture is smooth and thick. Add salt and pepper to taste.

Cafe Flora Caesar Salad

These days it seems that restaurants are required by law to offer a Caesar salad on their menu. Drive across the United States, and you'll probably find a Caesar salad as easily as a salad with ranch dressing. For chefs and creative people working at a restaurant known for its fabulous salads of unique, seasonal ingredients, it's a little disheartening to keep a particular salad on the menu year-round, especially one that every other restaurant in the world seems to serve. But we knew we were up to the challenge of creating a distinguished vegetarian Caesar salad—one with all the depth of a traditional Caesar. Sure enough, this is one that our guests constantly request. I've heard that people often make just one recipe from a cookbook they've purchased, and this may be the one for you. (But please, try some of the others, too!)

For a less traditional but equally delicious Caesar, garnish the finished salad with ½ cup crumbled Gorgonzola cheese instead of Parmesan.

Serves 4 as a main course, 8 as a side salad

TIMING

Make the croutons first. While they're baking, fry the capers, and then blend up the Caesar Dressing.

In this dish

- **Caesar Salad**
- **Caesar Dressing**
- **Herbed Croutons**
- **Fried Capers**

Caesar Salad

8 cups loosely packed, coarsely cut romaine

½ to ¾ cup Caesar Dressing (recipe follows)

2 cups Herbed Croutons (recipe follows)

¼ cup Fried Capers for garnish (recipe follows)

¼ cup grated Parmesan cheese for garnish

Toss the romaine in a large bowl with ¼ cup of the Caesar Dressing, adding more dressing if needed to coat the leaves fully. Toss the dressed greens with the Herbed Croutons. Divide the salad among 6 chilled plates, sprinkling each salad with the Fried Capers and Parmesan and serve.

Caesar Dressing

Our Caesar dressing is truly addictive, so we specify a quantity that will dress salads for several meals. It also makes an excellent sandwich spread and dip for vegetable crudité. Using fresh ingredients is key: squeeze lemons for the juice, and peel fresh cloves of garlic and chop them just before you add them. Use a light olive oil so each flavor shines. We substitute arame, a kind of dried seaweed, for the anchovies.

Makes 3 cups

1 heaping tablespoon arame (seaweed [see page 238])

1 egg (see below)

6 tablespoons freshly squeezed lemon juice

3 tablespoons chopped garlic

1 teaspoon freshly ground pepper

About Undercooked Eggs

You may have heard or seen warnings about the possibility of salmonella infection from eating raw or eggs cooked less than seven minutes (as is the case in this Caesar dressing). The Centers for Disease Control and Prevention (CDC) now estimate that one egg in 20,000 may be contaminated with *Salmonella enteritidis*, a harmful bacterium. Although the number of eggs affected is quite small, there have been a number of cases of foodborne illness related to infected eggs.

A solution for this salad is to use the eggs we use in the restaurant, pasteurized eggs. These have been heated rapidly and held at a minimum required temperature for a specified time to protect against the threat of a salmonella infection. Pasteurization destroys salmonella, but it doesn't cook the eggs or affect their color, flavor, or nutritional value. You may be able to find pasteurized eggs in the refrigerated section of a large supermarket as pasteurized liquid eggs; in some parts of the country, you maybe even find them still in their shells sold among the other eggs.

If you can't find pasteurized eggs in this form, look for "real egg product" in the dairy case. (At Trader Joe's, for example, these are marketed as ReddiEgg.) These are often primarily egg whites developed for use by people who must watch their cholesterol intake. Read the label, but you'll often find that they've been pasteurized for safety and can reliably be used in recipes that call for uncooked eggs, like our Caesar Salad Dressing.

1½ teaspoons salt
½ cup grated Parmesan cheese
1 tablespoon Fried Capers (recipe follows)
1½ cups olive oil

GET READY. Put a pot of water on to boil the egg. Prepare a small bowl of ice water to cool the egg after it is cooked.

PREPARE THE ARAME. Coarsely grind the arame in a spice or coffee grinder. (Hold your breath when you remove the lid because grinding arame creates dust that can make you sneeze or cough.) Put the arame in a small bowl, cover with 2 tablespoons warm water, and soak for 10 minutes.

COOK THE EGG. When the water boils, gently add the egg, and cook for 45 seconds to 1 minute. Remove the egg, and plunge it immediately into the ice water.

MAKE THE DRESSING. When the egg is cold, scoop the egg out of the shell—it will be runny. Put the egg and all the remaining ingredients (including any arame water that's left), except the olive oil, in a blender or food processor.

Turn on the machine, and when the egg mixture is thoroughly blended, drizzle in the olive oil as the machine runs. If the mixture is too thick, add cold water, a few drops at a time, until the mixture moves freely again. Store in a sealed container in the refrigerator for up to a week.

Herbed Croutons [V]

Croutons from a box are truly a waste of money. They have a strange flavor and a curiously long shelf life. You may as well do without. Luckily, making croutons is easy, and because stale bread makes the best croutons, it will make you feel good to use bread you might otherwise have thrown away. So whenever you have ends of a baguette or another crusty loaf that are getting stale, wrap them well in plastic and freeze until you have time to make croutons. You only have to thaw the bread until it's soft enough to cut, and then follow along with the recipe.

Makes 4 cups

4 cups bread from a rustic loaf or baguette, cut in ½-inch cubes
2 teaspoons assorted dried herbs (for example, basil, oregano, thyme, rosemary)
2 cloves garlic, minced
3 tablespoons olive oil
½ teaspoon salt

GET READY. Preheat the oven to 350 degrees.

TOSS ALL OF THE INGREDIENTS. In a large bowl, toss the bread cubes with the dried herbs and garlic until they're mixed well. Then drizzle the olive oil over the cubes of bread, tossing all the while, until the bread cubes are fully coated. Sprinkle on the salt, and toss once more.

TOAST THE BREAD CUBES. Spread the cubes on a baking sheet in a single layer, and bake for 20 minutes, stirring them halfway through the baking time. Cool completely before using in the salad or storing. Croutons will stay fresh for a week in a sealed container or plastic bag.

Fried Capers [V]

Makes about ½ cup

1 (3.5-ounce) jar capers (about ½ cup)
1 cup vegetable oil

RINSE THE CAPERS. Put the capers in a mesh strainer and rinse under running water. Shake the strainer to remove any excess water and then lay the capers on paper towels. Blot the capers with additional paper towels until they are very dry.

FRY THE CAPERS. Heat the oil in a deep, 1-quart saucepan to 375 degrees. (If you don't have a thermometer, see page 199 for alternative instructions.)

Put in half of the capers. They will pop open like blossoms, and they will turn a dark greenish brown. (Don't let them get brown.) This will happen quickly, so be ready to remove them with a strainer or slotted spoon.

Drain the fried capers on paper towels. Repeat this for the remaining capers. Use immediately, or cool, cover lightly, and store in a cool, dry place.

TIP

For suggestions about how to save oil for later use, read "Saving Oil," on page 199.

Salad of Grilled Portobello Carpaccio with Arugula

Although the dish named *carpaccio*, developed at Harry's Bar in Venice, consists of thinly shaved raw beef, today it can mean virtually anything sliced paper thin. Here we grill meaty portobello mushroom caps, slice them thinly, add some traditional carpaccio accompaniments, and then put them all together as a salad. If you make this as a supper salad, the Summer Vegetable Soup with Polenta (see page 50) and a good loaf of bread would make a satisfying combination.

Serves 4 as a side salad, or 2 as a main course

In this dish

- **Grilled Portobello Carpaccio with Arugula**
- **Dijon Caper Sauce**

Grilled Portobello Carpaccio with Arugula

2 tablespoons balsamic vinegar
¼ cup olive oil
1 tablespoon minced garlic
2 portobello mushrooms (about 1 pound)
Salt and freshly ground pepper
1 teaspoon freshly squeezed lemon juice
6 cups arugula, tough stems removed
Dijon Caper Sauce (recipe follows)
½-pound block Parmigiano-Reggiano cheese or other good Parmesan cheese

MIX THE MARINADE. In a small bowl whisk together the vinegar, 2 tablespoons of the olive oil, and the garlic.

MARINATE THE MUSHROOMS. Remove the stems from the mushrooms. Brush the mushroom caps generously on both sides with the oil and vinegar mixture, sprinkle with salt and pepper, and marinate for 15 minutes.

GRILL THE MUSHROOMS. When the grill is hot, put the mushroom caps on the grill, and cook for 5 to 7 minutes per side. Remove from the grill, and when they are cool enough to handle, cut diagonally in very thin slices, keeping the slices together in the shape of the mushroom cap. Set aside.

DRESS THE GREENS. In a large bowl, whisk together the remaining 2 tablespoons of olive oil, the lemon juice, and a pinch of salt. Toss this dressing with the arugula until well coated.

PUT THE SALAD TOGETHER. Mound the arugula in the center of 4 chilled plates. Slightly fan the slices of half of a mushroom cap, and place atop the dressed arugula. Drizzle with one-fourth of the Dijon Caper Sauce. Repeat for the remaining 3 salads.

SHAVE THE PARMESAN CHEESE. Using a vegetable peeler or cheese plane, shave about 20 to 25 paper-thin slices from the block of cheese. Scatter each salad with equal amounts of cheese. Grind fresh black pepper over all, and serve.

TIPS

- If you don't have access to a grill or the time to set it up, you can broil the portobellos for this salad in your oven (although they're not quite as good). Turn your broiler on, and set the oven rack in the middle position. Brush both sides of each portobello cap with olive oil, and broil until tender, about 5 minutes per side.

- Freeze the mushroom stems until you're ready to make a mushroom stock, like our Mushroom Essence (see page 172).

Dijon Caper Sauce [v]

Makes about 3 tablespoons

1 tablespoon capers, rinsed, drained, and finely chopped
1 garlic clove, minced
2 teaspoons Dijon mustard
1 teaspoon freshly squeezed lemon juice
1 tablespoon olive oil

Combine all the ingredients but the olive oil in a small bowl. Dribble in the olive oil, whisking constantly, until the mixture is thoroughly blended.

Soba Salad with Spicy Peanut Sauce and Vegetables [v]

Rather than tossing all the elements of the Soba Salad together, at Cafe Flora we present it as a composed plate—that is, an arrangement on each plate of peanut-sauced noodles, Pickled Red Cabbage, and blanched vegetables.

One of the components of the plate is a marinated seaweed salad (sometimes called Ocean Salad), which you can buy at larger Asian grocers, fish markets, and some food co-ops and natural-food stores. Although you don't have to include this on your plate—perhaps you live in a place where it's unavailable—it is a colorful, nutritious, and flavorful complement to the noodles and simply cooked vegetables.

To make this a completely filling meal, serve it with Sesame Vegetable Soup with Miso (see page 49).

GET A HEAD START

Make the Pickled Red Cabbage several hours ahead (or even the day before) to give the cabbage time to pickle. While you're at it, make the Spicy Peanut Sauce then, too (although you can wait to make it while the noodles cook).

Serves 4 for dinner

Soba Salad

Serves 4 as a main course, 6 as a side salad

8 ounces dried soba noodles (see About the Ingredients)

1 teaspoon sesame oil

½ to 1 cup Spicy Peanut Sauce (recipe follows)

COOK THE SOBA NOODLES. Bring 3 quarts of water to a boil in a large pot, and cook the soba noodles until al dente, 8 to 10 minutes. Drain, and rinse under cold, running water to cool them. Toss with the sesame oil to keep them from sticking to each other, and to make it easier for the peanut sauce to coat the noodles. Set aside.

DRESS THE NOODLES. If the Spicy Peanut Sauce has been refrigerated for a while, it may be too thick to coat the noodles easily. If so, warm it in its container under hot running water, and then toss ½ cup of the sauce with the noodles. Add more to taste.

Spicy Peanut Sauce [v]

This is good tossed with any kind of noodle or with hot steamed vegetables—potatoes, blanched green beans, and carrots—served over brown rice. Or drizzle it over hot spinach and fried tofu, a vegetarian version of the Thai dish, Bathing Rama. This keeps a week in your refrigerator. If it's too thick to pour, warm the container in hot water to get the sauce moving.

Makes about 1½ cups

1 tablespoon chopped garlic (about 3 cloves)

1 tablespoon sugar

2 tablespoons sesame oil

1 tablespoon peeled chopped ginger

½ teaspoon red pepper flakes

¼ cup tamari (see page 240)

2 tablespoons rice vinegar

½ cup peanut butter

¼ cup sesame tahini

Put all the ingredients in a blender or food processor, and purée thoroughly. If it's thicker than you want, add water, 1 tablespoon at a time, until you get a pourable consistency.

Pickled Red Cabbage [v]

Make this several hours ahead—or even a day or two before—to fully pickle the cabbage. This salad keeps for three days if refrigerated. You can also strain the marinade and use it for the next time you pickle cabbage.

Makes about 3 cups

½ medium red cabbage, core removed and very thinly sliced (about 6 cups)

½ cup raspberry vinegar

½ cup mirin (seasoned rice wine [see page 239])

½ cup rice vinegar

Optional: ½ teaspoon red pepper flakes

1 tablespoon kosher salt

MIX THE PICKLE. Put the sliced cabbage in a wide shallow bowl (or a deep narrow container) with all the remaining ingredients, and mix well. (You want as much cabbage as possible to be submerged in the marinade.) Cover the bowl tightly, and refrigerate for several hours or overnight.

SERVE THE PICKLE. Take it out of the marinade with tongs or drain it in a colander over a bowl (so you can save the dressing).

Put the Salad Together

4 cups broccoli or cauliflower florets, or a mix of both

¼ cup chopped pistachios, toasted (see page 150) and chopped

2 tablespoons black sesame seeds (see About the Ingredients), or white or brown sesame seeds

Pickled Red Cabbage (recipe above)

Optional: 4 ounces commercial marinated seaweed salad (if available)

Optional garnish: Pickled ginger (see About the Ingredients)

BLANCH THE VEGETABLES. Put a handful of ice cubes in a large bowl of water. Bring 3 quarts of water in a pot to a boil. Add the vegetables, and cook for 2 minutes. Drain in a sieve, and then plunge them into the ice water to stop the cooking. When they're cool, drain, and set aside.

SERVE THE SALAD

- **Family style.** Pile the dressed noodles in the center of a large platter, and sprinkle with the pistachios and sesame seeds. Around the perimeter of the plate, alternate mounds of drained Pickled Red Cabbage, blanched broccoli and cauliflower, marinated seaweed salad (if you're using it), and pickled ginger (if you're using it).

- **Individual plates.** Put one serving of the dressed noodles off center on a chilled salad plate, and sprinkle with some of the pistachios and sesame seeds. Next to the noodles, nestle a small pile of drained Pickled Red Cabbage, and then one pile each of broccoli and cauliflower, marinated seaweed salad (if you're using it), and pickled ginger (if you're using it). Repeat for the other plates.

About the Ingredients

You'll find many of the ingredients for this dish at an Asian grocer or large specialty-food store.

SOBA are Japanese noodles made from buckwheat and wheat flour that look a bit like whole wheat spaghetti. In fact, if you can't get soba, the salad would be good with whole wheat spaghetti.

BLACK SESAME SEEDS can be used for contrast on the pale noodles. (White or brown sesame seeds will taste just the same.)

PICKLED GINGER is the pickle that is usually served with sushi; it comes in two colors—pink and white—and a shredded version.

Warm Spinach Salad with Smoked Mushrooms and Roasted Shallot Dijon Vinaigrette [v]

This is our take on the classic wilted spinach salad with one of our favorite ingredients, smoked mushrooms, used here as the obvious substitute for bacon. This would make a hearty autumn dinner with the Dutch Potato Soup (see page 42) and a loaf of good bread.

Serves 6 as a side salad, and 4 as a main course

GET A HEAD START

Smoking mushrooms can take time, so consider making them a day or so ahead. (They'll keep just fine for a few days in your fridge. Just make sure to store them in a tightly sealed container so everything in your fridge doesn't smell smoky.)

TIMING

Start with the dressing, which includes roasting the garlic and shallots for about 30 minutes. (You can do this while the mushrooms are smoking if you don't smoke them in advance.) Have the rest of your meal ready to go before you start to sauté the mushrooms and leeks so you can serve the salad immediately after you add the hot dressing.

½ cup raw green pumpkin seeds, hulled

Salt

1 medium leek, white and pale green part only

1 teaspoon olive oil

½ pound shiitake and crimini mushrooms, stems removed, smoked (see "Smoking Foods") and sliced

¾ cup Roasted Shallot and Dijon Vinaigrette (recipe follows on page 80)

12 cups loosely packed spinach leaves

½ pint cherry tomatoes, halved

TOAST THE PUMPKIN SEEDS by tossing them in a dry sauté pan over high heat until they start to pop. Add salt to taste, and set aside.

WASH AND SLICE THE LEEK. Cut the leek in half lengthwise, and wash under running water, separating the layers and letting the water run through them to remove the dirt. Cut in ¼-inch slices.

COOK THE MUSHROOMS AND LEEKS. Heat the olive oil over high heat, and when it's very hot, carefully add the smoked mushrooms. Cook for about 3 minutes, stirring constantly.

Lower the heat, add the sliced leek, and cook until the leek is tender, about 5 more minutes.

Add the Roasted Shallot and Dijon Vinaigrette to the pan, bring just to a boil, and remove from the heat.

DRESS AND SERVE THE SALAD. Put the spinach leaves in a big bowl with plenty of room for tossing them. Pour the hot vinaigrette mixture over the spinach, and toss quickly. Divide the dressed spinach among 4 or 6 plates.

Toss the cherry tomato halves in the big bowl with any residue of dressing left in the bowl. Add a teaspoon more dressing if needed to coat the tomatoes.

Top each plate with the tomatoes and toasted pumpkin seeds, and serve immediately.

TIP

If you find toasted pumpkin seeds, use those and skip the toasting instructions.

Smoking Foods

We've smoked a wide variety of foods at Cafe Flora over the years. Although you can smoke just about anything, we most often smoke mushrooms, tofu, seitan, tempeh, tomatoes, garlic, onions, and peppers. Smoked mushrooms deepen the flavor of sautés, soups, and stews. Smoking jalapeño chiles, onions, and garlic adds a new dimension to their flavor, and in the case of the jalapeño, smoking seems to mellow the heat. A smoked jalapeño is especially good added to sour cream or crème fraîche, with salt and a little lime juice to balance the smokiness.

Since it's a hassle to set up a smoker to do just a few items, the next time you smoke something, smoke a dozen jalapeños, a few onions cut in wedges, and some peeled garlic cloves. Put a couple of jalapeño chiles and a couple of cloves of garlic in a plastic freezer baggie, throwing in a chopped up wedge or two of onion, and then put the bag in the freezer. Later, when you want to add some smokiness to a soup, sauce, or sauté, pull out a little "flavor packet" to cook with the other ingredients. You can keep anything you've smoked tightly wrapped in the freezer for a month.

Smoked Food

I recommend the mild smokiness you get with alder and apple wood chips; hickory produces a stronger flavor that tends to overpower most vegetables. Look for wood chips near the charcoal in a larger grocery store.

If you have a grill or a smoker, naturally you'll use that, following the manufacturer's instructions for soaking the wood, firing up the smoker, and smoking the food. But if you don't own a smoker, try our invention below. It's cheap and it works!

- Smoke mushrooms and tofu for 25 to 30 minutes. When they're smoked enough, tofu will have a brownish tinge to it, and the mushrooms will start to shrivel and have a brownish cast.

- Smoke tomatoes whole until the skin of the tomatoes begins to shrivel and has a brownish cast, about 25 minutes. When you remove the smoked tomatoes from the smoker, make sure to save any juices they release. They will add a depth of flavor to any sauce you put the smoked tomatoes in.

- Cut big bell peppers in half for smoking, but smoke smaller chiles, such as jalapeños, whole. Smoke them until the skin begins to shrivel and has a brownish cast, 18 to 20 minutes.

- When the vegetables are smoked to your liking, cool the smoked food in your refrigerator.

Make Your Own Smoker

Caution: For safety reasons, only do this in a kitchen ventilated with an exhaust fan and windows or a door open to the outside.

USE A PAN YOU DON'T MIND GETTING KIND OF BEAT UP. The smoldering wood chips ruin both the inside and outside of this pan; however, you can use this pan again and again for smoking. I find buying a cheap pan at a thrift or secondhand store. Choose a wide pan with a tight-fitting lid that will seal in as much smoke as possible. It must be deep enough to suspend the food in a perforated, heatproof container above the smoldering chips. I've used heavy-duty aluminum foil or foil baking pans that I've punched many holes in, or a metal strainer. One of those deep pots that include a steamer basket insert would be ideal.

SOAK THE CHIPS. Soak a cup of wood chips in a couple of cups of water for 20 minutes.

OPEN ALL THE WINDOWS, turn on the exhaust fan, turn off your smoke alarm, and warn your housemates (maybe even your neighbors) that you're going to smoke up the house for a bit.

FIRE UP THE WOOD CHIPS. Drain the water from the soaked wood chips, put them in the bottom of the pan, and cover it. (If the lid doesn't fit snugly, crimp aluminum foil over the top of the pan before you put the lid on.) Turn the heat to high. The chips will begin to smolder and smoke after 6 to 8 minutes.

SMOKE THE FOOD. When the chips are smoking steadily, put the items you want to smoke in the perforated container, and replace the lid. Lower the heat on the stove to medium so the chips continue to smolder and create smoke.

COOL THE SMOKER AND FOOD. Keeping the pan tightly covered, remove it from the heat. Take your "smoker" outside, or put it on the ledge of an open window. When the smoker has cooled, remove the lid—hold your breath!—and take out the smoked food.

Roasted Shallot and Dijon Vinaigrette [v]

This dressing would make a good French-inspired potato salad. Boil small red potatoes in their jackets, halve them, throw in some thinly sliced scallion, and toss them in this vinaigrette.

Makes about 1¾ cups

1 shallot, peeled

6 cloves garlic

1¼ cups olive oil

2 tablespoons brown sugar

3 tablespoons Dijon mustard

6 black peppercorns

3 tablespoons red wine vinegar

1 teaspoon salt

ROAST THE GARLIC AND SHALLOT. Preheat the oven to 375 degrees. Cut the shallot in half so it is about the same size as a garlic clove. Toss the garlic and shallot with 1 tablespoon of the olive oil, and put in a very small baking dish and cover with foil. Roast until soft, about 20 minutes. Remove the foil, stir, and roast until the shallot and garlic start to brown, another 5 to 10 minutes.

MAKE THE VINAIGRETTE. Combine everything but the oil in a blender or food processor. With the motor running, gradually add the remaining oil until the vinaigrette is smooth and thick.

Spring Pea Salad with Buttermilk, Goat Cheese, and Dill Dressing

This salad capitalizes on some of the first, locally grown produce we get in spring, peas and radishes. Snow peas and sugar snap peas are wonderful raw, but the shelled peas will need to be blanched and cooled first before being used in the salad. Freshly picked radishes are surprisingly sweet, so look for them at your local farmer's market.

Serves 4 to 6

½ cup freshly shelled English or shell peas (about ½ pound in the shell)

8 cups loosely packed mixed salad greens

Buttermilk, Goat Cheese, and Dill Dressing (recipe follows)

4 ounces snow peas, strings removed and thinly sliced (about 1 cup)

4 ounces sugar snap peas, thinly sliced (about 1 cup)

1 cup cherry tomatoes, cut in half

1 cup thinly sliced radishes (6 or 8 radishes)

Salt and freshly ground pepper

2 scallions for garnish, white and green parts, thinly sliced at a sharp angle

GET READY. Fill a medium saucepan with water, add 1 teaspoon salt, and bring to a boil. Fill a medium bowl with water and ice cubes.

BLANCH THE ENGLISH (OR SHELL) PEAS. Drop the peas in the boiling water, and cook until tender but crisp, about 2 minutes. Drain, as for pasta, into a colander or sieve, and then plunge into the ice water. When the peas are cool, drain well.

DRESS THE GREENS. Put the salad greens in a large bowl, and toss with ¼ cup of the dressing until all the leaves are coated. Add more dressing if you want. Divide the dressed greens among 6 chilled salad plates.

DRESS THE REMAINING INGREDIENTS (except the scallions). Put all three kinds of peas along with the tomatoes and radishes in the bowl you dressed the greens in. Toss with additional dressing to coat. Sample some of the pea mixture, and add salt and pepper to taste.

SERVE THE SALAD. Divide the pea mixture equally among the 6 salad plates, piling it on top of the greens. Sprinkle each plate with scallions.

> **TIP**
>
> If you can't find English (or shell) peas, just use a larger amount of snow or sugar snap peas.

Buttermilk, Goat Cheese, and Dill Dressing

This dressing has a thick consistency—ideally, that of mayonnaise—especially once refrigerated. That's the way it should be. Resist the temptation to thin it out too much; you want a lot of flavor to coat each leaf of lettuce. This dressing also makes a great sauce to serve with our Roasted Beets (see page 10) or as a dip with raw snow peas and sugar snaps.

Makes ¾ cup

1 (4-ounce) log goat cheese, at room temperature

¼ cup buttermilk

1 tablespoon minced onion or shallot

2 tablespoons freshly squeezed lemon juice

1 teaspoon grated lemon zest

3 tablespoons finely chopped fresh dill

Salt and freshly ground pepper

Combine all the ingredients, except the salt and pepper, together in a small bowl. Add salt and pepper to taste.

Waitin' for Spring Cabbage Salad

In early spring, we can see daffodils and tulips trying to come up, but the weather is still cold, wet, and gray. In the kitchen, we're also running out of salad ideas; we've used beets, pears, and apples in every way imaginable. So this was inspired by our desire for a fresh, crunchy, and light salad while we wait for spring to start and the bounty of produce it brings.

At the restaurant, we toss it to order, piled on a few lightly dressed butter lettuce leaves, and garnished with orange segments. However, you can forget the butter lettuce and the oranges if you wish. Without them this recipe makes a tasty slaw that can be made ahead of time, taken on an early spring picnic, or served as a side dish with many of our sandwiches.

Serves 6

½ large white cabbage, core removed and very thinly sliced (about 6 cups)

1 small fennel, core removed and very thinly sliced

1 red or yellow bell pepper, seeds removed, thinly sliced

1 cup snow pea pods, very thinly sliced at a sharp angle

½ small red onion, very thinly sliced

3 tablespoons capers, rinsed and drained

Yogurt Thyme Dressing (recipe follows)

3 oranges

1 small head butter lettuce (Bibb), leaves separated

DRESS THE VEGETABLES. Combine the cabbage, thinly sliced fennel, bell pepper, pea pods, onion, and capers in a large bowl. Reserving 2 tablespoons of the dressing for the lettuce, pour all the remaining dressing over the vegetables, and toss until they're completely coated.

SEGMENT THE ORANGES. Using a small serrated knife, peel the oranges, removing the outside thick white membrane. Using a seesaw motion, cut the membranes away from the orange segments, and set the segments aside in a small bowl. (Go ahead. Drink it up! It's not used in the recipe.)

DRESS THE LETTUCE. Put the butter lettuce leaves in another bowl, and drizzle with the reserved 2 tablespoons dressing. Very gently toss the lettuce leaves to moisten them.

SERVE THE SALAD. On each of 6 chilled salad plates, place 3 or 4 butter lettuce leaves in a cup shape. Fill the cup with the cabbage mixture, and scatter with orange segments.

Yogurt Thyme Dressing

Our inspiration for this dressing was—dare I say it?—ranch dressing! But we gussied it up a bit, and the fresh thyme really makes a difference.

Makes 1 cup

½ cup plain yogurt

¼ cup mayonnaise

1 tablespoon freshly squeezed lemon juice

1 tablespoon rice vinegar

1 tablespoon fresh thyme, chopped

1 tablespoon flat-leaf parsley, chopped

Salt and freshly ground pepper

Whisk all the ingredients until smooth. Add salt and pepper to taste.

Red Jewel Salad

Wild Mushroom Curry

Oaxaca Tacos with Black Bean Stew, and Tangy Swiss Chard

Curried Grain Salad [v]

We serve a version of this flavorful grain salad made with bulgur wheat alongside our Falafel Sandwich (see page 168), but I love this salad made with a combination of spelt and wheat berries along with quinoa. All are whole grains and high in nutrients.

Besides being good for you, these grains are nutty, chewy, and satisfying when dressed with our aromatic curry dressing and tossed with a variety of chewy dried fruits, crunchy toasted nuts, and thinly sliced scallions. Use a colorful combination of dried fruits, or whatever you have on hand. Raw pistachios can sometimes be hard to come by (check the bulk section at your local co-op or natural-food store), but slivered raw almonds or cashews taste good, too.

Makes about 5 cups

GET A HEAD START

This salad is especially good made ahead. It really tastes better the next day, when the curry dressing has had a chance to soak into the grains. Make the dressing and toast the nuts while the grains cook.

½ cup quinoa

1 cup spelt berries or wheat berries, soaked at least 8 hours and drained (see "About the Whole Grains")

¾ cup Dijon Curry Vinaigrette (see page 87)

¾ cup dried fruit (cranberries, cherries, apricots, currants, and golden raisins)

¾ cup raw pistachio nuts, cashews, or slivered almonds, toasted (see page 150) and roughly chopped

4 scallions, white and green parts, thinly sliced

Salt and freshly ground pepper

PREPARE THE QUINOA. Thoroughly rinse quinoa in a mesh strainer under running water until the water runs clear. This will remove the bitter powdery residue that coats each grain.

COOK THE QUINOA. In a medium saucepan, bring 1 cup of water to a boil. Add the rinsed quinoa, lower the heat to a simmer, and cook, covered, until all the water is absorbed, about 15 minutes. Remove the pan from the heat, leaving the lid on, and let the quinoa steam for 5 more minutes. Then fluff the grains with a fork.

COOK THE SOAKED SPELT OR WHEAT BERRIES. Put the grain in a medium saucepan with enough water to cover. Bring to a boil, lower the heat to a simmer, and cook, covered, until tender, 15 to 20 minutes.

MIX THE SALAD. Combine both grains in a bowl, and cool completely. Pour the dressing over all, and toss thoroughly. Add the dried fruit, nuts, and scallions, and mix well. Add salt and pepper to taste. If you can, store tightly covered in the refrigerator until you serve it. The flavors improve with time. Bring it to room temperature before serving.

About the Whole Grains

If you can't get any spelt or wheat berries, use 1½ cups quinoa instead. People will still beg you for the recipe.

QUINOA, a staple of the Incas (and a complete protein equivalent to milk), is the most widely available of all of these grains. (Technically it's not a grain, but the seed of a distant relative of spinach.) Look for it in boxes at your grocery store in the natural-food section or in the bulk-food section of a health-food store.

SPELT BERRIES AND WHEAT BERRIES have been a staple for millennia around the Mediterranean, perhaps as early as 6000 B.C. Look for them in natural-food stores with large bulk-food sections. Be sure you pick up spelt berries, not spelt flour.

TO COOK SPELT OR WHEAT BERRIES WITHOUT SOAKING: bring 3 cups of water to a boil in a medium saucepan, and add 1 cup of the grains. Cover the pan, and lower the heat to simmer. Cook the grains until tender, 50 to 60 minutes, and drain well.

Israeli Couscous Salad with Roasted Tofu, Yams, and Chermoula [v]

Inspired by a hot salad on our lunch menu, we created this to serve at room temperature for a light supper buffet. The addition of protein in the form of roasted tofu transforms this salad into hearty picnic fare or a welcome main dish at a potluck supper.

Serves 6

TIMING

Make the chermoula while you roast the yams and tofu. The finished salad needs to sit at room temperature for at least an hour to let the flavors develop.

2 teaspoons cumin seeds

2 teaspoons coriander seeds

1 (14- to 16-ounce) block pressed firm tofu (see page 22), or extrafirm tofu, cut into ½-inch cubes

½ pound yams (see page 241), peeled and cut into ½-inch dice (2 cups)

3 tablespoons olive oil

1 teaspoon pimenton (Spanish smoked paprika [see page 240]) or regular paprika

Salt and freshly ground pepper

1 small red onion, diced (about 1 cup)

1 cup Israeli (Middle Eastern) couscous

2 ears corn, kernels cut from the cob, or frozen whole-kernel corn (about 2 cups)

1 red bell pepper, seeded and cut into ¼-inch dice (about 1 cup)

3 scallions, sliced thinly on a diagonal

¾ cup Chermoula (recipe follows)

GET READY. Preheat the oven to 400 degrees. Bring 6 cups of water to a boil in a 2-quart pot.

TOAST THE CUMIN AND CORIANDER SEEDS together in a hot skillet until fragrant, stirring a few times. Grind them in a coffee grinder until they're the consistency of cornmeal (although uneven bits are fine).

PREPARE THE TOFU AND YAMS. In a large bowl, toss the tofu cubes and diced yams with 2 tablespoons of the olive oil. Gently toss the mixture with the cumin, coriander, and paprika until all the pieces are coated.

ROAST THE TOFU AND YAMS. Put the tofu and yams on a baking sheet, sprinkle with salt and pepper, and roast until the yams are tender, but not mushy, so that a sharp knife easily pierces them, for 25 to 30 minutes.

SAUTÉ THE ONION. In a large skillet with a tight-fitting lid, heat the remaining 1 tablespoon of oil over medium heat, and add the onion. Sauté until the onion is soft and translucent, about 10 minutes.

COOK THE COUSCOUS. Add the couscous to the skillet and toast the pearls, stirring often, until they begin to turn light brown. Put 2 cups of the boiling water into the skillet. Reduce the heat to medium-low. Cover the pan, and simmer the couscous until most of the liquid evaporates and the couscous is tender, about 12 minutes. Set aside.

BLANCH THE CORN. Prepare a bowl of ice water big enough to hold the corn. Drop the corn kernels into the remaining boiling water in the pot, and cook for 2 minutes. Drain, as for pasta, into a colander or sieve, and then plunge into the ice water. When the corn is cool, drain well, and set aside.

PUT THE SALAD TOGETHER. In a large bowl, gently mix the tofu-yam mixture, the couscous-onion mixture, corn, red pepper, scallions, and the Chermoula. Allow the salad to sit at room temperature for at least an hour before serving so the couscous absorbs the flavors.

> ## About Israeli Couscous
>
> Israeli couscous (also called Middle Eastern couscous) is actually pasta—little pearls of pasta—the perfect size to go with bite-size pieces of roasted tofu, peppers, and corn. If you can't find Israeli couscous in your area (for example, in a store that specializes in Middle Eastern foods), substitute orzo pasta.

Chermoula [v]

Chermoula is an aromatic blend of seasonings used in Moroccan cooking and can be a bit on the spicy side. If you're concerned about the spiciness, reduce the amount of cayenne to ⅛ teaspoon; you can always add more to the finished dish. Put the leftover chermoula to good use: spoon it over rice. Or toss it with a veggie stir-fry dished over brown rice for a homey supper.

Makes 1½ cups

½ cup chopped onion
1 tablespoon chopped garlic
1 teaspoon paprika
½ teaspoon cumin seeds, toasted and then ground (see page 52)
¼ teaspoon cayenne pepper
1 tablespoon freshly squeezed lemon juice
¼ cup water
1 cup loosely packed fresh parsley
1 cup loosely packed fresh cilantro
¼ cup canola oil
Salt and freshly ground pepper

Put all the ingredients except the oil, salt, and pepper in a food processor, and pulse until finely chopped. Scrape down the container. With the machine running, add the oil in a steady stream and process until the thick mixture is very smooth. Season with salt and pepper to taste.

Janine's Wasabi Potato Salad [v]

Janine came up with this combination of potatoes because that's what we had on hand when we invented this salad, but use any variety in any combination for a balance of color and sweetness. We added sliced, raw snow pea pods for crunch, but you could substitute blanched, sliced green beans. Without the greens, this makes an interesting alternative to the traditional potato salad for a summer supper.

Serves 4

TIMING

Make the Wasabi Dressing and toast the cashews while you cook the potatoes.

4 or 5 purple potatoes, unpeeled and cut in 1-inch chunks (2 cups)

1 medium to large sweet potato, peeled and cut in 1-inch chunks (2 cups)

4 cups loosely packed hearty salad greens, such as chard, kale, or curly endive

¾ cup Wasabi Dressing (recipe follows)

1 cup snow pea pods, thinly sliced at a sharp angle

½ cup cashews, toasted (see page 150)

COOK THE POTATOES in separate saucepans so the purple potatoes don't stain the sweet potato. Cover them with water, bring to a boil, and then reduce the heat to medium-low. Gently cook until the potatoes are tender, about 15 minutes. Drain and cool.

DRESS THE GREENS. When you're ready to eat the salad, tear the salad greens into bite-size pieces. In a large bowl, toss them with ¼ cup of the Wasabi Dressing until well coated, adding more if you want. Divide the dressed greens among 4 chilled salad plates.

DRESS THE POTATOES AND PEAS, AND SERVE. In the same bowl, gently toss the potatoes and raw pea pods with ½ cup more Wasabi Dressing. Divide the dressed potato mixture into 4 servings, sprinkle with the toasted cashews, and serve immediately. (The potatoes absorb the dressing so fast that if you hold it for long, the salad loses its spark.)

TIP

If the potato salad lacks sparkle, mix in another tablespoon (or two) of rice vinegar, tasting after each addition.

Wasabi Dressing [v]

This dressing is on the thick side and would make a great dip for raw vegetables.

Makes about 1 cup

2 teaspoons wasabi powder (see "About Wasabi")

¼ cup soft silken tofu

2 cloves garlic

2 tablespoons rice vinegar

1 tablespoon tamari (see page 240) or soy sauce

¼ cup plain soy milk

¼ cup vegetable oil

1 tablespoon dark (toasted) sesame oil

Mix the wasabi powder with enough water, 1 to 2 tablespoons, to form a paste. Put the wasabi paste with all the remaining ingredients except the oils in a blender or food processor. While the machine is running, drizzle in the olive and sesame oils. If the dressing is too thick, blend in more soy milk or water, a tablespoon at a time, until you get the consistency you want.

Cafe Flora Herb Balsamic Vinaigrette [v]

This is Cafe Flora's "house" dressing, developed by our first chef, Jim Watkins. We blend this dressing so it is satiny smooth and quite thick. Getting a creamy vinaigrette can be tricky, especially with such a small quantity, but don't worry if your dressing separates. Just shake or whisk it thoroughly before you toss it with the greens.

Use a variety of herbs depending on what you have on hand or in your garden. We generally use rosemary, oregano, and thyme, and for this recipe you'll need about one sprig of each. Dried herbs can be substituted; just reduce the quantity to one teaspoon for each tablespoon of fresh herbs.

Makes about 1½ cups

1 shallot, peeled

6 cloves garlic

1 cup olive oil

1 tablespoon Dijon mustard

1 tablespoon chopped fresh herbs (rosemary, oregano, and thyme, for example), or 1 teaspoon dried

¼ cup balsamic vinegar

½ teaspoon salt

¼ teaspoon freshly ground pepper

GET READY. Preheat the oven to 375 degrees. Cut the shallot in half so it is about the same size as a clove of garlic.

ROAST THE GARLIC AND SHALLOT. Toss the garlic and shallot with 1 tablespoon of the olive oil in a very small baking dish, and cover with foil. Roast until soft, about 20 minutes. Remove the foil, give it a stir, and roast uncovered until the shallot and garlic start to brown, another 5 to 10 minutes. Cool completely.

MIX THE DRESSING. Put everything but the oil in a blender. With the motor running, drizzle in the remaining olive oil until the dressing is thick and creamy.

Dijon Curry Vinaigrette [v]

If you have leftover dressing, this is great on any salad that includes apples or beets.

Makes 1 cup

2 teaspoons Dijon mustard

2 teaspoons curry powder

Juice of 1 lime

1 tablespoon honey, brown rice syrup, or brown sugar

½ teaspoon salt

¼ teaspoon freshly ground pepper

¾ cup olive oil

In a small bowl, whisk together all the ingredients except the oil. Dribble in the olive oil, whisking constantly, until the mixture is thoroughly blended.

DINNERS
AND SUPPERS

THE CREATION OF DISHES AT Cafe Flora is truly a collaborative effort, and there is no meal where this is more evident than at dinner. Looking through the dinner menus from years past is like looking at a scrapbook of people who have worked in our kitchen. The dishes recall many wonderful cooks from different backgrounds who love to cook and, more importantly, who love to eat.

Some of our cooks come from other countries and cultural backgrounds and bring to our kitchen the foods and cooking methods that they grew up with. I value the tips on wrapping tamales, making dumplings, or my introduction to an exotic ingredient through collaboration with a fellow cook from a different culture.

We love to eat, too, and we're lucky to live in a city like Seattle where there is so much good food from around the world. My excuse for dining out is that I am doing "research." Many times my fellow cooks and I have gotten together on a day off to discover a new ethnic eatery. Or we have dinner at a fancier place to be wowed and inspired by beautiful plate presentations.

As vegetarian cooks, we're inspired and directed by the seasons. Starting in late spring and into the fall, the fruits and vegetables that become available can overload us with ideas. Sometimes we're almost overwhelmed by the sheer abundance: how can we possibly fit into the menu all those huckleberries, fresh peas, figs, and other seasonal foods that delight us? There is so much available from our produce suppliers, small organic farms, and the many individual foragers we buy from that it's difficult to incorporate all of it into our menu in a few months' time.

On the other hand, it's also fun to create dishes when the choice of ingredients is limited and we're forced to be creative with what's available. Fall and winter challenge us to invent new and lively vegetarian dishes. The growing season for many favorites has come to an end and we're faced with limited supplies of local produce. As the days grow shorter and colder, we welcome the thought of warm, comforting stews and spicy curries. We're excited when we see the first hard winter squashes, root vegetables, wild mushrooms, and such fall fruits as apples and pears. Many of us save up menu ideas all year, awaiting the arrival of one of our favorite fall and winter ingredients, like delicata squash or parsnips.

Another serious influence on our menu is the feedback we get from our very vocal guests. On two separate occasions, we took a popular entrée off our menu to make room for another dish that we felt was a better demonstration of our kitchen's culinary talent. A letter-writing campaign demanding that the entrée be returned to the menu restored it. Some might see this as limiting our creativity, but I think of it as focusing our creativity. People dine out for many reasons, but ultimately restaurants exist to nourish and satisfy their guests.

Autumn Stroganoff

Delicata squash have the texture and flavor of hard winter squash, but they're easier to work with because of their thinner skin. Slicing into rounds or half moons is a snap compared to cutting other winter squash, like a butternut. This versatile squash has a shape perfect for stuffing. And you don't even need to peel it. The skin is tender and tasty when roasted.

All you need to make a complete meal with this rich, luscious pasta is a simple salad—wild greens or salad mix tossed with a balsamic vinaigrette.

Serves 4

GET A HEAD START

This dish calls for Mushroom Essence, a rich mushroom broth which takes an hour or more to make. However, you can make it days (or even weeks) beforehand and keep it in the freezer.

1 to 1½ pounds delicata squash, unpeeled

1 pound crimini mushrooms, quartered or thickly sliced

¼ teaspoon dried thyme

¼ cup plus 1 teaspoon olive oil

Salt and freshly ground pepper

1 tablespoon unsalted butter

2 medium yellow onions, thinly sliced

2 cups Mushroom Essence (see page 172)

½ cup dry red wine

2 tablespoons dry sherry

1 (12-ounce) package wide egg noodles, or fresh pappardelle (⅝ inch wide, like wide fettuccine)

¾ cup crème fraîche

¼ cup snipped fresh chives

GET READY. Preheat the oven to 400 degrees. Cut the squash in half lengthwise, remove the seeds, and cut into ¼-inch slices.

ROAST THE SQUASH AND MUSHROOMS. In a large bowl, combine the squash, mushrooms, thyme, 2 tablespoons of the olive oil, and a big pinch of salt and pepper. Toss to mix well.

Spread the squash-mushroom mixture on a rimmed baking sheet large enough to accommodate the vegetables in a single layer without crowding. (If you crowd them, you will steam rather than roast them.) Roast until the squash is tender but not mushy, so that a sharp knife easily pierces it, for 20 to 25 minutes.

SAUTÉ THE ONIONS. While the vegetables are roasting, put a heavy-bottomed saucepan or Dutch oven large enough to accommodate all the vegetables over medium heat. Heat 2 tablespoons olive oil with the butter. Add the onions, and cook, stirring once or twice, until they have reduced in volume and begun to soften, about 5 minutes.

Turn down the heat to low, and cook the onions for 15 to 20 minutes, stirring occasionally. If the onion starts to stick, add 1 to 2 tablespoons water, and stir to remove any bits of onion from the bottom of the pan. When done, the onions should be various shades of brown, soft and sweet. Remove from the heat, and set aside.

START THE SAUCE. To the onions, add the Mushroom Essence, wine, and sherry. Bring to a boil, lower the heat, and simmer until the liquid has been reduced by half, to about 1⅓ cups, about 20 minutes. While you're reducing the liquid, put 6 quarts of lightly salted water on to boil for the pasta.

COOK THE NOODLES. Cook the dried noodles for 6 to 8 minutes, less time if you're using fresh pasta. Drain, and toss with the remaining 1 teaspoon olive oil to prevent sticking.

FINISH THE SAUCE. Add the roasted vegetables to the onion mixture, stir in the crème fraîche, and simmer gently for 5 minutes. If you want a thicker sauce, simmer it longer to reduce it further. Stir in 3 tablespoons of the chives, and add salt and pepper to taste. (If need be, keep the sauce warm in a double boiler over, not in, hot water.)

SERVE THE STROGANOFF. Divide the noodles among 4 plates, and ladle the stroganoff over them. Garnish with the remaining 1 tablespoon chives.

TIPS

- Freeze mushroom stems until you're ready to make Mushroom Essence (see page 172).

- We use crème fraîche here because it is rich, creamy, and has just the right amount of tang. You may substitute sour cream, but it will diminish the intensity of the mushroom flavor. If you use it, make sure to whisk it in after you take the pot off the stove, at the very end, to avoid curdling the sauce. If you can't find crème fraîche at your local supermarket or if you have the time to experiment, you can make your own following the instructions on page 230. Just note that it takes about 24 hours.

Wild Mushroom Curry [v]

For the mushrooms, use a mix of domestic and wild such as shiitake, crimini, chanterelle, hen of the woods, oyster, puffball, enoki, or portobello. If you're lucky enough to come across some lobster mushrooms, definitely include them, as their unique flavor is perfect in this curry.

Serve this soupy curry piping hot over a bowl of rice or reconstituted dried rice stick noodles. Top it with cilantro and Thai basil sprigs (or sweet basil if you can't find the Thai variety), bean sprouts, chopped peanuts, and scallions. Tuck a wedge of lime on the side, and you have a meal-in-a-bowl.

Serves 6

1 pound mixed mushrooms, cut in thick slices or halved, depending on the size

2 medium carrots, peeled

1 tablespoon vegetable oil

2 tablespoons Cafe Flora Red Curry Paste (see page 93), or commercially prepared red curry paste

1 medium yellow onion, thinly sliced

1 red bell pepper, seeds removed and cut in strips

¼ cup tamari (see page 240) or soy sauce

3 tablespoons tamarind concentrate (see page 240), or 3 tablespoons lemon or lime juice

2 (14-ounce) cans coconut milk

½ teaspoon ground turmeric

CLEAN THE MUSHROOMS by brushing off any excess dirt with a towel or pastry brush. If the mushrooms are especially dirty, quickly rinse them under running water, and let dry for several hours on paper towels.

Cafe Flora Red Curry Paste [v]

The many Thai curry pastes available today have made cooking a Thai curry at home incredibly easy. However, it surprises many people to learn that some prepared curry pastes are not vegetarian because they almost always contain fish or shrimp paste. So we make our own using ground arame (a kind of seaweed) to supply the flavor of the sea. This paste is medium hot; if that's too hot for you, just reduce the amount of crushed red pepper.

Make this ahead of time and store it in a sealed container in your refrigerator up to one week. Or because our recipe makes enough for server meals freeze the leftovers in an ice cube tray so it's ready to use when you want it.

Makes 2 cups

¼ cup coriander seeds

2 tablespoons cumin seeds

½ cup red pepper flakes

2 tablespoons arame (seaweed [see page 238])

2 tablespoons water

2 stalks lemongrass (see Tip)

¼ cup chopped, peeled, fresh ginger (about a 6-inch piece)

½ cup chopped shallots

½ cup chopped garlic

6 lime leaves or the zest of 2 limes

2 tablespoons salt

¼ cup vegetable oil

PREPARE THE SPICES. Toast the coriander and cumin seeds in a hot dry skillet, tossing a few times until fragrant. Coarsely grind them with the red pepper flakes in a spice or coffee grinder, and set aside.

PREPARE THE ARAME. Coarsely grind the arame in the same grinder. You don't need to clean the grinder beforehand. (Hold your breath when you remove the lid because grinding arame creates dust that will make you sneeze and cough.) Put the ground arame in a small bowl with the water, and soak for 10 minutes.

PREPARE THE LEMONGRASS. Trim the white bottom as well as the dry hollow top of the lemongrass, and discard. Peel away a few of the tough outer leaves, and slice what remains very thinly.

BLEND THE PASTE. Put all the ingredients but the oil in a food processor and process by first pulsing a few times. Then, with the machine running, drizzle in the oil, and process until a smooth paste forms.

About Lemongrass and Lime Leaf

We use lemongrass and lime leaf for the aroma and fragrance of the lemon or lime without the sourness of the juice, just as the Thai and Vietnamese do.

LEMONGRASS is a long stalklike tropical grass that looks a bit like a large scallion with layers of pale green or yellow leaves and a white root. Lemongrass owes its bright lemony flavor and fragrance to the essential oil, citral (also an element in lemon peel). Look for lemongrass in the produce section of large Asian (especially Thai) markets; you may occasionally find it in a large grocery store's produce department near the fresh ginger. Choose blemish-free gray-green stalks with white ends.

LIME LEAVES (or kaffir lime leaves) are dark, glossy, green leaves which are joined in pairs; we count these as two leaves. You'll rarely find fresh lime leaf—its flavor is most intense in that form—but you'll find it frozen in most Asian markets. Asian cooks simmer the whole leaf in curries, soups, and sauces in the way Western cooks use bay leaves.

CUT THE CARROTS in half lengthwise, and then cut each half in ¼-inch slices at a sharp angle.

STIR-FRY THE VEGETABLES. Heat the oil in a wok over high heat. Add the carrots and curry paste, and cook for 1 minute. Add the onion, mushrooms, and bell pepper, and stir-fry for 3 more minutes.

ADD THE SEASONING AND COCONUT MILK. Add the tamari, tamarind concentrate, 1 can of the coconut milk, and turmeric. If you want the curry to be soupier (as we serve it at Cafe Flora), add the coconut milk from the second can until it's the consistency you want. Bring to a boil, remove from the heat, and serve.

TIPS

- If the mushrooms are really dirty, and you have to clean them with water, they could take several hours to dry.

- Rice stick noodles, long, translucent white strands, are a slightly thicker variation of Chinese rice flour noodles. To use them in this dish, cover in very hot (but not boiling) water for 5 minutes, drain, and serve. In Asian markets look for these sold in coiled nests packaged in cellophane.

Indian Chickpea Stew [v]

This stew is incredibly easy to make, hearty, and vegan. Plus it's low in fat and has a lot of flavor. What more could you want?!

Here we use cooked potatoes and chopped greens, but you can add a variety of almost any other vegetables you like: blanched cauliflower, carrots, or green beans, or a source of protein like tempeh (a nutty-flavored soybean cake), roasted or fried tofu, or hard-cooked eggs. (This stew would be a great way to use up leftovers.) I don't find this dish to be spicy, but if you're heat sensitive, reduce the jalapeño chile by half or leave it out entirely.

For a full meal, start with samosas—perhaps takeout from a local Indian restaurant or frozen from a specialty store like Trader Joe's. Serve the stew over basmati rice with the Coconut Raita (see page 225) or plain yogurt, and a quick sauté of green beans, asparagus, or snow peas. As the finishing touch, serve a fruit chutney like our Apricot Chutney (see page 35) or any of the excellent salty and hot chutneys made by Patak.

Serves 4 to 6

GET A HEAD START

If you're using dried chickpeas, start them soaking at least 3 hours ahead. (It's also OK to start them the night before.) At the restaurant we make the sauce a day or two ahead, up to the point of adding the chickpeas and additional vegetables (which we add to order). (You could even freeze the sauce.) This not only saves time at the last minute, but it tastes even better the next day when the flavors have had a chance to mellow.

1 cup dried chickpeas (garbanzos), soaked for 3 to 8 hours, or 1 (15-ounce) can (about 2 cups cooked)

2 tablespoons vegetable oil

1 tablespoon brown mustard seeds

1 tablespoon whole cumin seeds

1 large onion, thinly sliced in crescents

1 (2- to 3-inch) piece fresh ginger, peeled and minced

1 jalapeño chile, ribs and seeds removed and finely diced

1 (28-ounce) can diced tomatoes with juice

1 tablespoon ground turmeric

2 teaspoons salt

2 cups water

1 pound small red potatoes

3 cups washed and roughly chopped greens such as spinach, beet greens, kale, or chard

½ cup chopped fresh parsley

½ cup chopped fresh cilantro

COOK THE CHICKPEAS. If you're using dried chickpeas drain them, and cover generously with fresh water in a pot. Bring to a boil and lower the heat. Cover the pot, and cook at a gentle simmer until the chickpeas are very tender, 1 hour or more (depending on how old the beans are). (You may need to add more water if they get dry.) Drain the chickpeas.

If you're using canned chickpeas, rinse them under cold water, and drain well.

START THE SAUCE. Heat the oil in a 3-quart (or larger) saucepan, add the mustard and cumin seeds, and sauté over medium heat until fragrant and the mustard seeds start to pop.

Add the onion and sauté until it's soft and translucent, about 10 minutes. Then add the ginger and jalapeño chile and sauté for 2 minutes more.

Stir in the tomatoes and their juice, turmeric, salt, and water. Bring the mixture to a boil, lower the heat, and simmer for 20 minutes.

COOK THE POTATOES. While the sauce simmers, drop the potatoes into a small pot of boiling water to cover. Cook them, covered, until they are barely tender, about 20 minutes. Drain the potatoes and cut them in half. (You cook the potatoes separately so they don't break apart in the stew.)

ADD THE VEGETABLES AND HERBS. Add the chickpeas, potatoes, and greens to the tomato mixture. Simmer, stirring occasionally, until the vegetables are hot, 3 to 5 minutes. If you find the stew is getting thicker than you like, add more water to keep it saucy. Just before serving, add the herbs, and season to taste with salt.

Macaroni and Cheese with Warm Tomato Salsa

It's almost embarrassing to include this "fat bomb" of a recipe in this book, but it's one of our most requested recipes even though it only appears on our kid's menu. (A lot of parents must be eating their kids' food!)

This is not your typical macaroni and cheese casserole that requires mixing a white sauce with cheese and cooked macaroni and then popping it in the oven for an hour or so. We make this dish to order in the restaurant, so it has to cook quickly. Very simply, you reduce heavy cream to make it thicker, add cheddar cheese, and then mix that sauce with cooked macaroni. Add a tossed green salad, and in a flash, you have a comforting dinner.

Serves 4 to 6

1 pound penne pasta, or your favorite pasta shape
Salt
1 teaspoon olive oil
2 cups heavy cream
3 cups grated sharp Cheddar cheese (12 ounces)
Freshly ground pepper
Warm Tomato Salsa (recipe follows)

GET READY. In a large pot over high heat, bring 6 quarts of water and a pinch of salt to a boil.

SIMMER THE CREAM. While the pasta water is heating, heat the heavy cream in a saucepan over medium-low heat. (Watch the pot to make sure it doesn't boil over.) Simmer the cream until it thickens and is reduced by one quarter, about 20 minutes.

COOK THE PASTA. Add the pasta to the boiling water and cook until it's tender, yet firm to the bite, about 13 minutes. Drain the pasta well, toss it with the oil, and return it to the empty pot.

ADD THE GRATED CHEESE to the reduced cream, 1 cup at a time, stirring after each addition until the cheese is melted.

MIX AND SERVE THE MACARONI AND CHEESE. Add the cheese sauce to the hot pasta, and combine. Add salt and pepper to taste, and serve immediately with ½ cup or more of the warm salsa on top of each serving.

Warm Tomato Salsa [v]

This is really just my take on old-fashioned stewed tomatoes, a dish my mother always serves with macaroni and cheese. The acidity and natural sweetness of tomatoes and the chunkiness of the salsa contrast nicely with this rich and soothing dish.

If you want a little more heat in this salsa, use canned tomatoes with mild or hot green chiles, such as Rotel Original Diced Tomatoes and Green Chilies or Muir Glen Fire Roasted Diced Tomatoes with Green Chilies. Or you could chop up a tablespoon of those pickled jalapeño chiles (people sometimes use them in nachos), and add them after you sauté the vegetables.

Makes 2½ cups

1 teaspoon olive oil
1 small onion, diced
1 rib celery, diced
½ green bell pepper, seeds removed and diced
1 clove garlic, minced
1 (15-ounce) can diced tomatoes in juice, preferably no salt added
½ can water
1 tablespoon chopped fresh parsley
Salt and freshly ground pepper

In a large saucepan, heat the olive oil over medium heat. Add the onion, celery, green pepper, and garlic, and sauté until the onion is soft and translucent, about 10 minutes. Add the tomatoes with juice and the water, and simmer until a saucelike consistency, about 20 minutes. Add the parsley, and salt and pepper to taste.

Smoked Mushroom Gumbo [V]

This distinctive gumbo has never appeared on our menu but we have served it at benefits and catered events, and I have personally served it at dinner parties attended by "mixed company" (carnivores, vegetarians, and vegans). The intense smokiness of the mushrooms, the seafood essence of the arame, and the kick of the red pepper flakes leave everyone satisfied. (That's why we've suggested a party-size amount.)

This is spicy as a gumbo should be. If you're unsure about your guests' love for spicy food, cut the amount of red pepper flakes in half and offer a bottle of hot sauce on the side.

Serve up the gumbo in a bowl over a scoop of hot rice. For a sprightly accompaniment, toss a green salad dressed with Lemon Garlic Vinaigrette (see page 134) or make our Waitin' for Spring Cabbage Salad (see page 82). If you want a more wintry accompaniment, serve the Tangy Swiss Chard (see page 134).

Makes 12 cups, or about 16 servings

GET A HEAD START

To make quick work of this gumbo, you can smoke the mushrooms at least 2 or 3 days ahead. In fact the mushrooms taste better a day or two later. (Plus they freeze well.) You can also make the whole gumbo the day before as its flavors improve over time, too.

¼ cup (about ½ ounce) arame (seaweed [see page 238])

½ cup olive oil

½ cup unbleached all-purpose flour

1 pound crimini mushrooms, smoked (see page 79), and then quartered or thickly sliced

1 large yellow onion, diced

2 tablespoons minced garlic

1 teaspoon red pepper flakes

1 red bell pepper, seeds removed and diced

1 green bell pepper, seeds removed and diced

2 stalks celery, diced

1 (28-ounce) can diced tomatoes in juice

2 cups Vegetable Stock (see page 39), or prepared vegetable stock

¼ cup chopped fresh parsley

1 tablespoon chopped fresh oregano

1 tablespoon chopped fresh thyme

2 cups frozen cut okra or ½ pound fresh okra, sliced

Salt

PREPARE THE ARAME. Rinse the arame in a strainer under running water. Put it in a bowl and add enough cold water just to cover. Soak for 10 minutes. Drain well, coarsely chop, and set aside.

MAKE THE ROUX. Heat the olive oil in a large, heavy-bottomed pot over medium-high heat. Stir in the flour, and reduce the heat to low. Cook, stirring constantly, until the roux is coffee colored, 20 to 30 minutes.

ADD THE VEGETABLES. Add the smoked mushrooms, onion, garlic, and red pepper flakes to the roux. Cook until the onion softens, about 10 minutes. Add the bell peppers and celery, and cook for 5 minutes more.

Add the arame and the remaining ingredients except the okra and salt. Bring to a boil, lower the heat, and simmer, covered, for 15 minutes. Add the okra, and cook for 5 more minutes. Add salt to taste.

Seitan and Vegetables Mu Shu Style [v]

We really like to serve food that guests can put together at the table, an acceptable way to "play with your food." In this dish you roll up some stir-fried vegetables in a warm tortilla with a dab of sweet hoisin sauce and eat it like a burrito.

Feel free to substitute ingredients in this recipe according to your taste, or what you have on hand—for example, marinated, baked tofu for the seitan. Make a complete meal with the addition of nutty brown rice and the Avocado Grapefruit Salad with Ginger Miso Dressing (see page 63).

Serves 4 to 6

1 to 2 tablespoons vegetable oil

8 ounces seitan (1 cup), cut in thin strips

1 large carrot, peeled and thinly sliced at a sharp angle

3 cups sliced shiitake mushrooms (8 ounces)

2 tablespoons chopped, peeled, fresh ginger

2 tablespoons chopped garlic

1 red bell pepper, seeds removed and cut in strips

4 cups thinly sliced napa cabbage (about 1 pound)

1 cup mung bean sprouts

2 tablespoons tamari (see page 240)

8 scallions, white and green parts, thinly sliced at a sharp angle

Flour tortillas, warmed

½ cup hoisin sauce (see "About Hoisin")

STIR-FRY THE VEGETABLES. Heat 1 tablespoon vegetable oil in a large skillet or wok over medium-high heat. Add the seitan, carrot, mushrooms, ginger, and garlic, and stir-fry until the seitan begins to brown, about 5 minutes.

Drizzle more oil into the pan if the vegetables are starting to stick, and add the bell pepper, cabbage, and bean sprouts. Continue to stir-fry until the cabbage just begins to soften.

Add the tamari and half of the scallions, stir-fry just until combined, and remove from the heat.

SERVE THE STIR-FRY in a covered bowl to keep it warm at the table. Accompany it with the tortillas, a small bowl of hoisin sauce, and the remaining scallions. Have your guests spread their tortillas with hoisin sauce, spoon on some of the seitan stir-fry, sprinkle on some scallions, and roll them up like burritos.

About Hoisin

Hoisin is a dark, thick Chinese sauce, at once sweet and spicy. It's made of soybeans, garlic, chile peppers, and spices. Look for it in the Asian food section of your supermarket. Refrigerated, hoisin can last indefinitely. (If you buy it in a tin, make sure to transfer it to a plastic or glass bottle and seal it tightly.)

Seitan Jambalaya [v]

Traditionally, jambalaya has chicken, shrimp, or other protein cooked in the "stew" and raw rice added during the last hour of cooking time. In our version, we sauté the protein (spicy marinated seitan) and add it right before serving over a mound of steaming rice. Because seitan develops a "wheaty" flavor when it sits in a stew or sauce for awhile, it's always best to add seitan at the last minute, just before serving.

Serve this quick jambalaya with Smoky Collard Greens (see page 211) and Basil Corn Relish (see page 212), or Black-Eyed Pea Salad with Grilled Corn (see page 70).

Serves 4 to 6

TIMING

The seitan needs at least an hour to marinate, but you can also start marinating it the day before.

Jambalaya Stew [v]

12 ounces seitan (1½ cups), cut in chunks

Jambalaya Seitan Marinade (recipe follows)

2 tablespoons vegetable oil

1 large yellow onion, diced

2 tablespoons chopped garlic

2 stalks celery, diced, plus the leaves, chopped

1 large green bell pepper, seeds removed and diced

1 large red bell pepper, seeds removed and diced

1 jalapeño chile, diced

½ cup chopped fresh parsley

1 tablespoon chopped fresh thyme, or 1 teaspoon dried thyme

2 scallions, white and green parts, chopped

1 (28-ounce) can diced tomatoes in juice

Salt and freshly ground pepper

1 tablespoon olive oil

MARINATE THE SEITAN. Toss the seitan in the marinade to coat it fully. Marinate in the refrigerator for at least an hour or overnight.

COOK THE VEGETABLE STEW. Heat the vegetable oil in a large, heavy saucepan over medium heat. Add the onion and sauté until it is soft and translucent, about 10 minutes.

Add the garlic, celery, all bell peppers, chile, herbs, and scallions, and sauté for another 5 minutes. Add the tomatoes with juice, lower the heat, and simmer for 20 minutes. Season with salt and pepper to taste.

SAUTÉ AND ADD THE SEITAN. Heat the olive oil in a skillet or a wok over high heat. Drain the seitan and reserve the marinade. Add the seitan and sauté just until hot.

Just before serving, mix the seitan and its marinade to the vegetable stew. Add salt and pepper to taste, and serve immediately. If you want this to be soupier, add some water (or vegetable stock if you have it on hand).

TIP

If you have easy access to a grill, grill the seitan slices over hot coals before you marinate them. (They're still full of flavor, however, even if you don't grill them.)

Jambalaya Seitan Marinade [v]

Makes ½ cup

¼ cup tamari (see page 240) or soy sauce

1 tablespoon hot pepper sauce, such as Tabasco or Frank's Red Hot Sauce

1 tablespoon pimenton (smoked Spanish paprika [see page 240])

1 tablespoon dried oregano

1 tablespoon chopped garlic

In a small bowl mix all the ingredients well.

Spicy Seitan Fajitas [v]

In the restaurant, we grill plain seitan chunks on our charbroiler, slice and marinate them, and then sauté them to order with the vegetables. We do this to get a "seared" flavor into the seitan, which can't always be achieved in a hot pan in a hurry on a busy night. Hopefully, you'll never have 200 people coming over for dinner, and you can get the desired flavor in a skillet or wok at a more leisurely pace.

Serves 6

GET A HEAD START

If you're starting with dried pinto beans in the Chipotle Pinto Purée, they'll need to soak for several hours, if not overnight. You can also make this dish a day or two ahead.

Marinate the seitan for at least an hour, or overnight in the refrigerator, before you sauté it for the stew. The rest of the dish is best made the day you're serving it.

In this dish

- Spicy Vegetable Sauté
- Fajitas Seitan Marinade
- Chipotle Pinto Purée (see page 224)
- Pico de Gallo Salsa (see page 226)
- Guacamole (see page 226)

Spicy Vegetable Sauté [v]

Serves 6

8 ounces seitan (1 cup), cut in ½-inch slices

Fajitas Seitan Marinade (recipe follows)

Vegetable oil for the sauté

2 yellow onions, sliced into crescents

2 tablespoons chopped garlic

1 small red bell pepper, seeds removed and cut in strips

1 small green bell pepper, seeds removed and cut in strips

2 cups sliced crimini mushrooms

2 tablespoons chopped fresh cilantro

1 tablespoon chopped fresh oregano, or 1 teaspoon dried oregano

1 tablespoon chopped fresh basil, or 1 teaspoon dried basil

2 tablespoons tamari (see page 240)

1 tablespoon hot sauce

½ teaspoon cumin seeds, toasted and ground (see page 52)

MARINATE THE SEITAN. Add the seitan to the marinade, and toss to coat thoroughly. Marinate in the refrigerator for 1 hour or overnight. Drain the seitan, reserving the marinade.

SAUTÉ THE SEITAN. In a large wok on high heat, heat 1 tablespoon oil until very hot, and put in the seitan to the pan. (It will splatter, so be careful!) Sauté the seitan, turning, until it's well browned, about 10 minutes. Remove the seitan from the pan and return it to the marinade.

SAUTÉ THE VEGETABLES. Add more oil to the pan if the seitan absorbed all of the oil, and put in the onions, garlic, bell peppers, and mushrooms. Sauté, stirring, over high heat until they begin to brown, but the peppers still have some crunch to them, about 5 minutes.

Add the seitan back to the pan and add the herbs, tamari, hot sauce, and cumin, and cook until the entire mixture is very hot, about 2 minutes.

TIP

If you have easy access to a grill, grill the seitan slices over hot coals before you marinate them. (They're still full of flavor, however, even if you don't grill them.)

Fajitas Seitan Marinade [v]

Makes about ½ cup

3 tablespoons tamari (see page 240)

3 tablespoons lime juice

1 tablespoon minced garlic

1 tablespoon hot pepper sauce (like Frank's Red Hot)

In a small bowl thoroughly combine all the ingredients.

Serve the Fajitas

Spicy Vegetable Sauté (recipe above)

12 flour tortillas, warmed

Chipotle Pinto Purée (see page 224)

Pico de Gallo Salsa (see page 226)

Guacamole (see page 226)

Serve the sauté as soon as it's done. Have your guests spoon some on their tortillas. Top with a dab of Chipotle Pinto Purée, a dollop of Pico de Gallo Salsa, and a spoonful of Guacamole. Roll up like a burrito.

Spicy Grilled Polenta with Provençal Fennel Sauce [v]

This elegant yet rustic vegetarian entrée makes a delicious summer supper, and it can easily be made vegan simply by omitting the goat cheese garnish. To round out the meal, adapt the White Bean and Roasted Garlic Purée as a salad following the instructions in the introduction on page 28.

For a variation in late summer or early fall, when figs are plentiful (and less expensive), try the Provençal Fennel Sauce with Balsamic Roasted Figs.

Serves 6

TIMING

Start by cooking the polenta because it must cool in the refrigerator for an hour before you can use it in this dish. (It's also fine if you make it a day or two before.) Then, braise the fennel. (If you're making the balsamic roasted fig version, this would be the time to roast the figs.) Finish the fennel sauce and keep it warm over low heat while you grill the polenta.

Spicy Grilled Polenta [v]

Polenta tastes fantastic when grilled outdoors, but broiling it in the oven also works well. You can even make this polenta the day before, and then do the last step, grilling or broiling, when you put the dish together.

Makes about 12 triangles

Toasting and Soaking Dried Chiles

We use all kinds of dried chiles at Cafe Flora, especially ancho (dried poblano) and chipotle (dried jalapeño) chiles. (Turn to page 238 for information about the kinds of chiles we use in this cookbook and suggestions about where to find them.) Toasting adds a hint of smokiness to balance a chile's natural spiciness. We use them to make a spicy purée for seasoning—for example, our Chipotle Chile Purée (see page 225)—or we soak them and then chop up the reconstituted chiles for a sauce or sauté.

But toasting chiles isn't a very exact science; in fact, you could skip it altogether and your dish would come out all right, though a bit less rich. Overtoasting is a greater problem than not toasting at all, because chiles that have been toasted too long have an acrid flavor.

Whenever you work with chiles, either fresh or dried, it's a good idea to wear plastic or latex gloves. The substance in chiles that causes them to be hot, capsaicin, will adhere to the skin on your fingers and cause extremely unpleasant burning to whatever part of your body you touch afterwards. (Contact lens wearers in particular beware: rub your eyes with chile-stained hands, and you'll have to toss out your lenses.) We also instruct you to remove the ribs and seeds from the chiles to help control the heat of a dish. The ribs contain the most capsaicin, but because of the seeds' proximity, they also have a high concentration.

TOAST THE CHILES. There are two ways to toast chiles.

- ON THE STOVE TOP. Heat a heavy skillet over high heat. Add the chiles to the pan, and stir them to prevent burning, until they become puffed up and fragrant, 30 seconds to 1 minute.

- IN THE OVEN. Preheat the oven to 300 degrees. Toast chiles on a baking sheet until they're puffed up and fragrant, about 5 minutes.

When the chiles are cool enough to handle, pull off the stems, slice them open, and shake out the seeds. There's one exception: you don't need to bother with chipotle seeds.

SOAK TOASTED CHILES. Put the cool, toasted chiles in a bowl, and cover with boiling water. Soak the chiles until they are soft, about 20 minutes. Drain the chiles, reserving some of the flavorful water if you're going to purée them. You'll get a smoother, tastier sauce as a result.

GRIND TOASTED CHILES. Remove the stems and seeds. Roughly chop. Thoroughly clean your coffee grinder. Grind the chiles until a powder. When you're done, clean the grinder meticulously. (Grinding chiles is a great use for that old coffee grinder.)

1 tablespoon olive oil, plus extra for oiling the pan and grilling

½ large yellow onion, diced

1 tablespoon salt

2 tablespoons chopped garlic

1 teaspoon red pepper flakes

2 teaspoons fennel seeds, toasted and ground (see page 52)

7 cups water

2 cups coarse yellow cornmeal (polenta)

GET READY. Thoroughly oil a 13 × 9-inch baking dish with olive oil or cooking spray.

SAUTÉ THE ONION AND SPICES FOR THE POLENTA. Heat 1 tablespoon olive oil in a 3-quart pot over medium heat. Add the onion and ½ teaspoon of the salt, and sauté until the onion is soft and translucent, about 10 minutes. Add the garlic, red pepper flakes, and fennel, and cook for 1 minute longer.

COOK THE POLENTA. Add the water and the remaining 2½ teaspoons salt to the onion mixture, and bring to a boil. Pour the polenta into the boiling liquid in a thin stream, stirring constantly. (You're trying to avoid lumpy polenta.)

Lower the heat to medium, and cook, stirring, until the polenta pulls away from the sides of the pan, 10 to 15 minutes.

COOL THE POLENTA. Immediately pour the polenta into the prepared pan, using an oiled rubber spatula to spread it evenly. Cool in the refrigerator until firm, about 1 hour.

GRILL OR BROIL THE POLENTA TRIANGLES. Cut the cold polenta into 6 squares, and then cut the squares diagonally into 12 triangles. Brush both sides of the polenta triangles with olive oil.

Grill or broil them until they are lightly browned and heated through, 4 to 6 minutes per side. Keep the triangles warm in a 200-degree oven until ready to serve.

Provençal Fennel Sauce [v]

Makes about 2¾ cups

1 large fennel bulb (about 1 pound)
3 tablespoons olive oil
Salt and freshly ground pepper
½ large yellow onion, sliced
1 tablespoon chopped garlic
¼ cup white wine
2 cups diced Roma tomatoes
¾ cup kalamata olives, pitted and halved
1 tablespoon finely chopped fresh rosemary

GET READY. Preheat the oven to 350 degrees.

CUT THE FENNEL. Trim the root end and stalks of the fennel bulb, reserving some of the wispy fronds for garnish. Lay the bulb on its flatter side, and cut in half lengthwise, from the root to the stem. (This makes for more even browning.)

BROWN THE FENNEL. Heat 1 tablespoon of the oil in a deep saucepan or Dutch oven over medium heat. When the oil is hot, add the fennel. Turn each half over several times in the hot pan until it begins to brown. Salt and pepper each side as you do this.

BRAISE THE FENNEL. Put the browned fennel in a lidded baking dish (or cover with foil) with 1 cup water. Bake about 30 minutes, or until tender. When cool enough to handle, slice the cooled fennel bulb into ¼-inch slices. Reserve the cooking liquid.

SAUTÉ THE ONION. While the fennel is braising, heat the remaining 2 tablespoons olive oil over medium heat in the pan you used to brown the fennel. Add the onion and sauté, stirring often, until tender, about 5 minutes. Add the garlic and wine, and cook for 1 minute more.

FINISH THE FENNEL. Stir in the fennel slices and their braising liquid.

- Add the tomatoes, olives, and rosemary. Add salt and pepper to taste. Cook until hot, about 3 minutes.

- If you're making the version using Balsamic Roasted Figs (recipe follows), add the figs and the rosemary. Add salt and pepper to taste. Cook until hot, about 1 minute. Take off the heat, and add a splash of balsamic vinegar.

Serve the Polenta with Provençal Fennel Sauce

Spicy Grilled Polenta (see page 101)
Provençal Fennel Sauce (see page 103)
Optional: 6 ounces goat cheese, chilled
Fennel fronds, for garnish

Place a triangle of warm polenta on each plate, and top with a few spoonfuls of the fennel sauce. Place another triangle on top of the fennel, at an opposing angle, and top with more fennel sauce, crumbling the goat cheese over it, if you're using it. Garnish with some fennel fronds.

Variation: Balsamic Roasted Figs [v]

Figs are great in savory dishes and go very well with fennel. Try this variation in the late summer or early fall when figs are less expensive. For this fennel sauce, you'll replace the tomatoes and olives with these roasted figs and their juice. Add a splash more of balsamic vinegar to the final sauté.

Makes about 3 cups

1½ pints large, firm, black Mission figs, sliced in half (a little over 3 cups)
3 tablespoons balsamic vinegar, plus a splash
1½ tablespoons olive oil
½ teaspoon salt
Pinch of ground pepper

GET READY. Preheat the oven to 350 degrees. In a bowl, lightly toss all the ingredients until the fig halves are fully coated.

ROAST THE FIGS. Put the figs on a baking sheet, and roast until they're soft, but still hold their shape, for 20 to 30 minutes. (The riper the fig, the faster it will cook, so start checking for doneness after 20 min-

utes.) Add the figs and their juice to the final sauté, along with a splash of balsamic vinegar.

Polenta with Roasted Butternut Squash and Kale Sauté, Brown Butter, and Fig Balsamic

This dish makes a satisfying vegetarian entrée or a beautiful side dish in a larger feast. You ladle deep orange squash sautéed with brown butter and deep green kale onto grilled (or broiled) slices of triangle-shaped golden polenta. Top with a little bit of blue cheese, and drizzle with the complex sweetness of figs. Although this is rich and luscious comfort food, keep in mind that it also includes a healthy dose of nutrition-packed winter kale.

Round out a perfect autumn dinner with Braised Black Lentils (see page 121) and a salad of mixed greens, slices of ripe pear, toasted hazelnuts, and our Herbed Sherry Vinaigrette (see page 63).

Serves 6

GET A HEAD START

You can make the Brown Butter and Fig Balsamic Reduction days or even weeks ahead. You can also cook the polenta a day or two ahead of time and then refrigerate it until you need it.

TIMING

If you make this dish in a day, cook the polenta first because it must cool in the refrigerator for an hour before you can use it. Then start the Fig Balsamic Reduction; it will need to simmer for at least an hour. Put the butternut squash in the oven to roast, and brown the butter. Then you can finish the squash by adding the kale, and grilling or broiling the polenta while the kale cooks.

Onion Parsley Polenta [v]

Makes 12 triangles

1 tablespoon olive oil, plus extra for oiling the pan and grilling

½ large yellow onion, diced

1 tablespoon salt

2 teaspoons chopped garlic

¼ cup white wine

7 cups water

2 cups coarse yellow cornmeal (polenta)

1 cup chopped fresh parsley

GET READY. Thoroughly oil a 13 × 9-inch baking dish with olive oil or cooking spray.

SAUTÉ THE ONION AND GARLIC. Heat the 1 tablespoon olive oil in a deep, heavy saucepan over medium heat. Add the onion and ½ teaspoon of the salt, and sauté until the onion is soft and translucent, about 10 minutes. Add the garlic, and cook for 1 minute longer.

ADD THE WINE and cook, stirring and scraping the bottom of the pan to remove all cooked bits, until most of the wine has evaporated.

COOK THE POLENTA. Add the water and the remaining 2½ teaspoons salt to the onion mixture, and bring to a boil. Pour the polenta into the boiling liquid in a thin stream, stirring constantly. (You're trying to avoid lumpy polenta.)

Lower the heat to medium, and cook, stirring, until the polenta is very thick and begins to pull away from the sides of the pan, 10 to 15 minutes.

COOL THE POLENTA. Fold the chopped parsley into the polenta, and immediately pour it into the prepared pan, using an oiled rubber spatula to spread it evenly. Cool in the refrigerator until firm, about 1 hour.

GRILL OR BROIL THE POLENTA TRIANGLES. Cut the cold polenta into 6 squares, and then cut the squares diagonally into 12 triangles. Brush both side of the polenta triangles with olive oil.

Grill or broil them until they are lightly browned and heated through, 4 to 6 minutes per side. Keep the triangles warm in a 200 degree oven until ready to use.

Roasted Butternut Squash and Kale Sauté [v]

Serves 6

1 butternut squash (about 2 pounds), peeled, seeded, and cut into ½-inch cubes

1½ teaspoons olive oil

Salt and freshly ground pepper

Brown Butter (recipe follows)

1 tablespoon chopped garlic

6 cups winter kale, tough stems removed, leaves torn or roughly chopped

1 cup white wine

ROAST THE SQUASH. Preheat the oven to 400 degrees. Toss the squash cubes with the olive oil, season with salt and pepper, and toss again.

Spread the squash on a rimmed baking sheet large enough to accommodate it in a single layer without crowding. (If you crowd the squash, you'll steam rather than roast it.) Roast until tender, about 30 minutes. Remove from the oven.

HEAT THE ROASTED SQUASH WITH GARLIC. Warm the Brown Butter in a large skillet that has a lid over medium heat. Add the garlic, and cook for 1 minute. Add the squash and heat through, about 3 minutes.

ADD THE KALE. Pile the kale into the pan with the squash, and add the wine. Cover the pan and steam the kale until it is tender. This could take anywhere from 2 to 15 minutes depending on the maturity of the kale. When the kale is tender, remove the lid, and continue to cook by gently stirring the contents of the pan until enough of the wine has evaporated to make a sauce that's not too soupy.

Brown Butter

Brown butter keeps a very long time in your refrigerator and is delicious for scrambling eggs or sautéing mushrooms.

Makes 6 tablespoons

½ cup (1 stick) unsalted butter

Melt the butter in a heavy saucepan over medium heat. Cook until the butter turns a golden, nut brown, 8 to 10 minutes. Remove from the heat, and pour through a strainer lined with cheesecloth or a thin cotton dish towel. Set the brown butter aside until ready to use.

Serve the Dish

Onion Parsley Polenta (see page 105)
Butternut Squash and Kale Sauté (see page 105)
6 ounces blue cheese, crumbled
Fig Balsamic Reduction (see page 234), warmed until pourable

In a deep oval platter, overlap the warm polenta triangles down the center by placing the pointed tip of one piece of polenta onto the flat side (or base) of the preceding triangle. Spoon the Butternut Squash and Kale Sauté and pan juices over the overlapping polenta slices. Scatter the blue cheese over the dish, and drizzle with warmed Fig Balsamic Reduction. Serve additional Fig Balsamic Reduction on the side.

Roasted Vegetable Vindaloo [v]

Vindaloo is a spicy curry from the Goa region in western India, and the inclusion of garlic reflects the influence of Portuguese traders in that area. Roasting the vegetables intensifies their rich flavors and makes the vegetables sturdy enough for their bath in a very spicy curry. We also add a mixture of spices, panchphoron, to deepen the flavors. Panchphoron is found in the cooking of Bengal in eastern India—a completely different region of India than Goa (my apology to purists)—which tends to emphasize lighter dishes of vegetables and fish.

In spite of the long list of ingredients, this vindaloo is actually quite simple. You roast the vegetables and then mix them with the Spicy Goan Curry in the last instant before you serve atop hot rice (we prefer basmati). Puddle Coconut Raita (see page 225) on the side. I also love this dish with roasted beets—either our tart and fresh Red Jewel Salad (see page 67) or the Roasted Beets (see page 10).

First start cooking the chickpeas for the Spicy Goan Curry, if you're not using canned. Make the Vindaloo Paste and then roast the vegetables. While they're roasting, mix up the Panchphoron Spice mixture and continue with the curry.

In this dish

- Roasted Vegetables
- Spicy Goan Curry
- Vindaloo Paste
- Panchphoron Spice Mixture

Roasted Vegetables [v]

This is also a great way to use leftovers—roast the vegetables you want, and then mix in the leftover vegetables at the end.

Makes about 6 cups

2 cups fingerling or small red or white potatoes

2 cups sliced carrots (about 2 medium), cut in $\frac{1}{2}$-inch coins

2 cups cauliflower (about $\frac{1}{2}$ head), cut in 1-inch florets

1 (about 1 pound) eggplant, unpeeled and cut in $\frac{3}{4}$-inch dice

2 tablespoons Vindaloo Paste (recipe follows)

Salt and freshly ground pepper

Vegetable oil

GET READY. Preheat the oven to 400 degrees.

CUT THE FINGERLING POTATOES in $\frac{1}{2}$-inch coins. If you're using small red or white potatoes, cut them in $\frac{1}{2}$-inch wedges.

MIX THE VEGETABLES WITH VINDALOO PASTE. Put all the vegetables in a large bowl; add the Vindaloo Paste and a few pinches of salt and pepper. Toss the vegetables, adding a few dribbles of vegetable oil to help stretch the paste and fully coat the vegetables.

ROAST THE VEGETABLES. Spread the vegetables on a rimmed baking sheet large enough to accommodate everything in a single layer. Cover with foil, and roast for 15 minutes. Remove the foil, and roast until tender but not mushy, so that a sharp knife easily pierces the potatoes, 15 to 20 minutes.

Spicy Goan Curry [v]

Makes about 6 cups

$\frac{1}{2}$ cup dried chickpeas (garbanzos), soaked for 3 to 8 hours, or 1 (15-ounce) can (about 2 cups cooked)

2 tablespoons vegetable oil

1 tablespoon Panchphoron Spice Mixture (recipe follows)

2 large yellow onions, thinly sliced

1 tablespoon miso (Japanese bean paste [see page 239])

2 cups Vegetable Stock (see page 39), purchased vegetable stock, or water

6 tablespoons Vindaloo Paste (recipe follows)

1 (28-ounce) can diced tomatoes

1 teaspoon salt

COOK THE CHICKPEAS. If you are using dried chickpeas drain them, and cover with fresh water in a pot. Bring to a boil, lower the heat, cover the pot, and cook at a gentle simmer until the chickpeas are very tender, 1 hour or more (depending on how old the beans are). Drain the chickpeas.

If you're using canned chickpeas, rinse them under cold water, and drain well.

SAUTÉ THE ONIONS. In a very large heavy-bottomed pan, heat the oil over medium heat. (The pan needs to be big because later you'll be adding the roasted vegetables to the curry in this pan.) Add the Panchphoron Spice mixture, and heat until the mustard seeds sputter. Add the onions, and sauté until the onions are soft and translucent, about 10 minutes.

DISSOLVE THE MISO in the vegetable stock, and add it to the pan, stirring and scraping to remove any bits from the bottom.

ADD THE VINDALOO PASTE, CHICKPEAS, AND TOMATOES. Add the Vindaloo Paste to the pan and stir for about 30 seconds. (It will begin to stick.)

Add the chickpeas, tomatoes with juice, and salt. Lower the heat, cover, and simmer for 20 minutes. If the sauce is finished before the vegetables are roasted, keep it warm.

Vindaloo Paste [v]

This paste will keep for a week in the refrigerator covered with a thin layer of foil. Use it as the basis for a simple curry. Or, stir fry veggies like onions, carrots, bell peppers, green beans, and mushrooms with a couple of tablespoons of Vindaloo Paste. Add some baked or fried tofu chunks, a splash of tamari or soy sauce, a squeeze of lime or lemon juice, and a can of coconut milk. Add a little water or vegetable broth if you like it saucier and serve over basmati rice.

Makes about 1 cup

1 teaspoon coriander seeds
2 teaspoons cumin seeds
6 tablespoons chopped, peeled, fresh ginger
6 cloves garlic
2 teaspoons paprika
1 teaspoon ground turmeric
1 teaspoon red pepper flakes
1 teaspoon ground cardamom

1 teaspoon ground cloves
1 teaspoon salt
6 tablespoons vegetable oil

TOAST THE SPICES. Toast the coriander and cumin seeds in a hot dry skillet until fragrant, tossing a few times, and then grind in a spice or coffee grinder.

MIX THE PASTE. Put all the ingredients except the oil in a food processor. Process the mixture until it is combined, and then, with the machine running, drizzle in the oil until a smooth paste forms.

Panchphoron Spice Mixture [v]

Fennel and cumin are easy to find in most any grocery store. You'll most likely find fenugreek seeds at larger grocers or food co-ops with bulk-spice departments or at Mediterranean and Middle Eastern markets. Look for black mustard seeds and black onion seeds at Indian markets. You might also hit the jackpot at an Indian market, which sometimes sells packets of panchphoron spice already mixed up. If the ingredients are the same (or close), go for it!

This spice mixture is so versatile that we always have some stored in a jar in the restaurant. It turns a simple stir-fry of vegetables into something special. Add a teaspoon or two of the spice mix to hot oil, and cook until the seeds begin to sputter and become fragrant. Then add vegetables to the pan, and stir-fry as you would ordinarily.

Fennel seeds
Cumin seeds
Brown (or black) mustard seeds
Black onion seed (also known as nigella)
Fenugreek seeds (see page 239)

Mix equal portions of each spice, for this recipe, you probably need only 1 teaspoon each. Store the spice mixture in a jar or container with a tight-fitting lid away from the heat.

About Black Onion Seed (Nigella)

Nigella (or *kolonji*, its Indian name) is the tiny black seed of the *Nigella sativa* plant with a nutty, peppery flavor. Nigella is also known as black onion seed because of its resemblance to the seeds of an onion (although it is *not* the seed of an onion plant), and sometimes mistakenly called *kalo jeera*, which is black cumin seed. We've taken it from Indian cuisine. For example, you may have eaten it sprinkled on Indian breads, like naan.

Put the Vindaloo Together and Serve It

Roasted Vegetables (see page 107)
Spicy Goan Curry (see page 107)
¼ cup freshly squeezed lemon juice

Just before you're ready to serve the vindaloo, add the Roasted Vegetables to the Spicy Goan Curry. If you made the vegetables and the curry ahead, add the vegetables to the curry, and cook only long enough to heat through. Stir in the lemon juice, and serve immediately.

Pumpkin Enchiladas with Roasted Tomatillo Sauce [v]

Our dishes with a Mexican theme are always popular because they're both nourishing and tasty. For these enchiladas, we roast the

mushrooms to concentrate their flavor. You could also use smoked mushrooms here (see instructions for smoking foods on page 79), or you can add a little smokiness to the dish by topping it with a smoked cheese.

All the hard winter squashes suggested here have a naturally sweet flesh in common. Sugar pie pumpkins (not jack-o'-lanterns) are probably the most familiar squash because they're used to make pies. Kabocha, a Japanese pumpkin with a dark green skin, has a texture that's a cross between sweet potato and pumpkin. Red kuri looks like a reddish pumpkin, and its flesh has a distinctive chestnut flavor and a texture similar to butternut squash.

For a feast that celebrates fall and winter, serve these enchiladas with green-flecked rice, Black Bean Stew (see page 133), and Roasted Tomatillo Sauce on the side if you have some left over. (Room temperature is fine.) To make the rice, cook rice as you normally would. When you fluff it, toss in two tablespoons of roughly chopped cilantro and one very thinly sliced scallion to every two cups of cooked rice.

Serves 6

GET A HEAD START

You can make the Tomatillo Sauce and roast the squash and mushrooms 1 or 2 days before.

TIMING

If you're making this in a day, the pumpkin or squash will take about an hour to bake, and it must cool before you can use it. Roast the squash and mushrooms at the same time. Next roast the tomatillos and the poblanos for the Roasted Tomatillo Sauce.

2 tablespoons vegetable oil, plus oil for the pan and cooking the tortillas

4 pounds pumpkin, kabocha, or red kuri squash, unpeeled

½ pound button mushrooms

2 tablespoons tamari (see page 240)

1 medium yellow onion, coarsely chopped

1 medium zucchini, cut in ½-inch dice

5 cloves garlic, minced

1 teaspoon cumin seeds, toasted and ground (see page 52)

½ teaspoon ground cinnamon

½ teaspoon ground nutmeg

1 teaspoon chili powder

1 teaspoon pimenton (smoked Spanish paprika [see page 240])

1 teaspoon salt

12 thin corn tortillas

Roasted Tomatillo Sauce (recipe follows)

Optional: 2 cups grated cheese (8 ounces), such as Monterey Jack, smoked mozzarella, or vegan cheese

GET READY. Thoroughly oil a 13 × 9-inch baking dish with some oil or cooking spray. Preheat the oven to 350 degrees.

ROAST THE SQUASH. Split the pumpkin or squash in half, and scrape out the seeds and fiber. Put the cut sides down on a lightly greased baking sheet, and roast until tender and you can pierce the squash easily with a fork, 45 minutes to 1 hour. Remove from the oven and cool.

ROAST THE MUSHROOMS. Toss the mushrooms in a medium bowl with the tamari and 1 tablespoon of the oil, and spread on a lightly greased baking sheet. You can put the mushrooms in the oven with the squash; just leave some space between the racks. Roast for 30 minutes.

SAUTÉ THE ONION AND ZUCCHINI. While the squash and mushrooms are in the oven, heat 1 tablespoon vegetable oil in a large skillet over medium heat. Add the onion and sauté until the onion is soft and translucent, about 10 minutes.

Add the zucchini and garlic, and sauté for 5 more minutes. Add the spices and salt, and sauté for 1 minute more. Set aside to cool.

MIX ALL THE VEGETABLES. When the pumpkin is cool enough to handle, scoop out the flesh. When the mushrooms are cool, quarter or slice them thickly. Combine the squash, mushrooms, and onion-zucchini mixture in a large bowl, and mix thoroughly.

OIL THE TORTILLAS. Heat ⅛ inch oil in a skillet over medium heat. When the oil is hot, put a tortilla in the hot oil and fry until it is soft, 8 to 10 seconds; flip and repeat with the other side. Do not let the tortilla get crisp by letting the oil bubble up around its edges; reduce the heat to medium-low or low if this occurs. (It's important for the tortillas to be oily so they get crisp when roasted in the oven.)

KEEP THE TORTILLAS WARM. Put the tortilla on a plate and cover with foil to keep warm. Continue to heat the tortillas, piling them one on top of the other under the foil cover. (Keep the tortillas warm so they're pliable enough to stuff and roll without breaking.)

ASSEMBLE THE ENCHILADAS. Divide the squash filling equally among the 12 tortillas. Roll them up like tacos, and place them seam side down in the prepared baking dish.

ASSEMBLE AND BAKE THE ENCHILADAS. Bake until the edges of the tortillas have begun to crisp, about 20 minutes. Remove the pan from the oven, and just cover each enchilada with the tomatillo sauce. (This shouldn't be a bath of sauce.) Sprinkle with the cheese (if you're using it), and bake for 10 minutes more, or until the cheese is melted.

Roasted Tomatillo Sauce [v]

You'll be lucky if you have any of this left over. But if you do, it's terrific on scrambled eggs (or tofu).

Makes about 4 cups

12 tomatillos, husks and any stems removed

½ cup raw green pumpkin seeds, hulled

1 teaspoon vegetable oil

1 yellow onion, diced

3 cloves garlic, chopped

2 poblano chiles, roasted (see page 212) and roughly chopped

1 cup water

½ cup chopped fresh cilantro

Salt and freshly ground pepper

ROAST THE TOMATILLOS. Preheat the oven to 400 degrees. Put the tomatillos on a rimmed baking sheet, and roast, uncovered, for 15 minutes. The tomatillos will collapse and be browned and soft.

TOAST THE PUMPKIN SEEDS in a hot dry skillet, tossing until most of the seeds pop and are fragrant, 3 or 4 minutes. (Be careful not to burn them!) Set the toasted seeds aside.

SAUTÉ THE VEGETABLES. In a large heavy-bottomed saucepan, heat the oil over medium heat. Add the onion, and sauté until it is soft and translucent, about 10 minutes. Add the garlic and poblano chiles, and cook for 2 more minutes.

Add the tomatillos, their juice, and the water, and bring to a boil. Lower the heat and simmer until the tomatillos are tender, about 10 minutes.

PURÉE THE SAUCE. Put the toasted pumpkin seeds and cilantro in a blender with a few spoonfuls of the liquid from the onion-tomatillo sauté, and purée. Add the remaining onion-tomatillo mixture to the blender, and purée again until smooth. Add salt and pepper to taste.

Roasted Yam Enchiladas with Smoky Tomato Sauce [v]

The sweet flesh of roasted yams and the smoky flavor of chiles and cumin comes to us from the Mexican kitchen. We make these enchiladas meatier by adding roasted mushrooms, and bathe the whole dish in a smoky tomato-based sauce. Serve this with rice, Black Bean Stew (see page 133), our Pico de Gallo Salsa (see page 226) and your own guacamole or ours (see page 226).

Serves 6

1 tablespoon vegetable oil, plus extra for oiling the pan and cooking the tortillas

1 tablespoon onion powder

1 tablespoon cumin seeds, toasted and ground (see page 52)

1 tablespoon chili powder

Salt and freshly ground pepper

1½ pounds yams (see page 241), peeled and cut into ½-inch dice

1 pound domestic or crimini mushrooms, thickly sliced or quartered

12 thin corn tortillas

3 cups lightly packed raw spinach leaves, roughly chopped

1 poblano chile, roasted (see page 212) and diced

Smoky Tomato Sauce (recipe follows)

Optional: 2 cups grated Monterey or pepper jack, cheddar, or another cheese that melts (8 ounces)

GET READY. Thoroughly oil a 13 × 9-inch baking dish with olive oil or cooking spray. Preheat the oven to 400 degrees.

MIX THE SPICES. In a small bowl, mix the onion powder, cumin, chili powder, and a sprinkling of salt and pepper. Divide the spice mix in half.

ROAST THE YAMS. Toss the yams with ½ tablespoon of the oil, and then toss them with half of the spice mix. Spread the yams on a rimmed baking sheet large enough to accommodate them in a single layer without crowding. (If you crowd them, you will steam rather than roast them.) Roast until the yams are very tender but not mushy, about 30 minutes. Set aside to cool.

ROAST THE MUSHROOMS. Toss the mushrooms with the remaining ½ tablespoon oil, and then toss with the remaining half of the spice mix. Roast as for the yams on another rack in the oven until the mushrooms are tender, about 20 minutes. Set aside to cool. Lower the oven temperature to 350 degrees.

PREPARE THE TORTILLAS. Heat ⅛ inch oil in a skillet over medium heat. When the oil is hot, put a tortilla in it, and heat until soft, 8 to 10 seconds; flip and repeat with the other side. Do not let the tortilla get crisp by letting the oil bubble up around its edges; reduce the heat to medium-low or low if this occurs. (It's important for the tortillas to be oily so they get crisp when roasted in the oven.)

KEEP THE TORTILLAS WARM. Put the oiled tortilla on a plate and cover with foil to keep warm. Continue to heat the tortillas, piling them one on top of the other under the foil cover. (Keep the tortillas warm so they're pliable enough to stuff and roll without breaking.)

MIX THE ENCHILADA FILLING. When the yams and mushrooms are cool enough to work with, combine them with the spinach and roasted poblano. Season to taste with salt and pepper.

ASSEMBLE THE ENCHILADAS. Put a scoop of the yam-spinach mixture in the center of a tortilla. Use as much filling as you can; you want the enchiladas to be stuffed full. (Remember that the spinach will shrink as it cooks.)

Roll them up like tacos, and place them seam side down in the prepared baking dish. Repeat with remaining tortillas and filling.

BAKE THE ENCHILADAS. Bake until the edges of the tortillas have begun to get crisp, about 20 minutes. Remove from the oven, and just cover each enchilada with the Smoky Tomato Sauce; this shouldn't be a bath of sauce. Scatter with grated cheese, if you're using it.

Bake at 350 degrees for 10 to 20 minutes, until the sauce is bubbling and the cheese has melted.

Smoky Tomato Sauce [v]

This sauce is the perfect complement to any Mexican dish that calls for a tomato-based sauce like enchiladas or a wet burrito. It's mild, but if you want to turn up the heat, add a minced jalapeño or chipotle chile when you sauté the onion and garlic.

Makes about 3 cups

2 tablespoons olive oil

1 yellow onion, diced

2 tablespoons chopped garlic (about 4 or 5 cloves)

1 teaspoon cumin seeds, toasted and ground (see page 52)

1 teaspoon chili powder

2 teaspoons dried oregano

2 pounds ripe medium tomatoes (about 8 tomatoes), smoked (see page 79)

1½ teaspoons salt

¼ teaspoon freshly ground pepper

1 cup water

COOK THE SAUCE. In a medium saucepan, heat the olive oil over medium heat. Add the onion and sauté until it is soft and translucent, about 10 minutes. Add the garlic, cumin, chili powder, and oregano, and sauté for 1 minute longer. Add the smoked tomatoes, salt, and pepper, and break them up with a spoon to release their juices. Add the water, bring the pot to a boil, and simmer for 20 minutes.

PURÉE THE SAUCE in a blender, stopping the blender occasionally to scrape down the sides. If the sauce is too thick to keep the blender blade moving, add more water, 1 tablespoon at a time, until it moves freely. (The juiciness of the tomatoes affects the thickness of the sauce.) If it's too thick, it's very hard to strain.

STRAIN THE SAUCE. When the sauce is smooth and pourable, pour it through a mesh strainer to remove the tomato seeds and skins

TIP

I like to use Mexican oregano in Mexican-style dishes because of the subtle difference in its fragrance and flavor compared to the more common Greek oregano. Look for it (along with the chiles) in the Mexican or Latino food section of your local supermarket.

English Pea Pancakes with Colorful Vegetable Sauté and Basil Butter

Here's a terrific savory dish for a pancake supper, especially in springtime, when you can sometimes get fresh English peas—plump and sweet little pearls of green goodness. (These are also referred to as shelling peas because the pod, unlike that of the sugar snap or snow pea, cannot be eaten.) Even though it's rainy and cool until July here in the Northwest, a dish like this helps us pretend we have a season called spring.

For an elegant dinner, start with Linda's Marinated Goat Cheese (see page 7) or our Hazelnut-Crusted Goat Cheese Salad with Roasted Pear and Herbed Sherry Vinaigrette (see page 62).

Serves 6

GET A HEAD START

You can make the Basil Butter up to a week before. Just store it tightly wrapped in the refrigerator or freezer.

TIMING

This is the kind of dish you serve as soon as you finish making it, so make the Basil Butter at least an hour ahead so there's time enough for the butter to firm up for slicing. Have all the vegetables prepped and ready to cook before you cook the pancakes. Cook the pancakes, keeping them warm in the oven. Make the Colorful Vegetable Sauté last. It only takes a few minutes.

In this dish

- **English Pea Pancakes**
- **Colorful Vegetable Sauté**
- **Basil Butter**

English Pea Pancakes

Makes about 18 (5-inch) pancakes

3 cups shelled English (or shelling) peas, fresh or frozen and defrosted

1 shallot, minced

¼ cup finely chopped fresh mint

2 tablespoons finely chopped fresh basil

2½ cups milk

2 eggs, lightly beaten

3 tablespoons unsalted butter, melted and cooled

2 cups unbleached all-purpose flour

2 teaspoons baking powder

1 teaspoon baking soda

1 teaspoon salt

½ teaspoon freshly ground pepper

2 teaspoons sugar

Vegetable oil for the griddle

MAKE THE PANCAKE BATTER. In a blender, purée the peas with the shallot, mint, basil, and milk. Add the eggs and butter to the blender, and blend until combined.

Sift together the flour, baking powder, baking soda, salt, pepper, and sugar into a medium bowl. Add the pea mixture to these dry ingredients, and stir just until all the dry ingredients are incorporated. Be careful not to overbeat.

COOK THE PANCAKES. Heat a lightly greased griddle or nonstick skillet over medium heat. When it is hot, drop 3 tablespoons batter per pancake onto the hot skillet. Cook until bubbles form, about 3 minutes, and then flip to brown the other side, about 1 minute.

Stack the pancakes on a plate, cover with a damp towel, and keep warm in a 200-degree oven until all the pancakes are done.

Colorful Vegetable Sauté

Feel free to substitute other vegetables to get the most colorful sauté possible: small radishes cut in half, thinly sliced carrots or blanched baby carrots, yellow summer squash (in season), or orange or red bell peppers.

Makes 6 cups

1 tablespoon olive oil

2 cups asparagus, cut at a sharp angle in 1-inch pieces

1 cup snow or sugar snap peas, cut at a sharp angle in ½ inch pieces

1 yellow bell pepper, seeds removed and cut in 1-inch pieces

1 cup smallish cherry tomatoes, or 1 cup diced tomatoes

1 cup shelled fresh English (or shelling) peas, only if available

3 tablespoons white wine or vegetable stock

1 to 2 thick slices Basil Butter (recipe follows)

Salt and freshly ground pepper

SAUTÉ THE VEGETABLES. In a skillet, heat the olive oil over high heat. Add the asparagus, snow or sugar snap peas, and bell pepper, and sauté for 2 minutes. Add the tomatoes, English peas, and wine, and lower the heat. Cover the pan, and cook for 1 more minute.

SEASON THE SAUTÉ. Stir in the slices of Basil Butter, and add salt and pepper to taste. Remove the pan from the heat, and cover to keep it warm while you plate the pancakes. (But serve this dish quickly as the vegetables lose their sparkle if you hold them too long.)

TIP

If fresh English (shelling) peas are not available, you can make this anyway. Just increase the fresh sugar snap or snow peas to two cups.

Basil Butter

This butter is great on hot corn on the cob, too. Make this at least one hour ahead so there is time for the butter to firm up for slicing. You can even make this days ahead, because it freezes well, too. Just make sure to wrap the log tightly in foil so it doesn't absorb the flavors of the freezer.

Makes about 1 cup

½ pound (2 sticks) unsalted butter, at room temperature
2 cloves garlic, minced
1 small shallot, minced
¼ cup finely chopped Italian parsley
10 big basil leaves, finely chopped
1½ teaspoons salt
1 tablespoon freshly squeezed lemon juice
A few cranks of freshly ground pepper

COMBINE ALL THE INGREDIENTS in a food processor. Process until completely mixed, scraping down the sides of the bowl if necessary.

SHAPE THE BUTTER. Roll the butter into a log about 2 inches in diameter using plastic wrap or parchment paper to help you roll it. Twist each end tightly, and refrigerate until firm.

Serve the Pancakes

English Pea Pancakes (recipe above)
Basil Butter (recipe above)
Colorful Vegetable Sauté (recipe above)
Parsley, mint, and basil, finely chopped, for garnish

TO SERVE INDIVIDUALLY, place 3 pancakes overlapping in a circle on a warm plate. Put 2 slices of Basil Butter on them, and top with some of the sautéed vegetables. Scatter the chopped herbs over the entire plate.

TO SERVE FAMILY STYLE, overlap the pancakes around the edges of a warm platter. Top every 2 pancakes with a slice of Basil Butter, and pile the sautéed vegetables in the middle. Scatter the chopped herbs over the entire platter.

Black-Eyed Pea Fritters with Spiced Coconut Sauce and Turmeric Basmati Rice [v]

This dish is what the food at Cafe Flora is all about: the flavors of several cuisines, colorful and visually appealing, hearty and delicious. Served with steamed or sautéed vegetables, it's a savory and filling dinner. A platter of these fritters, with a small bowl of Spiced Coconut Sauce on the side for dipping, makes great party fare as well.

Serves 5

TIMING

If you're using dried black-eyed peas, start them soaking at least 2 hours ahead. (It's also OK to start them the night before.) Begin making the fritters by cooking the black-eyed peas. While they're cooking, start the coconut sauce. Mix up the fritters, and just before you start to fry them, put on the rice.

In this dish

- Black-Eyed Pea Fritters
- Spiced Coconut Sauce
- Turmeric Basmati Rice

Black-Eyed Pea Fritters

Makes about 15 fritters

1 cup dried black-eyed peas, soaked for 2 hours or up to 8 hours, or 2 (15-ounce) cans (about 2½ cups cooked)

2 tablespoons chopped garlic

3 stalks celery, finely diced

4 scallions, trimmed and chopped

1 teaspoon chili powder

½ teaspoon chipotle chile, toasted and ground (see "Toasting and Soaking Dried Chilies" page 102)

1 teaspoon pimenton (smoked paprika [see page 240])

1 teaspoon salt

½ teaspoon pepper

1 tablespoon Egg Replacer (see page 239), thoroughly mixed with 4 tablespoons water, or other egg substitute equal to 2 eggs

1 cup panko (Japanese-style bread crumbs [see page 239]), or unseasoned bread crumbs

½ cup vegetable oil

COOK THE BLACK-EYED PEAS. If you're using dried peas, drain them, and cover with about an inch of fresh water in a pot. Bring to a boil, lower the heat, and simmer, uncovered, until tender, 45 minutes to 1 hour. Check the pot during cooking to see if it needs more water. Drain and set aside to cool.

If you're using canned black-eyed peas, rinse them under cold water, and drain well.

MAKE THE FRITTER MIX. When the peas are cool enough to work with, put them in a food processor with the garlic, celery, scallions, spices, salt, and pepper. Pulse the contents 3 or 4 times to chop evenly, and then scrape down the sides of the bowl. Add the Egg Replacer mixture, and process for 1 minute.

Remove the pea mixture from the food processor, and put it in a large bowl. Add the panko, ¼ cup at a time, mixing with your hands after each addition, until the mixture holds together.

SHAPE THE FRITTERS. Using 2 tablespoons of the pea mixture for each fritter, shape the mixture into balls. Gently flatten each ball with your fingertips into a patty about 1½ inches in diameter. Smooth

out the jagged edges so they don't break off when you cook them.

DEEP-FRY THE FRITTERS. Put oil into a heavy pot to a depth of 2 inches. (Make sure the pot is at least 4 inches tall to reduce spattering.) When the oil reaches 350 to 360 degrees, gently drop in fritters, a few at a time so the temperature of the oil doesn't drop. (If you don't have a thermometer, see page 199 for alternative instructions.)

Cook on each side about 3 minutes. Use a slotted spoon or small strainer to remove fried bits from the pan between each batch as you fry them (so they don't burn). Drain the fritters on paper towels. Keep them warm in a 200-degree oven while you fry the remaining fritters.

TIPS

- If you're using canned black-eyed peas, read the label carefully to make sure they're vegetarian. Because black-eyed peas are such a staple in Southern cooking, they often contain ham or bacon.

- If the fritters fall apart as you shape or fry them, see "Tips for Making Sturdy Patties and Burgers," on page 177.

- For suggestions about how to save oil for later use, read "Saving Oil" on page 199.

Spiced Coconut Sauce [v]

Star anise is critical to the distinctive flavor of this sauce. But if you can't find fenugreek seeds, don't let that stop you from making this rich and spicy accompaniment to the fritters. This sauce is thin, so if you want it thicker, simply cook it longer to reduce it to a consistency you like.

Makes about 3 cups

3 star anise (see page 240)

1 teaspoon fennel seeds

1 teaspoon yellow mustard seeds

8 whole cloves

1 teaspoon fenugreek seeds (see page 239)

2 (14-ounce) cans coconut milk

1 tablespoon tamari (see page 240) or soy sauce

2 tablespoons dry sherry

1 tablespoon molasses

1 tablespoon tomato paste

1 bay leaf

½ teaspoon chili powder

½ teaspoon onion powder

TOAST THE SPICES. In a saucepan over medium heat, toast the 5 spices until the mustard seeds begin to pop.

ADD ALL THE REMAINING INGREDIENTS, and bring to a boil. Lower the heat, and simmer for 30 minutes. Pour the sauce through a mesh strainer, and serve hot.

Turmeric Basmati Rice [v]

The turmeric gives this rice a bright yellow color, which makes a nice contrast with the black-eyed pea fritters and tan coconut sauce. A member of the ginger family, turmeric imparts a slight gingery flavor and aroma.

Makes 3 cups

1 cup basmati rice, rinsed twice

1⅓ cups water

1 bay leaf

1½ teaspoons ground turmeric

½ teaspoon salt

Put the rice in a pot with the water and bay leaf. Stir in the turmeric and salt. Bring the pot to a boil, cover, and cook over low heat until the rice is tender and the water is absorbed, about 15 minutes. Let rest for 10 minutes, and fluff the rice with a fork.

Serve the Dish

For visual appeal and crunch, you could also top each plate with thinly sliced jicama and radicchio.

Spiced Coconut Sauce (see page 116)

Turmeric Rice (recipe above)

Black-Eyed Pea Fritters (see page 115)

Ladle one-fifth of the Spiced Coconut Sauce in the center of a pasta or shallow soup bowl. Mound some Turmeric Rice on top of it, and top with 3 Black-Eyed Pea Fritters. Repeat for the remaining 4 bowls.

Ocean Cakes with Gingery Mashed Sweet Potatoes and Tamarind Cilantro Sauce [v]

We drizzle Tamarind Cilantro Sauce over these crispy-crusted panfried cakes and serve them hot with mashed sweet potatoes redolent with pickled ginger. The Ocean Cakes are also good with our Spicy Rémoulade (see page 23) or your favorite tartar sauce.

For a substantial and delicious sandwich, make the cakes bigger and serve them on a soft roll. But whether you make them for dinner or lunch, Waitin' for Spring Cabbage Salad (see page 82) and Smoky Collard Greens (see page 211) make a tasty addition.

Serves 6

GET A HEAD START

You need an hour to soak the arame and press the tofu before you start mixing up these ocean cakes. (You can also do these two things the day before.)

Ocean Cakes

Don't let the long list of ingredients in this recipe intimidate you because these cakes are relatively simple to make. Most ingredients are spices, condiments, or prepared foods that you merely need to measure out and combine. (You can cut back on the time even further by using a commercial vegan mayonnaise instead of making it yourself.) The arame seaweed gives these cakes a distinctive taste of the sea, and a flavor and texture similar to crab cakes.

Serves 6 generously

½ cup (about 1 ounce) arame (seaweed) [see page 238])

1 tablespoon olive oil

1 yellow onion, finely diced

1 red bell pepper, seeds removed and finely diced

2 stalks celery, finely diced

2 tablespoons chopped garlic

1 (14- to 16-ounce) block firm tofu, pressed (see page 22), or extra firm

½ cup chopped fresh parsley

2 tablespoons Dijon mustard

¼ cup Cafe Flora Vegan Mayonnaise (see page 231), or purchased vegan mayonnaise

1 tablespoon pimenton (smoked Spanish paprika [see page 240])

1 teaspoon salt

1 teaspoon onion powder

1 teaspoon dry mustard

2 large basil leaves, minced, or ½ teaspoon dried basil

1 teaspoon picked and chopped thyme, or ½ teaspoon dried thyme

¼ teaspoon cayenne pepper

½ teaspoon freshly ground black pepper

2 cups panko (Japanese bread crumbs [see page 239]), or unseasoned bread crumbs

¼ cup vegetable oil

PREPARE THE ARAME. Rinse the arame in a strainer under running water. Put it in a bowl and add enough cold water just to cover. Soak for 10 minutes. Drain well, coarsely chop, and set aside.

SAUTÉ THE VEGETABLES WITH THE ARAME. Warm the olive oil in the skillet over medium heat. Add the onion, bell pepper, celery, and garlic, and sauté until the onion is soft and translucent, about 10 minutes.

Lower the heat to medium, add the arame, and cook for 2 minutes. Remove from the heat and cool. If the mixture is wet, drain off any liquid before combining with the remaining ingredients.

MIX ALL THE INGREDIENTS. Crumble the pressed tofu into a medium bowl, and then mix in the cooled arame-vegetable mixture and all the remaining ingredients except the panko and vegetable oil.

Sprinkle on 1 cup of panko, and mix well. Add more panko, 1 tablespoon at a time, until the mixture holds together.

SHAPE THE PATTIES. Using 3 tablespoons of mixture for each patty, shape the mixture into balls. Gently flatten each ball with your fingertips into a patty about 2½ inches in diameter. Smooth out the jagged edges so they don't break off when you cook them.

BREAD THE PATTIES. Just before you're ready to fry the patties, put the remaining panko on a plate or in a bowl. Press the breading onto each patty until it is well coated.

PANFRY THE PATTIES. Heat 2 tablespoons oil in a large nonstick skillet over medium-high heat. (If you don't have a nonstick pan, any heavy skillet works well.) Put several patties in the pan, leaving enough room to flip them easily. (Go easy when you flip them over; they're fragile.)

Cook the patties until light brown, about 2 minutes per side. Remove bits from the pan between batches so they don't burn. Add more oil as needed between batches.

> **TIP**
>
> If the patties fall apart as you shape or fry them, see "Tips for Making Sturdy Patties and Burgers," on page 177.

Tamarind Cilantro Sauce [v]

There's really no substitute for the tangy tamarind concentrate, so if you can't get it, try Spicy Rémoulade (see page 231) instead; it's different than the sauce here, but equally good.

Makes about 1 cup

1 bunch fresh cilantro

½ cup tamarind concentrate or pulp (see page 240)

1 tablespoon light brown sugar

1 tablespoon mirin (seasoned rice wine [see page 239]), or to taste

Combine all the ingredients in a blender, and blend until smooth. Taste and add another 1 tablespoon mirin if you want.

Gingery Mashed Sweet Potatoes [v]

Makes about 4 cups

2 pounds sweet potatoes, peeled and cut into 1-inch chunks

½ cup rice or soy milk

1 to 2 tablespoons pickled ginger (see page 239), minced

1 teaspoon salt

½ teaspoon pepper

COOK THE SWEET POTATOES in salted, boiling water until tender, about 12 minutes. Drain the potatoes in a colander. Return the cooked potatoes to the pot, turn the heat on low to evaporate any excess water, and then turn off the heat.

MASH THE SWEET POTATOES. Using a potato masher, add rice milk as you mash, until the potatoes are smooth. Add the pickled ginger, salt, and pepper, and mash again to combine. Keep the mashed potatoes warm until ready to serve.

Serve the Ocean Cakes

Gingery Mashed Sweet Potatoes (recipe above)
Ocean Cakes (recipe on opposite page)
Tamarind Cilantro Sauce (recipe above)

Put a scoop of mashed potatoes on a plate, and rest 3 Ocean Cakes against it. Drizzle with the Tamarind Cilantro Sauce.

Artichoke Croquettes with Lemon Cream Sauce and Braised Black Lentils

We often design dishes so all our guests, vegans and nonvegans alike, will be able to eat them; these croquettes are an example. The croquettes are prepared without dairy or eggs as are the lentils, the Lime Chile Sauce, and the salad topping. If you're serving this to someone who is vegan (or watching fat intake), simply omit the Lemon Cream Sauce.

At Cafe Flora, we mound Braised Black Lentils in a pool of pale yellow Lemon Cream Sauce. On top of that we lay three crispy, tart, Artichoke Croquettes teepee style, top with a little bit of green salad, and dribble Lime Chile Sauce over all.

This dish was a popular entrée on our dinner menu for quite a long time. But when we needed to make room for new dishes, we decided to serve a scaled-down version as an appetizer. To make this dish as a first course, omit the black lentils. Place one or two croquettes on a small pool of Lemon Cream Sauce, drizzle with a tablespoon of Lime Chile Sauce, and top with the small salad of baby greens. Serves 4 for dinner. Serves 6 to 12 as an appetizer.

GET A HEAD START

You can make the croquettes, cream sauce, lentils, and chile sauce the day before. You can also make the patties ahead, but stop short of coating them with panko. Leave this step until you are ready to fry the patties so the coating doesn't get soggy.

TIMING

Start by making the Artichoke Croquettes. While they chill for an hour, start the cream sauce. When that's simmering, braise the lentils.

Panfrying the croquettes will take 30 minutes or less, and once cooked they can be kept warm in a 200-degree oven for up to half an hour. While you're panfrying the croquettes, warm up the lentils and cream sauce.

In this dish

- **Lemon Cream Sauce**
- **Braised Black Lentils**
- **Artichoke Croquettes**
- **Lime Chile Sauce**

Lemon Cream Sauce

Omit this sauce if you want to make this a vegan dish.

Try this luscious sauce tossed with hot linguine or fettuccine. Balance its rich creaminess by then tossing the pasta with a sauté of colorful vegetables cut into 1-inch pieces. To finish the dish, grate more Parmesan over it and sprinkle with chopped Italian parsley.

Makes 1¾ cups

2 tablespoons unsalted butter
¼ cup minced shallot
1 clove garlic, minced
1 cup white wine
2 cups heavy cream
1 tablespoon grated lemon zest
2 tablespoons freshly squeezed lemon juice
½ cup finely grated Parmesan cheese
Salt and freshly ground pepper

SAUTÉ THE SHALLOT AND GARLIC. Heat the butter in a medium saucepan over medium heat until foamy.

Add the shallot and garlic and cook until translucent, 5 to 7 minutes.

ADD THE LIQUIDS. Add the wine and cook at a low boil until reduced by half, about 15 minutes.

Add the cream and cook at a low boil until reduced by about one-third and the sauce thickly coats the back of a spoon, about 15 minutes. (You should have about 1⅔ cups sauce after this second reduction.)

BLEND IN THE LEMON AND PARMESAN CHEESE. Pour the hot sauce into a blender and add the lemon zest and juice. With the blender running at medium speed, add the cheese 2 tablespoons at a time, and blend until it's completely incorporated.

FINISH THE SAUCE. Pour the sauce through a mesh strainer back into the saucepan, and add salt and pepper to taste. Keep it warm over low heat until ready to serve. If you're not serving the sauce right away, refrigerate it. Later, reheat gently over medium-low heat just until hot.

TIP

If you prefer a thicker sauce, dissolve ½ teaspoon cornstarch in 1 teaspoon cold water, and whisk into the strained sauce. Stir over medium heat until the sauce has thickened slightly.

Braised Black Lentils [v]

We use black lentils because their deep color contrasts with the citrus cream sauce and the Artichoke Croquettes, and because they keep their shape when cooked. For equally good results, you can substitute French green (Le Puy) lentils. If you need to reheat these, warm them in a saucepan with one or two tablespoons water or vegetable broth over low heat, giving them an occasional gentle stir.

Makes about 2 cups

1 tablespoon olive oil

2 cloves garlic, minced

1 shallot or small red onion, minced

1 cup black (Beluga) lentils, or French green (Le Puy) lentils (see page 239)

1 bay leaf

1 tablespoon fresh thyme leaves, or 1 teaspoon dried thyme

4 cups water

¼ teaspoon salt

¼ teaspoon freshly ground pepper

SAUTÉ THE GARLIC AND SHALLOT. Heat the olive oil in a medium saucepan over medium heat. Add the garlic and shallot, and cook, stirring constantly, until the shallot is translucent, 5 to 7 minutes.

COOK THE LENTILS. Add the lentils, bay leaf, and thyme, and give the lentils a stir to coat them with the oil. Cover with the water, turn up the heat, and bring the pot to a boil. Lower the heat, cover, and simmer the lentils until tender, 20 to 25 minutes.

Drain off the remaining liquid, discard the bay leaf and add the salt and pepper. Keep the lentils warm until ready to use.

Artichoke Croquettes [v]

Makes 12 croquettes

1 (14-ounce) can artichoke hearts, rinsed, drained, and roughly chopped

½ cup Vegan Mayonnaise (see page 231), or purchased vegan mayonnaise

2 cups panko (Japanese bread crumbs [see page 239]), plus 1 cup for breading, or unseasoned bread crumbs

¼ cup finely diced celery

¼ cup finely diced onion

½ cup finely diced red bell pepper

1 tablespoon capers, rinsed, drained, and chopped

1 tablespoon chopped fresh cilantro

¼ cup chopped scallions, white and green part, about 2 scallions

⅛ teaspoon cayenne pepper

½ teaspoon chili powder

½ teaspoon salt

Vegetable oil for panfrying croquettes

MIX THE CROQUETTES. Combine all the ingredients in a bowl except the 1 cup of panko you've reserved for breading the croquettes and the oil. Mix well. Refrigerate for at least an hour.

SHAPE THE CROQUETTES. Using 2 tablespoons of the mixture, shape it into balls. Gently flatten each ball with your fingertips into a patty about 1½ inches in diameter. Smooth out the jagged edges so they don't break off when you cook them.

COAT THE CROQUETTES WITH PANKO. Put the remaining 1 cup panko in a shallow bowl. Completely coat all the croquettes with panko, and lay them on an ungreased baking sheet until you're ready to fry them.

PANFRY THE CROQUETTES. Heat 2 tablespoons oil in a large nonstick skillet over medium-high heat. (If you don't have a nonstick pan, any heavy skillet works well.) When the oil is hot, put several patties in the pan, leaving enough room to flip them easily. Cook on each side until browned and heated through, 3 to 4 minutes per side.

Between batches wipe out the pan to remove any burned bits, and use additional 2 tablespoons oil per batch. Keep the croquettes warm in a 200-degree oven until you're ready to serve them.

> **TIP**
>
> If the croquettes fall apart as you shape or fry them, see "Tips for Making Sturdy Patties and Burgers," on page 177.

Lime Chile Sauce [v]

Sometimes we don't mess with a good thing, at least not too much. This recipe uses as its base sweet chile sauce, a Vietnamese-style bottled sauce that is most often served with rice-paper-wrapped spring rolls. It is sweet, syrupy, and remarkably unspicy considering all the chile flakes it contains. We add fresh lime juice and zest for a contrasting tart flavor.

Makes about ½ cup

½ cup bottled sweet chile sauce

Grated zest and juice of one lime

Combine the sweet chile sauce with the zest and lime juice.

Serve the Croquettes [v]

2 cups loosely packed baby mixed salad greens

1 tablespoon olive oil

1 teaspoon sherry vinegar

Pinch of salt and pepper

Optional: Lemon Cream Sauce (recipe above)

Braised Black Lentils (recipe above)

Artichoke Croquettes (recipe above)

Lime Chile Sauce (recipe above)

MAKE THE SALAD. In a small bowl, toss the baby salad greens with the olive oil until the leaves are coated. Toss again with the sherry vinegar, and then toss one last time with the salt and pepper.

SERVE THE CROQUETTES. If you're not serving vegans, pool one-fourth of the warm Lemon Cream Sauce on each plate. Mound one-fourth of the Braised Black Lentils in the center of the sauce in a high, neat pile. Place 3 croquettes up against the pile of lentils in a circle, at approximately 12 o'clock, 4 o'clock, and 8 o'clock positions. Top with one-fourth of the salad, and drizzle 2 tablespoons of the Lime Chile Sauce over the entire plate. Serve at once.

Spinach, Mushroom, and Gorgonzola Puff Pastry Rolls with Roasted Red Pepper Coulis

The vegetables are sautéed and then rolled up in puff pastry, baked until golden and puffy, and served in a pool of Roasted Red Pepper Coulis. These delectable puff pastry rolls don't need much to make a complete dinner. Try them with steamed or roasted asparagus in season, sautéed zucchini and yellow squash, or steamed broccoli and cauliflower florets.

Serves 6

GET A HEAD START

Toast the pine nuts before you begin, and make the Roasted Red Pepper Coulis while the puff pastry bakes.

1 (17.3-ounce) box Pepperidge Farm puff pastry (see Tip)

2 tablespoons olive oil

½ pound mushrooms, crimini or domestic, cut in ¼-inch thick slices

Salt and freshly ground pepper

½ yellow onion, medium dice

2 cloves garlic, minced

1 bunch spinach (about 1½ pounds), stems removed and leaves left whole

2 tablespoons white wine

4 to 6 ounces Gorgonzola cheese, crumbled

¼ cup pine nuts, toasted (see page 150)

GET READY. Remove the frozen puff pastry from the box. (The pastry works best when it's thawed but still cold; this takes about 20 minutes.) Thaw it uncovered and folded (just as it comes out of the box) on a lightly floured surface.

SAUTÉ THE MUSHROOMS. In a skillet large enough to accommodate all the spinach, heat 1 tablespoon of the olive oil over medium-high heat. Add the sliced mushrooms, and cook until they are browned, about 4 minutes. Season with a pinch of salt and pepper, remove the mushrooms from the pan, and set aside.

COOK THE ONION AND GARLIC. Heat the remaining tablespoon of oil in the same pan over medium heat. Add the onion and garlic, and sauté until the onion is soft and translucent, about 10 minutes.

COOK THE SPINACH. Add the spinach to the skillet, and cook until it wilts. Add the white wine and cook until all the liquid evaporates, about 3 minutes. Season the onion-spinach mixture with a pinch of salt and pepper, and set aside to cool.

When the mixture is cool enough to handle, roughly chop it. Put it in a strainer, and gently press once or twice to remove the excess liquid.

ROLL OUT AND CUT THE PUFF PASTRY. Roll out each puff pastry sheet into a 12-inch square. Cut each square into fourths so you have eight 6-inch squares. (You'll need only 6 of these smaller squares, three-fourths of the package.) Preheat the oven to 350 degrees.

DIVIDE THE STUFFING AMONG THE 6 SQUARES. On the bottom half of each square, center one-sixth of the spinach and add a layer of mushrooms. Top with a tablespoon or less of Gorgonzola (depending on your love of blue cheese), and finish with pine nuts. Repeat this with all the squares.

ASSEMBLE THE ROLLS. Fold the top half of each pastry square over the filling. (You now have a stuffed rectangle with open ends.) Press the top and bottom edges together, and crimp with the tines of a fork to seal them. (The ends are still open.)

Coax the rectangle into a sausage-like shape with the crimped edge on top. Crimp the two open ends to seal them. (The finished product should look a bit like a sausage roll or a hot pocket.)

BAKE THE ROLLS on an ungreased baking sheet in the preheated oven until golden brown all over, 20 to 25 minutes. (This is a lower temperature than indicated on the Pepperidge Farm box because the contents need to cook as well.)

TIP

Pepperidge Farm puff pastry comes two sheets per package, each about ten inches square. Look for them in the frozen-food section of the supermarket along with the pies and crusts. A common commercial size package weighs about a pound, and measures 15 × 10 inches. Look for the Dufour brand at Whole Foods or specialty food stores.

Roasted Red Pepper Coulis [V]

Coulis is just another term for a thick purée of fruits or vegetables, and a great way to add an accent color to dishes.

Makes 2½ cups

1 teaspoon olive oil

½ yellow onion, chopped

2 tablespoons red wine

3 large red bell peppers, roasted (see page 212) and roughly chopped

Salt and freshly ground pepper

COOK THE COULIS. Heat the oil in a medium saucepan over medium heat. Add the onion, and sauté until it is soft and translucent, about 10 minutes.

Add the wine, and cook until it evaporates, about 1 minute. Add the peppers and ½ cup water, bring to a boil, and then reduce the heat to simmer for 15 minutes.

PURÉE THE COULIS. Remove the sauce from the heat, and purée in a blender until smooth. If the sauce seems too thick, add up to ¼ cup water as you blend it to keep it moving. Season with salt and pepper to taste.

If you're not serving the coulis immediately, return it to the saucepan, and keep warm over low heat.

Serve the Puff Pastry Rolls

Roasted Red Pepper Coulis (recipe above)

Gorgonzola Puff Pastry Rolls (recipe above)

Divide the Roasted Red Pepper Coulis among 6 plates. Cut each puff pastry roll in half on the diagonal. Set one half on the coulis, and lean the other half against it at an opposing angle, as if they were logs and you were building a fire.

Roasted Vegetable and Wild Rice Roulade with Parsnip Purée [v]

The culinary term *roulade* can mean different things, but generally it means something wrapped around a filling. Here we build six roulades by simply wrapping a couple of buttered sheets of phyllo dough around a savory filling, baking it, and serving it with a sweet, silky, parsnip purée. This dish would be great served with a salad of baby spinach, shaved fennel, and apple slices tossed with a sherry vinegar and olive oil vinaigrette.

Serves 6 generously

GET A HEAD START

You can roast the vegetables, cook the wild rice, and make the Parsnip Purée a day or two in advance.

TIMING

When you put the wild rice on to cook, put the squash, celery root, and carrots in the oven, and start the Parsnip Purée. You can finish it while the roulades bake.

12 sheets phyllo dough

1/3 cup wild rice

2 cups water

1 small butternut squash (about 1½ pounds), peeled, seeds removed, and cut into ½-inch dice

1 celery root (about 10 ounces), peeled and cut into ½-inch dice

2 carrots, peeled and cut into ½-inch dice

1 tablespoon plus 2 teaspoons olive oil

1 yellow onion, diced

2 ribs celery, diced

1 tablespoon chopped garlic

¼ cup chopped fresh parsley

1 tablespoon chopped fresh sage, or 1 teaspoon dried sage

1 tablespoon chopped fresh thyme, or 1 teaspoon dried thyme

Salt and freshly ground pepper

Soy margarine, melted, or olive oil for the phyllo

Parsnip Purée (recipe follows)

GET READY. If the phyllo is frozen, take it out of the freezer to thaw, leaving it in its box. Preheat the oven to 400 degrees.

COOK THE WILD RICE. Rinse the wild rice in a fine strainer under cold water. Put it in a small saucepan with the water, and bring to a boil. Lower the heat to a simmer, and cook, uncovered, until tender, stirring occasionally, about 40 minutes. (Add more water if most of it evaporates before the rice is tender.) Drain off any remaining liquid, and set aside to cool completely.

ROAST THE SQUASH, CELERY ROOT, AND CARROTS. While the wild rice cooks, toss the squash, celery root, and carrots with the 1 tablespoon olive oil in a large bowl until completely coated.

Spread the vegetables on a rimmed baking sheet large enough to accommodate all the vegetables in a single layer without crowding. (If you crowd them, you will steam rather than roast them.) Roast until tender, 25 to 30 minutes. Remove from the oven and lower the oven temperature to 350 degrees.

COOK THE ONION. While the vegetables roast, heat the remaining 2 teaspoons olive oil in a skillet over medium heat. Add the onion, celery, and garlic, and cook until the onion is soft and translucent, about 10 minutes. Set aside until the vegetables are out of the oven.

FINISH THE ROULADE FILLING. Combine the roasted vegetables with the onion mixture in a large bowl.

Mix in the wild rice, parsley, sage, and thyme. Season with salt and pepper to taste.

BRUSH THE PHYLLO WITH MARGARINE. Remove the phyllo from the box and unfold it, covering it with a damp towel to keep it from drying out. Lay out 1 sheet on your work surface with the short end (13 inches) closest to you, and brush it gently with some of the margarine. Lay 1 more sheet on top of the other sheet and brush with margarine.

ASSEMBLE THE ROULADES. Spread 1 cup of the filling (about one-sixth) evenly over the bottom third of the phyllo. Roll the phyllo into a tight cylinder (13 inches wide), open at both ends. Brush the cylinder with more margarine.

REPEAT THE LAST TWO STEPS. Repeat 5 more times the process of brushing the remaining sheets of phyllo with margarine, and then filling and rolling them.

BAKE THE ROULADES. Place the roulades on a baking sheet, and bake until golden brown, 20 to 25 minutes.

SERVE THE ROULADES. Ladle ½ to ⅔ cup warm Parsnip Purée on a warm plate. Cut each roulade in half at an angle. Place one half on the sauce, and lean the other half against it at an opposing angle, as if they were logs and you were building a fire.

Parsnip Purée [v]

Makes about 4 cups

6 sprigs fresh parsley
4 sprigs fresh thyme
kitchen twine
1 teaspoon olive oil
1 yellow onion, diced
2 ribs celery, diced
2 parsnips (about ¾ pound total), peeled and diced
¼ cup white wine
3 cups rice or soy milk
1 bay leaf
¼ cup silken tofu, drained if packed in water
Salt and freshly ground pepper

GET READY. Bundle the parsley and thyme together, and tie them tightly with kitchen twine, and set aside.

COOK THE VEGETABLES AND HERBS. Heat the olive oil in a medium saucepan over medium heat. Add the onion and celery and cook until the onion is soft and translucent, about 10 minutes.

Add the parsnips and wine, and continue cooking until most of the wine has evaporated. Add 2 cups of the milk, the bundle of herbs, and bay leaf. (The milk will curdle, but don't worry because you'll purée it in the next step.)

Simmer over low heat until the parsnips are tender, about 30 minutes.

PURÉE AND STRAIN THE SAUCE. Remove the bundle of herbs and bay leaf, and transfer the sauce to a blender. Add the tofu. Purée the sauce, adding the remaining 1 cup milk while the machine is running.

For a perfectly smooth sauce, pour it through a mesh strainer. (If you don't mind a little texture in the sauce, you can skip this step.) Add salt and pepper to taste. Keep warm until ready to serve, or refrigerate until ready to use.

Moussaka with Mushrooms, Lentils, and Walnuts

Moussaka always seemed perfectly suited for conversion to a vegetarian dish. The problem, however, was coming up with a substantial, "meaty" filling to replace the traditional lamb. A '70s party I planned with friends served up the solution to the problem. We were all to dress like flower children—tie-dye, headbands, frizzy wigs, bell bottoms—and eat hippie food. Vegetarian, of course.

Inspired by the vegetarian moussaka in the *Tassajara Cookbook*, I discovered that roasted mushrooms that have been finely chopped look a little like beef. To that I added lentils and toasted walnuts for body and texture, and then ground up the whole thing. The result? Something that not only *looked* like ground beef, but was a complete protein, too.

To make the moussaka, we layer the mushroom-lentil-walnut filling with roasted eggplant and an aromatic tomato sauce, top it with a rich ricotta béchamel, and bake to a golden brown. This dish has a few steps to it but it will feed a crowd or make lots of enticing leftovers. Serve it with something sprightly—an orzo salad, for example. Toss orzo, a rice-size, rice-shaped pasta, with Lemon Garlic Vinaigrette (see page 134) and garnish it with chopped parsley.

Serves 9 to 12

GET A HEAD START

Making this moussaka takes a few hours. But luckily you can make any or all parts of this sturdy dish the day or two before you plan to serve it. You can then assemble the dish an hour and a half before dinner, about the time it takes to bake. (You can also assemble the whole moussaka in advance, except for the made-ahead ricotta béchamel, which you put on just before you bake it.)

TIMING

- Prepare the eggplant for roasting. While it's draining, roast the mushrooms, and start the lentils.

- Roast the eggplant. While it is roasting, start the tomato sauce.

- While the tomato sauce cooks, make the ricotta béchamel sauce.

In this dish

- **Mushroom-Lentil-Walnut Mixture**
- **Roasted Eggplant**
- **Cinnamon Tomato Sauce**
- **Ricotta Béchamel**

Mushroom-Lentil-Walnut Mixture [v]

I'm in love with this rich, savory, slightly crunchy mixture. In addition to filling our moussaka, it makes a wonderful stuffing for vegetables such as zucchini, portobello mushroom caps, or bell peppers. I sometimes mix in cheese, such as feta or Parmesan, before stuffing the vegetables. Once stuffed, the vegetables are roasted in a 350-degree oven until they're tender and the stuffing is hot. This mixture would also be a nice addition to lasagna or another baked pasta dish.

Makes 3½ cups

1 pound crimini whole mushrooms
2 tablespoons olive oil
½ cup French green (Le Puy) lentils (see page 239)
1½ cups cold water
1 bay leaf
1 cup broken walnuts, toasted (see page 150)
½ cup chopped fresh parsley
1 tablespoon chopped fresh oregano, or 1 teaspoon dried oregano

1 teaspoon pimenton (smoked Spanish paprika
[see page 240])

1 teaspoon salt

¼ teaspoon freshly ground pepper

ROAST THE MUSHROOMS. Preheat the oven to 350 degrees. Toss the mushrooms with the oil to coat them. Put them on a rimmed baking sheet in a single layer, and roast for 20 minutes. The mushrooms will shrink and their juices will become more concentrated. Set them aside.

COOK THE LENTILS. Rinse the lentils, and put them in a medium saucepan with the water and bay leaf. Bring to a boil and then lower the heat. Simmer, covered, until tender, 20 to 25 minutes. Drain the lentils, remove the bay leaf, and set aside.

PROCESS THE MUSHROOMS, LENTILS, AND WALNUTS. When the mushrooms are cool enough to handle, put them in a food processor. Pulse 3 or 4 times, and scrape down the bowl. Add the walnuts and pulse several more times, until the mushrooms and walnuts are evenly chopped and the texture of cooked ground beef.

MIX ALL THE REMAINING INGREDIENTS. Put the mushroom-walnut mixture in a medium bowl. Thoroughly mix in the lentils, parsley, oregano, pimenton, salt, and pepper. Set aside.

Roasted Eggplant [v]

Makes 4 to 4½ cups

3 large eggplants, 3 to 3½ pounds

2 tablespoons kosher salt

¼ cup olive oil

PREPARE THE EGGPLANT FOR ROASTING. Peel the eggplant, and slice into ½-inch-thick rounds. Put the slices in a colander, sprinkle with the salt, and let them drain for 30 minutes. Preheat the oven to 350 degrees.

ROAST THE EGGPLANT. Rinse the eggplant slices thoroughly, and pat dry. Brush 2 baking sheets with oil. Brush the eggplant with the remaining oil and spread the slices on the baking sheets. Roast until tender, about 30 minutes.

Cinnamon Tomato Sauce [v]

Makes 3½ cups

1 tablespoon olive oil

½ teaspoon salt

1 large yellow onion, diced

1 tablespoon chopped garlic

1 teaspoon ground cinnamon

⅛ teaspoon ground cloves

½ cup red wine

1 (28-ounce) can diced tomatoes in purée

2 cups water

½ cup chopped fresh parsley

1 tablespoon chopped fresh oregano

COOK THE ONION, GARLIC, AND SPICES. Heat the oil in a large heavy-bottomed pot over medium heat. Add the salt and the onion, and sauté until the onion is soft and translucent, about 10 minutes. Add the garlic, cinnamon, and cloves, and cook for 1 minute more, stirring constantly.

ADD THE REMAINING INGREDIENTS, AND SIMMER. Add the wine and deglaze the pan by stirring and scraping to remove any bits from the pan bottom. Cook until most of the wine has evaporated, 2 to 3 minutes.

Add the tomatoes with juice, water, parsley, and oregano. Lower the heat, and simmer gently for 30 minutes.

Ricotta Béchamel

Makes 2½ cups

2 cups milk

2 tablespoons unsalted butter

¼ cup unbleached all-purpose flour

¼ teaspoon ground nutmeg

¼ teaspoon salt

¼ teaspoon ground white pepper

½ cup ricotta cheese

SCALD THE MILK in a small pot by heating it over low heat until just before it boils; look for small bubbles around the edge of the pot, and take it off the heat.

MAKE THE ROUX. Melt the butter in a second small saucepan over low heat, and stir in the flour. Cook, stirring constantly, until the mixture is bubbling but not brown, about 2 minutes.

FINISH THE SAUCE. Slowly add the scalded milk, and cook, continuing to stir as the sauce thickens. Add the nutmeg, salt, and white pepper. Cook for 5 minutes over low heat, stirring constantly to prevent scorching. Remove from the heat, fold in the ricotta cheese, and refrigerate until ready to use.

Put the Moussaka Together

Cinnamon Tomato Sauce (recipe opposite)

Roasted Eggplant (recipe opposite)

Mushroom-Lentil-Walnut Mixture (recipe page 127)

1½ cups grated Asiago cheese, or Parmesan or Romano cheese (6 ounces)

Ricotta Béchamel (recipe above)

½ cup bread crumbs, toasted (see below)

Toasting Bread Crumbs

We serve a lot of bread at Cafe Flora, and inevitably we end up with a lot of bread ends (or butts, as we affectionately call them). We don't throw them out; we save them throughout the week and make bread crumbs (or croutons) from them. Four cups of bread pieces will make about one cup of bread crumbs.

SAVE YOUR BREAD! Any time you have leftover bread, let the bread sit out a day or two in a paper bag to get stale, and then store it in the freezer until you're ready to make bread crumbs.

CUT UP THE BREAD. Cut the stale bread into pieces about 2 inches square before toasting. (Smaller pieces are easier to pulverize in the food processor.)

TOAST THE BREAD. Preheat the oven to 250 degrees. Spread the chunks of bread on a rimmed baking sheet large enough to accommodate them in a single layer without crowding. Bake the bread pieces until they are hard and dry, about 1 hour.

MAKE THE BREAD CRUMBS. Put some of the toasted bread pieces in the food processor, leaving enough room for the processor blade to move freely. Pulse several times to break up the bread pieces into smaller bits, and then process at full power to grind them into small crumbs. Repeat this procedure with the remaining pieces of bread.

STORE THE BREAD CRUMBS. In a tightly covered container, the crumbs will keep in your pantry for 2 weeks. Or put them in a self-sealing plastic freezer bag, squeezing out all the air as you seal it, and freeze for up to 3 months.

GET READY. Preheat the oven to 350 degrees. Grease a 13 × 9-inch baking dish.

BUILD THE MOUSSAKA. Spread half of the Cinnamon Tomato Sauce on the bottom of the prepared pan. Then layer half of the Roasted Eggplant slices, one half of the Mushroom-Lentil-Walnut Mixture, and ¾ cup of the grated cheese. Repeat this layering process one more time finishing with cheese.

BAKE THE MOUSSAKA. Cover with the Ricotta Béchamel, and sprinkle with bread crumbs. Bake until golden brown on top, 50 to 60 minutes. Let the moussaka rest for 15 minutes before you serve it.

Black Forest Stew with Sage Bread Pudding

We concocted this rich and comforting dish from some interesting ingredients. For the sauce, we use porter, a heavy, dark, strongly flavored beer, and fruits, like apple and prune, which thicken the stew and balance some of the beer's bitterness. To make the Black Forest Stew, we mix the sauce with roasted root vegetables, mushrooms, and French lentils, and serve it, moatlike, around Sage Bread Pudding.

This stew is also delicious without the bread pudding over wide noodles or simply in a bowl with crusty bread on the side. In either case, round out your meal with a salad of beets and baby spinach leaves tossed in a sherry vinegar vinaigrette.

Serves 6

GET A HEAD START

This dish does take time, but one of its beauties is that you can make almost everything ahead of time except the Sage Bread Pudding. Make the sauce in advance and keep the roasted vegetables and the lentils separate.

When you're ready to serve the dish, make Sage Bread Pudding, and heat the roasted vegetables and the lentils with the Black Forest Sauce. The bread pudding takes about an hour to bake and needs a 10-minute rest before you serve it.

In this dish

- Lentils and Roasted Vegetables
- Black Forest Sauce
- Sage Bread Pudding

Lentils and Roasted Vegetables [v]

Roasted vegetables and simple lentils form the sturdy base for the stew.

Makes about 6½ cups

2 medium carrots, peeled and cut in ½-inch dice

1 small celery root (about ½ pound), peeled and cut in ½-inch dice

1 parsnip (about 6 ounces), peeled and cut in ½-inch dice

2 or 3 fingerling, Yellow Finn, or Yukon Gold potatoes (about ½ pound), cut in ½-inch chunks

10 ounces fresh or frozen pearl onions, peeled if fresh

½ pound large crimini or button mushrooms, quartered

2 tablespoons olive oil

1 teaspoon salt

½ teaspoon freshly ground pepper

½ cup French green (Le Puy) lentils (see page 239)

1½ cups water

1 bay leaf

2 cloves garlic

PREPARE THE VEGETABLES FOR ROASTING. Preheat the oven to 400 degrees. In a large bowl toss the carrots, celery root, parsnip, potatoes, pearl onions, and mushrooms with the olive oil, salt, and pepper.

ROAST THE VEGETABLES. Spread the vegetables on a rimmed baking sheet large enough to accommodate everything in a single layer. Cover with foil, and roast for 15 minutes. Remove the foil, and roast until all the vegetables are tender, an additional 10 minutes.

COOK THE LENTILS. Meanwhile, put the lentils in a saucepan with the water, bay leaf, and garlic. Bring to a boil, lower the heat, and simmer until most of the liquid evaporates and the lentils are tender, 20 to 25 minutes. Remove the bay leaf and garlic cloves.

> **TIP**
> Freeze any mushroom stems until you're ready to make Mushroom Essence (see page 172).

Black Forest Sauce [v]

This deep, rich, savory gravy would be good on many things, especially mashed potatoes.

Makes 5½ cups

6 sprigs fresh parsley
4 sprigs fresh thyme
2 sprigs fresh rosemary
Kitchen twine or cheesecloth
1 tablespoon olive oil
2 carrots, peeled and thinly sliced
1 yellow onion, thinly sliced
2 tablespoons chopped garlic
1 (12-ounce) bottle porter beer
4 cups Mushroom Essence (double the recipe on page 172)
1 bay leaf
1 large apple, peeled, cored, and diced

¼ cup pitted prunes, chopped
1 teaspoon salt
¼ teaspoon freshly ground pepper
Sherry vinegar to taste

BUNDLE THE HERBS. Bundle the parsley, thyme, and rosemary with kitchen twine, or tie them in cheesecloth.

SAUTÉ THE VEGETABLES. Heat the olive oil in a large, heavy-bottomed saucepan or Dutch oven over medium heat. Add the carrots, and cook, stirring occasionally, until they begin to brown, about 3 minutes. Add the onion and garlic, and cook until the onion is soft and translucent, about 10 minutes.

ADD THE REMAINING INGREDIENTS, EXCEPT THE VINEGAR. Add the bundled herbs, porter, Mushroom Essence, bay leaf, apple, prunes, salt, and pepper.

SIMMER THE SAUCE. Bring to a boil, lower the heat, and simmer until you've reduced the sauce by about one-fourth. This will take about 30 minutes.

PURÉE AND STRAIN THE SAUCE. Remove the bundled herbs and bay leaf, and purée the sauce in a blender or food processor. Pour the sauce through a mesh strainer, and return it to the large pot. Taste it, and if it seems a bit flat, add a splash of sherry vinegar. Set the pot aside, covered, to keep it warm until the vegetables are finished roasting.

Sage Bread Pudding

This savory bread pudding offers all the comfort of the sweet dessert, except you get to eat it for dinner.

Makes 6 servings

4 eggs, lightly beaten
4 cups half-and-half
2 teaspoons salt, plus a pinch

½ teaspoon freshly ground pepper

1 tablespoon unsalted butter

1 yellow onion, finely diced

3 tablespoons chopped fresh sage, or 1 tablespoon dried sage

2 tablespoons white wine

6 cups (1-inch) rustic bread cubes (see Tip)

GET READY. Preheat the oven to 350 degrees. Grease a 2-quart baking dish.

PREPARE THE EGG AND CREAM MIXTURE. In a large bowl, mix the eggs, half-and-half, 2 teaspoons salt, and pepper, and set aside.

COOK THE ONION. Heat the butter in a skillet over medium heat. Add the onion, sage, and the pinch of salt. Cook until the onion is soft and translucent, about 10 minutes.

ADD THE WINE, stirring to remove any bits of onion from the bottom of the pan, and cook until the wine evaporates, about 1 minute. Remove the onion mixture from the heat, and cool to lukewarm.

MIX THE BREAD WITH THE EGG MIXTURE AND ONIONS. Add the onion to the egg mixture and combine thoroughly. Add the bread cubes and mix gently. Let stand for 10 minutes so the bread can absorb the liquid.

BAKE THE BREAD PUDDING. Transfer the bread mixture to the prepared baking pan, pressing it gently into the pan. Cover with foil, and bake for 20 minutes.

Remove the foil, and bake an additional 30 minutes, or until the pudding is set and lightly browned. Remove from the oven, and let the pudding rest for 10 minutes before serving.

> **TIP**
>
> Make sure to use a sturdy bread here. If you use fresh or soft bread, the bread pudding will lose its nice chewy consistency and could be unpleasantly mushy.

Finish and Serve the Black Forest Stew

Lentils and Roasted Vegetables (page 130)
Black Forest Sauce (page 131)
Sage Bread Pudding (page 131)

Just before you serve the dish, mix the Lentils and Roasted Vegetables with the Black Forest Sauce to make the stew. Heat gently over low heat until all the vegetables are hot. If it doesn't seem saucy enough, add water, a tablespoon at a time, until you get the consistency you want.

Cut the Sage Bread Pudding into 6 squares. Put a square in the middle of a plate or large shallow bowl, and ladle the stew around it.

Oaxaca Tacos with Black Bean Stew and Tangy Swiss Chard

By far the most popular dish on our menu, Oaxaca Tacos clearly demonstrates what our guests find most appealing about Cafe Flora: hearty food with bold flavors and varied textures, beautifully presented.

Although you can serve Oaxaca Tacos with your favorite beans or salsas, the many guests who have requested this recipe want to serve this dish just as we do: two tortillas plump with mashed potatoes and cheese served up with a spicy black bean stew, chard tossed in a tangy, garlicky vinaigrette, and a fiery salsa.

Serves 4 generously

> **GET A HEAD START**
>
> You can make the Lemon Garlic Vinaigrette and the Black Bean Stew ahead. If you're planning to use dried black beans, start them the night before.

If you want to make everything the day you serve it, here's how to proceed:

- Soaked black beans will take anywhere from 45 minutes to 2 hours to cook depending on how dry (and old) they are. While they're cooking, start the potatoes, and make the vinaigrette.

- Then mash the potatoes (which must be cool before you can stuff the tortillas). Make the Pico de Gallo Salsa.

- Just before you're ready to serve the dish, while the tacos are baking, prepare and cook the chard.

In this dish

- Black Bean Stew
- Oaxaca Tacos
- Tangy Swiss Chard
- Lemon Garlic Vinaigrette
- Lime Crème Fraîche (see page 230)
- Pico de Gallo Salsa (see page 226)

Black Bean Stew [v]

This stew is so good, you could make a simple supper by dishing it up over steamed rice along with a green salad or your favorite slaw, and Pico de Gallo Salsa (see page 226).

Makes about 3 cups

1 cup dried black beans, soaked for 2 hours or up to 8 hours, or 1 (15-ounce) can black beans (about 2 cups cooked)

1 cup fresh or frozen corn kernels

2 cloves garlic, minced

¼ cup chopped fresh cilantro

½ teaspoon crushed red pepper flakes

½ teaspoon cumin seeds, toasted and ground (see page 52)

½ teaspoon chili powder

½ teaspoon dried oregano

¾ teaspoon salt

Optional: ½ tablespoon brown sugar

COOK THE BEANS. If you're using soaked dried beans, drain them. Put them in a 3- or 4-quart pot or Dutch oven with 5 cups water, and bring to a boil. Reduce to a simmer, and cook, partially covered, until the beans are tender, but still hold their shape, anywhere from 45 minutes to 2 hours (depending on how dry the beans were). You may need to add more water to keep them submerged.

If you're using canned black beans, rinse them under cold water, and add 1 cup of water before you go to the next step.

COOK THE BEANS WITH THE REMAINING INGREDIENTS. When the beans are tender, do not drain them, and add the remaining ingredients to the pot. (If you're using canned beans, you may want to taste the finished stew before you add salt.) Simmer for about 15 minutes to blend the flavors, adding more water or vegetable stock for a soupier consistency.

Oaxaca Tacos

Makes 8 tacos

1½ pounds russet potatoes, peeled and quartered

2 tablespoons unsalted butter

½ teaspoon salt

½ cup shredded, smoked mozzarella cheese (2 ounces)

½ cup shredded cheddar cheese (2 ounces)

Big pinch red pepper flakes

Vegetable oil for preparing tortillas

8 thin corn tortillas (see Tip)

1 small red or green bell pepper, seeds removed and cut into fine dice
Toothpicks

GET READY. Preheat the oven to 400 degrees.

COOK AND MASH THE POTATOES. Put the potatoes in a pot with water to cover. Cook them, covered, until tender, 20 to 40 minutes. (The time depends on the size of the chunks.) Drain the potatoes well, and mash with the butter and salt. Cool completely.

MIX THE CHEESES. In a small bowl, mix the cheeses with the red pepper flakes, and set aside.

OIL THE TORTILLAS. Heat ⅛ inch oil in a skillet over medium heat. When the oil is hot, put a tortilla in the hot oil and fry until it is soft, 8 to 10 seconds; flip and repeat with the other side. Do not let the tortilla get crisp by letting the oil bubble up around its edges; reduce the heat to medium-low or low if this occurs. (It's important for the tortillas to be oily so they get crisp when roasted in the oven.)

KEEP THE TORTILLAS WARM. Put the tortilla on a plate and cover with foil to keep warm. Continue to heat tortillas, piling them one atop each other under the foil cover. (Keep the tortillas warm so they're pliable enough to stuff and roll without breaking.)

ASSEMBLE EACH TACO. Place each tortilla on a flat surface. Using a ⅓-cup measure, put a scoop of mashed potatoes in the middle of each tortilla. Pat the potatoes with your hand to flatten them a little. Sprinkle with 1 tablespoon of the bell pepper and 2 tablespoons of the cheese mixture.

Roll the tortilla into a large tube so both edges overlap (but the ends are still open), and fasten with 1 or 2 wooden picks as if you were sewing with them.

BAKE THE TACOS. Put the filled tortillas in a roasting pan or on a baking sheet, toothpicks facing up. Bake until the cheese has melted and the tortillas start to brown and crisp around the edges, 15 to 20 minutes.

TIPS
Use thin corn tortillas for these tacos. The thick ones break easily when you roll them up, and they won't get as crispy as they should. (It's fine to use frozen tortillas. Just make sure that they're defrosted before you start.)

Tangy Swiss Chard [v]

Make this dish last, and serve it immediately after it has finished cooking because it deteriorates rapidly if you hold it.

Serves 4

1 big bunch red or green Swiss chard, most of the stems removed, leaves left whole
¼ cup Lemon Garlic Vinaigrette (recipe follows)

Steam the chard in a covered large pan with a little water (or use a steamer basket), until the leaves are wilted and tender, about 5 minutes. Toss with the Lemon Garlic Vinaigrette, and serve at once.

Lemon Garlic Vinaigrette [v]

This vinaigrette has been a staple in the Cafe Flora kitchen for years. It's thick and really clings to whatever you dress it with. I like to have a jar on hand to drizzle on steamed vegetables and greens, dress cold pasta salads, and spread on sandwiches.

It will keep for two weeks in your fridge. Bring to room temperature and shake well before serving.

Makes about 1½ cups

10 whole cloves garlic
⅓ cup freshly squeezed lemon juice (about 2 lemons)

¼ teaspoon salt

8 black peppercorns

1 cup olive oil

In a blender combine all the ingredients except the oil. With the motor running, slowly add the olive oil until the vinaigrette is thoroughly blended and emulsified. Taste for salt.

Serve the Oaxaca Taco Plate

Black Bean Stew (see page 133)

Oaxaca Tacos (see page 133)

Lime Crème Fraîche (see page 230)

¼ cup (2 ounces) crumbled feta cheese

4 sprigs cilantro for garnish

2 cups Pico de Gallo Salsa (see page 226)

Tangy Swiss Chard (see page 134)

ARRANGE THE BLACK BEAN STEW AND THE OAXACA TACOS ON A PLATE. Put ½ cup of the Black Bean Stew on one half of a plate.

Remove the toothpicks from the tacos. Place 1 taco in the middle of the beans, and lean another taco against it at an opposing angle, as if they were logs and you were building a fire.

FINISH THE DISH. Drizzle 1 or 2 tablespoons of the Lime Crème Fraîche over the tacos, and top with a tablespoon of feta and a cilantro sprig.

On the other half of each plate, put ½ cup Pico de Gallo Salsa and one-fourth of the dressed chard.

> **TIP**
>
> If you can't find crème fraîche at your local supermarket or you have the time to experiment, you can make your own following the instructions on page 230. Just note that it takes about 24 hours.

Portobello Wellingtons with Madeira Sauce

Celebrate a special occasion—a holiday dinner or a birthday party—with this classic dish. Although it takes time to prepare, the festive and sumptuous results will please everyone.

As the name implies, there are two main parts to this dish: the Wellingtons and the Madeira Sauce. The Wellingtons are crispy, golden packets of puff pastry stuffed with slices of Mushroom Pecan Pâté, Roasted Portobellos, and Pan-Braised Leek. They're served atop the sauce, a long-cooked, complex, velvety affair.

At Cafe Flora, we serve this dish with creamy mashed potatoes and a sauté of colorful seasonal vegetables such as baby carrots, tiny pattypan squash, green beans, or a combination. Finish your feast with a simple salad of the freshest mixed greens tossed with Cafe Flora Herb Balsamic Vinaigrette (see page 87).

Serves 8

Although there's nothing very complicated about any one part of this dish, each part does take time, and every element must be cool before you can assemble the Wellingtons. Luckily, most parts keep up to 2 days in the fridge so you can make them ahead of time.

You can also build the Wellingtons the day before. Refrigerate them on a baking sheet or something flat like that—don't stack them—and wrap the whole pan tightly with plastic wrap. Then you only have to pop them in the oven to bake while you're preparing the rest of the meal.

That said, here are some ideas for scheduling the making of this dish:

MAKE THE MADEIRA SAUCE AND THE MUSHROOM PECAN PÂTÉ AHEAD.

These are the most complex and time-consuming components of the dish, so consider making them a day or two before you plan to assemble the Wellingtons. Once you have them ready and waiting in your refrigerator (they can be held up to 2 days there), you can put the rest of the dish together in about 2 hours. The Madeira Sauce requires a mushroom broth (Mushroom Essence), which takes an hour, and the sauce itself takes another hour to cook. After you mix the pâté, it requires 45 minutes to bake and another hour or more to chill.

ROAST THE PORTOBELLOS, PAN BRAISE THE LEEKS, AND COOL THEM.

You can do this the day before you plan to put the Wellingtons together, and refrigerate.

In this dish

- Madeira Sauce
- Mushroom Pecan Pâté
- Roasted Portobellos
- Pan-Braised Leek

Madeira Sauce

The mushroom stock adds depth to the color and concentrated mushroom flavor to the sauce. You can substitute canned mushroom or vegetable broth, but the mushroom flavor will be less pronounced and the color of the finished sauce will be lighter.

The instructions call for reducing the sauce twice. (This concentrates as much flavor as possible and cooks off the alcohol that's added.) I've given approximate measurements for the volume of sauce you should have after each reduction, so don't bother with the mess of actually measuring. The volume doesn't have to be precise—½ cup either way won't make any difference. Just note the level of the sauce in the pan when you add the liquid and at the end of each reduction, and eyeball it from there.

Makes 3½ to 4 cups

Start this sauce by first making a rich mushroom broth, Mushroom Essence, a process that takes an hour or more to complete. Plan accordingly because you'll want to have the sauce ready to go when the Wellingtons come out of the oven.

1 tablespoon olive oil

1 yellow onion, thinly sliced

6 cloves garlic, chopped

Salt

½ pound button mushrooms, sliced

1 tablespoon tomato paste

2½ cups red wine

8 to 10 (5-inch) fresh thyme branches

10 to 12 parsley sprigs with stems

1 bay leaf

6 whole peppercorns

4 cups Mushroom Essence (double recipe on page 172)

3 tablespoons unsalted butter

3 tablespoons all-purpose flour

½ cup Madeira wine

Freshly ground pepper

COOK THE ONIONS AND MUSHROOMS. In a heavy-bottomed 4-quart sauce pan, heat the olive oil over medium heat. Add the onion, and sauté until the onion is soft and translucent, about 10 minutes.

Add the garlic and a pinch of salt, and sauté until the onion begins to turn brown and soft, about 5 minutes.

ADD THE MUSHROOMS and cook, stirring and scraping the bottom of the pan, until the mushrooms are browned, about 5 minutes.

ADD THE TOMATO PASTE, RED WINE, AND HERBS. Add the tomato paste, continuing to stir and scrape the bottom of the pan. Then add the red wine, thyme, parsley, bay leaf, and peppercorns.

Cook at a low boil (lots of small bubbles just breaking on the surface of the sauce) until the sauce has been reduced by one-quarter (to about 3 cups). This will take about 15 minutes and is the first reduction. (It's still a thin sauce; it won't thicken until you add the roux.)

ADD THE MUSHROOM ESSENCE, and cook at a low boil until reduced by one-quarter again (to about 5½ cups), another 15 minutes. (This is the second reduction.)

MAKE A ROUX. Meanwhile, melt the butter in a small skillet over medium heat. Add the flour, and stir until the mixture is light brown and smells toasty. Set aside to cool.

ADD THE MADEIRA. After the sauce has been reduced the second time, add the Madeira, lower the heat, and simmer the sauce for 10 minutes.

STRAIN THE SAUCE. Remove from the heat, and pour the thin sauce through a mesh strainer into another saucepan, pressing the solids with the back of a large spoon. You should have about 4 cups strained sauce. Discard the solids in the strainer.

ADD THE ROUX. Bring the strained sauce to a simmer until all lumps disappear and the sauce begins to thicken. Season to taste with salt and pepper, and keep warm over low heat for up to 15 minutes. If you're going to hold the sauce any longer than that, refrigerate and reheat over medium-low heat.

Mushroom Pecan Pâté

You'll have about half a pan of this pâté left over after you make the Wellingtons. Good thing, because then you'll be able to make four scrumptious sandwiches with Green Peppercorn Aïoli (page 231), or a comforting classic American supper, vegetarian style, with mashed potatoes and steamed green beans. Or serve the leftover pâté as an appetizer or snack with crackers, mustard, and gherkins as you would a meat pâté.

Makes enough pâté for 8 Wellingtons, plus leftovers

½ pound button mushrooms

3 tablespoons olive oil

1 yellow onion, finely diced

2 cloves garlic, minced

¼ cup dry sherry

1 tablespoon chopped fresh thyme leaves, about 10 sprigs

1 teaspoon salt

½ teaspoon freshly ground pepper

1½ cups pecans, toasted (see page 150) and chopped into fine bits

4 eggs, beaten

2 cups shredded mozzarella (8 ounces)

GET READY. Grease an 8½ × 4½-inch loaf pan thoroughly, and line it with parchment paper.

CHOP THE MUSHROOMS. Fill a food processor bowl halfway with the mushrooms, and pulse until they're finely chopped, 3 to 4 pulses of 5 seconds each. (It's better to process the mushrooms in 2 batches rather than risk mushroom mush.)

COOK THE MUSHROOMS WITH THE ONIONS AND GARLIC. Using a heavy-bottomed deep saucepan, heat the olive oil over medium heat. Add the onion, and cook until the onion is soft and translucent, about 10 minutes. Add the garlic and mushrooms, and cook for 8 to 10 minutes while stirring and scraping the bottom of the pan to prevent sticking.

ADD THE SHERRY AND HERBS. Add the sherry, stirring to remove any bits from the bottom of the pan. Cook until most of the liquid has evaporated. The mixture should be moist and thick. (Don't worry about how it looks!) Mix in the thyme, salt, and pepper, and set aside to cool completely.

FOLD THE REMAINING INGREDIENTS INTO THE MUSHROOM MIXTURE. When the mushroom mixture is cool, fold in the pecans, eggs, and cheese until thoroughly combined. Pour into the prepared loaf pan.

BAKE THE PÂTÉ for 45 minutes to 1 hour, or until a sharp knife inserted into the center comes out clean. (The baking time depends on the moisture in the pâté.) While it bakes, the pâté will puff up and have a rounded top; this will flatten as it cools.

COOL IN THE PAN for about an hour. Cool it for the first 30 minutes on the countertop, and then move it to the refrigerator. Do not attempt to unmold the pâté until it is completely cold, or it may fall apart.

Roasted Portobellos [v]

TIMING

You can also roast the portobellos the day you plan to serve the Wellingtons, allowing about 1 hour for them to bake and cool.

Makes enough for 8 Wellingtons

3 portobello mushrooms (about 1¼ pounds)

¼ cup olive oil

Salt and freshly ground pepper

GET READY. Preheat the oven to 350 degrees. Remove the portobello stems. Using a pastry brush, brush the portobello caps on both sides with olive oil, and sprinkle each side of the cap with salt and pepper.

ROAST THE PORTOBELLOS. Put the portobello caps in a baking dish, and roast until they are completely tender, 20 to 25 minutes. When the caps are cool enough to work with, cut them into thin, ⅛-inch-thick slices at an angle.

TIP

Freeze the mushroom stems until you're ready to make a mushroom stock such as our Mushroom Essence (see page 172).

Pan-Braised Leek

TIMING

You can braise the leeks the day you plan to serve the Wellingtons, allowing about 30 minutes for them to cook and cool.

Makes about ½ cup

1 medium leek, white and pale green part

1 tablespoon olive oil

Salt and freshly ground pepper

¼ cup white wine

PREPARE THE LEEK. Remove the top dark-green part of the leek and the root end. Cut the leek in half lengthwise and clean the dirt from the layers under running water. Thinly slice both halves of the leek.

PAN BRAISE THE LEEK. Heat the olive oil in a skillet over medium heat. Add the leek and a pinch of salt and pepper, and cook until it's soft, about 10 minutes. Add the wine, and cook until most of the liquid evaporates. Remove from the heat, and set aside to cool completely.

Assemble and Bake the Wellingtons

The Wellingtons have three layers: first, a slice of Mushroom Pecan Pâté; then slices of Roasted Portobellos; and last, a bit of Pan-Braised Leek.

You can build the Wellingtons in a kind of assembly line. Cut all the puff pastry rectangles. Lay a pâté slice on each, fan the portobello slices on top of the pâté, and top each with a bit of leek. Then fold and crimp as instructed.

2 boxes Pepperidge Farm puff pastry, or other puff pastry (about 2 pounds) (see Tip)
8 (½-inch) slices Mushroom Pecan Pâté
Roasted Portobellos (page 138)
Pan-Braised Leeks (page 138)

THAW THE PUFF PASTRY. When you're about 20 minutes away from assembling the Wellingtons, remove the frozen puff pastry from the box. (The pastry works best when it's thawed but still cold.) Thaw it just as it is, folded and uncovered, on a lightly floured surface for about 20 minutes. Preheat the oven to 400 degrees.

CUT THE PUFF PASTRY. When the pastry is thawed, unfold it. Cut each square in half so you have 2 rectangles, 5 inches × 10 inches.

ASSEMBLE THE WELLINGTONS. With the short end of a puff pastry strip toward you, put a ½-inch slice of the pâté on the bottom half (the part closest to you), leaving a ½-inch border for crimping. Top it with 4 or 5 slices of portobello fanned out, and one-eighth of the pan-braised leek (about 1 tablespoon).

Fold the top half of the pastry over the filling, to make a 5-inch square. (You may have to stretch the pastry a bit over the filling when you fold it, so it will meet at the bottom.) Seal all 3 sides by pressing down with your fingers first. Crimp the 3 sides with a fork and then trim any edges with a sharp knife. Repeat this process with the remaining ingredients to make a total of 8 packets.

BAKE THE WELLINGTONS. Place the packets on an ungreased baking sheet, and bake on the middle rack of the oven until the pastry is golden brown, 25 to 30 minutes.

> **TIP**
>
> Pepperidge Farm puff pastry comes two sheets per package, each about ten inches square. Look for it in the grocery store frozen-food section next to the pies and crusts. A common commercial-size package weighs about a pound and measures 10 × 15 inches. Look for the Dufour brand at Whole Foods or Specialty food stores.

Serve the Wellingtons

Madeira Sauce (page 136)
Mashed potatoes to serve 8
Portobello Wellingtons (recipe above)
Sautéed vegetables to serve 8

If you've made the Madeira Sauce ahead, heat it up over medium-low heat. Puddle ⅓ to ½ cup of the Madeira Sauce on a warm plate, and mound ½ cup of your favorite mashed potatoes on one-third of the sauce. Put a Wellington in the sauce nestled against the mashed potatoes. Settle a serving of sautéed vegetables on the side.

PIZZA

MY INTRODUCTION TO MAKING PIZZA was over at my friend Anne's house with a Chef Boyardee boxed pizza kit, which her family always seemed to have in the cupboard. This kit had a little packet of flour and other things to which you added water to make a crust, a can of tomato sauce, and a miniature container of Kraft Parmesan cheese. You mixed up the crust and pressed it into a pan like piecrust, opened the can of sauce and spread it around, and then covered it all with "shaky cheese" (as we used to call it).

I remember it was a lot of fun to put all this together—playing pizza chef with Anne—but even then I thought that "pizza" was pretty gross! The pizza kit was obviously designed to keep in the pantry of your bomb shelter. I guess it would serve as pizza when absolutely nothing else was available, and you were tired of eating canned beans.

I still think making pizza is more fun than preparing just about any other kind of food. Making the dough doesn't really take that long, and it's so enjoyable to use your hands to knead and shape the dough. Because a pizza requires smallish quantities of ingredients, it's also fun to scrounge around for interesting tidbits of vegetables or fruits to combine as toppings. In addition, there is the satisfaction of using up the various bits of cheese that always seem to accumulate in the fridge. I'm not talking about using stuff headed for the compost heap or garbage can here, just being creative with what is on hand.

That spirit of fun extends to the recipes in this chapter. They are definitely not written in stone. At Cafe Flora we offer three or four types of pizza a week, and over the years we've created over 250 different pizzas. Some of them, like our Tropical Pizza, are completely unique and don't leave a lot of room for improvisation. But many times, a pizza featuring a seasonal ingredient like asparagus will be made almost exactly the same way as the year before, changing only the cheese or the pesto from week to week during asparagus season. Most of the time, a change is simply based on what cheese or herb we have in abundance that week. In these recipes we have made some suggestions for substitutions, but please don't feel locked into any of these either. If you think it will taste good, it probably will. And anyway, what's the worst that could happen?

You'll notice our recipes require the use of a pizza stone. Baking on a stone helps distribute the heat for a more evenly baked pizza and makes for a crispier crust. Pizza stones are widely available these days at most kitchen supply stores and even most large discount stores such as Target. They are usually well under $30, and I have seen some as cheap as $15.

A chief complaint about pizza stones is that they break easily. This usually occurs when moving the pizza stone out of the oven before it cools completely, so I suggest keeping the stone in your oven on a lower rack all the time. (I haven't found it to affect the baking of anything else, and it will remind you to make pizza more often.) However, if it's in your way and you must remove it, take the stone out of the oven only when it is completely cool. And if your stone does crack in two or three big pieces, don't throw it away. Just push the pieces together before you slide the pizza onto the stone. It will work just fine.

If you're using a pizza stone, another useful tool for making pizzas is a large, paddlelike pizza peel, which helps you get the uncooked pizza onto the stone. Generally these are made of a thin piece of wood with a long handle, but sometimes they are of metal. Our experience with metal peels at Cafe Flora has not been good. If you're making pizzas in quick succession, a metal peel gets hot from being in the oven even a short time, and it's very difficult to prepare your next pizza on a hot peel. A wooden peel does not conduct heat well, so this is not an issue.

Baking Pizza Using a Peel and Stone

To make a pizza on a peel, first sprinkle a teaspoon of cornmeal evenly over it. Put the circle of pizza dough on top, and add your toppings. Open the oven door, and slide the topped pizza in one smooth motion evenly onto the hot stone with no bunching or wrinkling of the dough. This process of sliding the pizza onto the stone from the peel may take a couple of tries to get used to, but you'll get the hang of it with practice.

If you're using a stone but don't have a peel, sprinkle a baking sheet with cornmeal, and assemble your pizza on it. Bake the pizza on the baking sheet until the crust is firm enough to lift with a big spatula, about halfway through the total baking time. Lift the pizza off the baking sheet, transfer to the preheated stone, and finish baking.

Herbed Pizza Dough [v]

Making pizza dough is easy, so don't let using yeast or waiting an hour for it to rise stop you from making it. This recipe is tried and true and should always result in a perfect crust.

Makes 2 (10-inch) pizza crusts

1 cup warm water (a tiny bit warmer than body temperature, 105 to 115 degrees)

2 teaspoons dry yeast (a bit less than 1 package)

1 teaspoon sugar

1 tablespoon olive oil plus oil for coating dough

2 teaspoons chopped fresh herbs (such as thyme, rosemary, parsley, basil)

1 teaspoon salt

3 cups unbleached all-purpose flour (You can substitute up to ½ cup whole wheat flour for the all-purpose flour.)

MIX THE DOUGH. Put the water in a large mixing bowl. Sprinkle in the yeast and sugar, stir, and let stand until foamy, 5 minutes.

Stir well, and add the olive oil, herbs, salt, and 1 cup of the flour, and mix well. Add the remaining flour a ½ cup at a time, mixing well after each addition. If this becomes too difficult with a spoon, mix in the flour with your hands.

KNEAD THE DOUGH. Dump the dough onto a lightly floured surface, and knead it with your hands until all the flour is incorporated.

Lightly coat the entire ball of dough with oil, return it to the (uncleaned) bowl, and cover the bowl with a towel. (Oiling the dough keeps it from clinging to the bowl; covering the dough keeps it from developing a crust.) Let sit in a warm place until the dough has doubled in bulk, about 1 hour.

ROLL OUT THE DOUGH. Punch down the dough and divide into 2 pieces. Form each piece of dough into a tight ball, and let it sit uncovered for 5 minutes on the counter. On a floured surface, roll each dough ball into a 10-inch circle. (If you prefer a thinner pizza, roll it out to 12 inches.)

PUT TOGETHER AND BAKE THE PIZZA. Refer to individual pizza recipes for these details.

Classic Pizza

This simple and delicious pizza was one of our first, and is still available on our menu year-round. You really can't beat the combination of tomatoes, basil pesto, and smoked mozzarella.

Makes 2 (10-inch) pizzas; each serves 3 to 4

Pizza Dough (see previous recipe)

Cornmeal for the pan or peel

½ cup Basil Pesto (see page 233)

4 Roma tomatoes, sliced ¼ inch thick

2 cups grated smoked mozzarella cheese (½ pound)

MAKE THE DOUGH, AND PREPARE THE OVEN. Make the pizza dough and set it aside to rise. Preheat the oven to 500 degrees. If you're using a pizza stone, preheat it on a lower rack in the oven for at least 30 minutes before you bake the pizza.

ROLL OUT THE DOUGH. On a floured surface, roll out half of the pizza dough into a 10-inch circle. Sprinkle a baking sheet or pizza peel with cornmeal to keep the pizza from sticking to it, and place the dough on it.

ADD THE TOPPING. Leaving a ¼-inch border, spread half the Basil Pesto on the dough, being careful not to tear it. (If the pesto is hard to spread, thin it with a bit of olive oil.)

Lay half the tomato slices on the pesto in a single layer, leaving spaces between them. (Do not overlap them.) Top with half of the shredded cheese.

BAKE THE FIRST PIZZA. Bake the pizza in the pan, or, if you're using a wooden pizza peel, slide the pizza directly onto the stone. Bake for 5 to 7 minutes, rotating the pizza halfway through baking, or until the cheese melts and the edges appear crisp and lightly browned.

BUILD AND BAKE THE SECOND PIZZA. While the first pizza is baking, roll out the dough for the second one, and add the topping. Bake it when the first pizza comes out of the oven.

Kid's Pizza with Not-So-Spicy Tomato Sauce

Getting an order for a Kid's Pizza on a busy night can be a little frustrating. First you have to haul from the fridge ingredients you don't regularly stock at your station. Then you have to transform a round of plain dough into a happy animal face that's good to eat. But by the time you're done, you're really happy and proud, realizing that the creative break from the hectic pace was just what you needed. The icing on the cake? When the server picks it up and says, "They're gonna love this!"

To make a kid's pizza at Cafe Flora, we start with a rolled-out round of dough (from the stack of pizza rounds we've rolled out when we prepped for dinner). We carve ears out of the dough, and use those scraps to shape the nose. We spread the tomato sauce over it and sprinkle with cheese and bake it. When it comes out of the oven, we cut it in slices, put it back together on a plate, and then make the happy animal face— my model was Smokey the Bear or sometimes Hello Kitty—with little bits of fruit or vegetable.

When you make the eyes, mouth, and whiskers, use morsels of whatever is on hand—for example, slices of Roma tomatoes with sliced olives or grapes in the center for the eyes. Half a Roma tomato slice makes a cute smiley mouth, as does half an orange slice. Chives cut into three- or four-inch lengths make good whiskers, as will ultrathin strips of bell pepper or carrot. Be creative!

This also makes a great participatory dinner for the whole family. Depending on the age of your children, they can help make the whole pizza (including the dough and the sauce), but even the littlest ones will enjoy making the face.

Makes 2 (10-inch) pizzas; enough for 2 kids and a couple of grownups to share

TIMING

While the dough is rising would be a good time to make the Not-So-Spicy Tomato Sauce.

Herbed Pizza Dough (see page 144)
Cornmeal for the pan or peel
1 cup Not-So-Spicy Tomato Sauce (recipe follows), or mildly seasoned prepared sauce
1½ cups shredded cheddar cheese (6 ounces)
Bits of vegetables and fruit for eyes, mouth, and whiskers for 2 pizzas

MAKE THE DOUGH, AND PREPARE THE OVEN. Make the pizza dough and set it aside to rise. Preheat the oven to 500 degrees. If you're using a pizza stone, preheat it on a lower rack in the oven for at least 30 minutes before you bake the pizza.

ROLL OUT THE DOUGH. On a floured surface, roll out half of the pizza dough into a 10-inch circle.

CUT OUT THE EARS AND SHAPE THE NOSE. Using a sharp knife, carve the dough away to create 2 pointed or round ears. Roll the dough you have removed into a ball, and pinch off a nose-size amount of dough. Shape it into a nose, poking 2 holes in it for nostrils. Set the nose aside.

Sprinkle a baking sheet or wooden pizza peel with cornmeal to keep the pizza from sticking to it, and place the dough-with-ears on it.

ADD THE TOPPING. Leaving a ¼-inch border, spread ½ cup of the pizza sauce over the dough, being careful not to tear the dough. Scatter half the cheese over the sauce.

BAKE THE FIRST PIZZA. Bake the pizza in the pan, or, if you're using a pizza peel, slide the pizza directly onto the stone. Put the little dough nose on the stone if there's room; otherwise, put it on another baking pan.

Bake for 5 to 7 minutes, rotating the pizza halfway through baking, or until the cheese melts and the edges appear crisp and lightly browned. Remove the pizza and the dough nose from the oven.

BUILD AND BAKE THE SECOND PIZZA. While the first pizza is baking, roll out the dough and cut out the ears and shape the nose for the second one. Add the topping, and bake it when the first pizza comes out of the oven. Then follow the instructions below for turning the pizza into a face.

CUT THE BAKED PIZZA into 6 or 8 pieces, and use a long thin-bladed metal spatula to lift half the cut pizza at a time onto a plate. Be careful! Melted cheddar seems to be drippier than other cheeses, so it can slide right off the pizza when it is just out of the oven. (You cut the pizza before you decorate it, because it's more difficult to cut the pizza once transformed into a cute animal).

MAKE THE FACE. Fit the pizza together on the plate. Press on the dough nose, and add the fruits or vegetables you've chosen for eyes, mouth, and whiskers.

SERVE THE PIZZA. Make sure the pizza has been out of the oven for at least 5 minutes before you serve it as the very hot cheese may drip off the pizza and burn your kids.

Not-So-Spicy Tomato Sauce [v]

This recipe makes a lot more sauce than you'll need for two pizzas, but this mildly seasoned tomato sauce is perfect for kid's spaghetti, too, and freezes well.

Makes 2 cups

1 tablespoon olive oil
1 small onion, finely diced
Salt
1 clove garlic, minced
¼ teaspoon dried oregano
1 (14.5-ounce) can diced tomatoes and their juice
Pinch sugar
1 cup Vegetable Stock (page 39), prepared vegetable stock, or water
Freshly ground pepper

SAUTÉ THE ONION, GARLIC, AND HERBS. Heat the olive oil in a medium saucepan over medium heat. Add the onion and a pinch of salt. Sauté until the onion is soft and translucent, about 10 minutes. Add the garlic and oregano, and cook for 5 minutes.

ADD THE TOMATOES, AND SIMMER. Add the tomatoes and their juice, sugar, and stock. Bring the mixture to a boil, reduce the heat to low, and simmer until the sauce is the consistency of spaghetti sauce, about 20 minutes.

PURÉE THE FINISHED SAUCE IN A BLENDER, adding a pinch of pepper and salt to taste.

Asparagus, Roasted Mushroom Pâté, and Jarlsberg Pizza

Asparagus-topped pizzas make their first appearance on our menu at the end of April, when we receive the first 25-pound bin of beautiful, fat, eastern Washington asparagus from our farmer friend, Merv Dykstra. They stay on the menu until sometime in July, when Merv starts bringing in his big bins of colorful mixed peppers—sweet and hot—and another pizza is born.

Jarlsberg cheese may seem like an odd choice for a pizza topping, but its nutty, mellow flavor seems to work really well with the mushroom pâté. Other good cheeses would be fontina, manchego, or a smoky provolone.

Makes 2 (10-inch) pizzas; each serves 1 to 2

TIMING

You'll need about least an hour to make the mushroom pâté, so start it first. (You can make the pâté ahead if you want. It keeps in the refrigerator for several days.) The mushrooms roast for 30 minutes and then require time to cool.

Herbed Pizza Dough (see page 144)

1 pound asparagus spears

Cornmeal for the pan or peel

1 cup Roasted Mushroom Pâté, at room temperature (recipe follows)

Salt and freshly ground pepper

2 cups grated Jarlsberg cheese (½ pound)

15 to 20 cherry or grape tomatoes, sliced in half

2 tablespoons olive oil

MAKE THE DOUGH, AND PREPARE THE OVEN. Make the pizza dough and set it aside to rise. Preheat the oven to 500 degrees. If you're using a pizza stone, preheat it on a lower rack in the oven for at least 30 minutes before you bake the pizza.

SLICE AND BLANCH THE ASPARAGUS. Bring a large saucepan of lightly salted water to a boil. Trim the tough ends of the asparagus and then slice the spears thinly at a very sharp angle, keeping the tips whole. Drop the asparagus into the boiling water, and blanch for 30 seconds to 1 minute. Drain under cold running water, and pat dry.

ROLL OUT THE DOUGH. On a floured surface, roll out half of the pizza dough into a 10-inch circle. Sprinkle a baking sheet or pizza peel with cornmeal to keep the pizza from sticking to it, and place the dough on it.

ADD THE TOPPING. Leaving a ¼-inch border, spread half of the pâté on the dough, being careful not to tear the dough. Drizzle or brush the pâté and dough with 1 tablespoon of the olive oil. Scatter half the asparagus over the pâté, sprinkle with salt and pepper, and then top with half of the cheese. Scatter half of the tomato halves evenly over the cheese.

BAKE THE FIRST PIZZA. Bake the pizza in the pan, or, if you're using a pizza peel, slide the pizza directly onto the stone. Bake for 5 to 7 minutes, rotating the pizza halfway through baking, or until the cheese melts and the edges appear crisp and lightly browned.

BUILD AND BAKE THE SECOND PIZZA. While the first pizza is baking, roll out the dough for the second one, and add the topping. Bake it when the first pizza comes out of the oven.

Roasted Mushroom Pâté [v]

Makes about 1 cup, enough for 2 pizzas

4 ounces crimini mushrooms

4 ounces shiitake or chanterelle mushrooms

3 tablespoons chopped garlic

1 tablespoon olive oil

¼ cup pecan bits, toasted (see page 150)

1 tablespoon fresh thyme, or 1 teaspoon dried thyme

2 teaspoons sherry vinegar

Salt and freshly ground pepper

CLEAN THE MUSHROOMS by brushing off any excess dirt with a towel or pastry brush. Remove any tough stems, and quarter them. If the mushrooms are especially dirty, quickly rinse them under running water, and let dry for several hours on paper towels. Preheat the oven to 350 degrees.

ROAST THE MUSHROOMS. Combine the mushrooms and garlic in a bowl. Toss the mushrooms and garlic with the olive oil, and then put in a baking dish. Roast, uncovered, until the mushrooms have begun to shrivel, about 30 minutes. Set aside to cool.

PROCESS THE MUSHROOMS WITH THE REMAINING INGREDIENTS. When the mushrooms are cool enough to handle, put them in a food processor with the pecan bits. Pulse several times until the mixture is finely and evenly chopped, but not turned to mush.

Remove the lid and scrape down the bowl. Add the thyme and sherry vinegar, and process until the mixture is smooth. Add salt and pepper to taste.

> **TIP**
> Freeze the mushroom stems until you're ready to make Mushroom Essence (see page 172).

Asparagus, Tarragon Parsley Pesto, Roasted Red Pepper, and Goat Cheese Pizza

For another way to enjoy more asparagus in season, try substituting halved cherry or grape tomatoes for the roasted red pepper; you'll need about 15 to 20 little tomatoes for two pizzas.

Makes 2 (10-inch) pizzas; each serves 1 to 2

Herbed Pizza Dough (see page 144)

1 pound asparagus spears

Cornmeal for the pan or peel

½ cup Tarragon Parsley Pesto (see page 233)

2 bottled roasted red bell peppers, or 1 fresh red bell pepper, seeds removed and sliced very thinly

Salt and freshly ground pepper

6 ounces goat cheese, crumbled

MAKE THE DOUGH, AND PREPARE THE OVEN. Make the pizza dough and set it aside to rise. Preheat the oven to 500 degrees. If you're using a pizza stone, preheat it on a lower rack in the oven for at least 30 minutes before you bake the pizza.

SLICE AND BLANCH THE ASPARAGUS. Bring a large saucepan of lightly salted water to a boil. Trim the tough ends of the asparagus and then slice the spears thinly at a very sharp angle, keeping the tips whole. Drop the asparagus into the boiling water, and blanch for 30 seconds to 1 minute. Drain under cold running water, and pat dry.

ROLL OUT THE DOUGH. On a floured surface, roll out half of the pizza dough into a 10-inch circle. Sprinkle a baking sheet or pizza peel with cornmeal to keep the pizza from sticking to it, and place the dough on it.

ADD THE TOPPING. Spread ¼ cup of the Tarragon-Parsley Pesto evenly over the dough, leaving a ¼-inch border. Scatter half of the asparagus over the pesto and then half of the bell pepper. Sprinkle with salt and pepper, and crumble half of the goat cheese over all.

BAKE THE FIRST PIZZA. Bake the pizza in the pan, or, if you're using a pizza peel, slide the pizza directly onto the stone. Bake for 5 to 7 minutes, rotating the pizza halfway through baking, or until the cheese melts and the edges appear crisp and lightly browned.

BUILD AND BAKE THE SECOND PIZZA. While the first pizza is baking, roll out the dough for the second one, and add the topping. Bake it when the first pizza comes out of the oven.

Apple and Roasted Delicata Pizza with Sage Walnut Pesto and Smoked Mozzarella

We love delicata squash and wait impatiently for its arrival each September. Topped with tender roasted delicata, apples, and sweet sautéed onions, this pizza is a perfect introduction to autumn.

Makes 2 (10-inch) pizzas; each serves 1 to 2

TIMING

While the pizza dough is rising, roast the squash. It takes about 20 minutes, and then a bit of time to cool. During this time, you can sauté the onions and make the Sage Walnut Pesto.

Herbed Pizza Dough (see page 144)
2 delicata squash, each about 6 inches long
Olive oil
Salt and freshly ground pepper
2 yellow onions, thinly sliced
Cornmeal for the pan or peel
Sage Walnut Pesto (recipe follows)
2 of your favorite apples, peeled and thinly sliced
1 cup grated smoked mozzarella cheese (4 ounces)
1 cup grated Parmesan or Asiago cheese (about 5 ounces)

MAKE THE DOUGH, AND PREPARE THE OVEN. Make the pizza dough and set it aside to rise. If you're using a pizza stone, preheat it on a lower rack in the oven for at least 30 minutes before you bake the pizza.

PREPARE AND ROAST THE SQUASH. Preheat the oven to 400 degrees. Peel the squash with a vegetable peeler; if you can't get to the skin hiding in the creases, that's OK. Cut it in half lengthwise, remove the seeds, and slice it in ½-inch crescents.

In a bowl, toss the squash pieces with 1 teaspoon olive oil and a sprinkling of salt and pepper. Spread on a baking sheet and roast until tender, about 20 minutes. Set aside to cool.

SAUTÉ THE ONIONS. Meanwhile, heat 1 tablespoon olive oil in a skillet over medium heat. Add the onions and sauté until the onions are soft and translucent, about 10 minutes.

Turn down the heat to low, cover the pan, and cook the onions until they begin to brown, about 5 minutes. Set the onions aside to cool.

ROLL OUT THE DOUGH. Turn up the oven to 500 degrees. On a floured surface, roll half of the pizza dough into a 10-inch circle. Sprinkle a baking sheet or pizza peel with cornmeal, and lift the dough onto it.

ADD THE TOPPING. Leaving a ¼-inch border, spread half of the Sage Walnut Pesto over the dough. Arrange half of the squash slices about ¼ inch apart on the pesto, and evenly distribute half of the onions and apple slices. Scatter half of the cheese over all.

BAKE THE FIRST PIZZA. Bake the pizza in the pan, or, if you're using a wooden pizza peel, slide the pizza directly onto the stone. Bake for 5 to 7 minutes, rotating the pizza halfway through baking, or until the cheese melts and the edges appear crisp and lightly browned.

BUILD AND BAKE THE SECOND PIZZA. While the first pizza is baking, roll out the dough for the second one, and add the topping. (You may have slices of squash left over if the squashes were large.) Bake it when the first pizza comes out of the oven.

Sage Walnut Pesto [v]

The leftover pesto would be perfect for spreading on a rustic bread, for roasted pear and Gorgonzola, or for Jarslberg sandwiches. This keeps refrigerated up to one week.

Makes about 1 cup, enough for 2 pizzas

¼ cup chopped fresh parsley

2 tablespoons chopped fresh sage

1 teaspoon chopped garlic

½ teaspoon salt

½ cup olive oil

½ cup walnuts, toasted (see "Toasting Nuts") and roughly chopped

Put the parsley, sage, garlic, and salt in a blender or food processor. With the machine running, drizzle in the oil. Turn the machine off, and scrape down the sides of the container.

Turn on the machine again, and add the walnuts. Process just until the walnuts are well combined, about 10 seconds. (Walnuts get gummy when processed too long, and you want a little nut texture.)

> **TIP**
>
> As with any pesto, you cannot substitute dried herbs for fresh herbs in this pesto.

Toasting Nuts

Toasting nuts before you add them to a dish not only crisps them up, but greatly enhances their flavor and aroma.

GET READY. Preheat the oven to 350 degrees, and spread the nuts in a single layer in a baking pan.

TOAST THE NUTS until they're fragrant and the nuts are beginning to brown. Check the nuts once or twice, and stir them or give the pan a shake to make sure they toast evenly. Approximate toasting times are as follows:

- Macadamia nuts and sliced or slivered almonds: 4 to 5 minutes
- Pine nuts: 6 to 8 minutes
- Pecans, whole almonds, walnuts, and other nuts: 8 to 10 minutes.

REMOVE THE NUTS FROM THE OVEN, and take them off the pan to cool. If you leave them in the hot pan, they will continue to cook and may scorch.

Spicy Rapini Pizza with Oil-Cured Olives and Smoked Mozzarella

Rapini, also known as broccoli raab, is something akin to a leafier version of broccoli that has begun to flower. It has a leafy green stalk with clusters of very small broccoli florets. It's generally available in late summer or early fall, so when you see it at your grocery store or farmer's market, give it a try.

The flavors in this pizza are pretty assertive; the addition of arame to the garlicky greens gives a faint whiff of the sea. Because a slender slice of this pizza packs a big wallop, it would make an especially good appetizer or first course.

Makes 2 (10-inch) pizzas; each serves 1 to 2

Herbed Pizza Dough (see page 144)
¼ cup arame (seaweed [see page 238])
2 bunches rapini (broccoli raab [about 2 pounds])
Olive oil
16 cloves garlic, roughly chopped (see tip)
1 teaspoon red pepper flakes
4 teaspoons finely chopped lemon zest
Cornmeal for the pan or peel
½ cup oil-cured olives, pitted and roughly chopped
1 cup grated smoked mozzarella cheese (4 ounces)

MAKE THE DOUGH, AND PREPARE THE OVEN. Make the pizza dough and set it aside to rise. Preheat the oven to 500 degrees. If you're using a pizza stone, preheat it on a lower rack in the oven for at least 30 minutes before you bake the pizza.

PREPARE THE ARAME. Rinse the arame in a strainer under running water. Put it in a bowl and add cold water just to cover. Soak for 10 minutes. Drain well, coarsely chop, and set aside.

PREPARE THE RAPINI. Separate the thicker stems of the rapini from the leafy, tender stems. (You may have to pull the bunch apart to get at all the thicker stems.) Slice the thick stems very thinly at a very sharp angle, and cut the leafy part into 2-inch pieces. (You're trying to get all the parts of the rapini about the same size so they cook evenly.)

SAUTÉ THE GARLIC. Warm 2 tablespoons olive oil in a large heavy skillet over medium heat. Tip the pan so the olive oil forms a pool to one side. Add the garlic and cook in the oil until it is golden brown and fragrant, watching that it doesn't burn.

COOK THE RAPINI WITH THE GARLIC. Flatten the pan, add the rapini stems and red pepper flakes, and cook until the stems are tender, about 7 minutes.

Add the rapini leaves and cook, stirring occasionally, until all the leaves are wilted, about 3 minutes. Stir in the arame and lemon zest. Remove from the heat and set aside.

ROLL OUT THE DOUGH. On a floured surface, roll out half of the pizza dough into a 10-inch circle. Sprinkle a baking sheet or pizza peel with cornmeal to keep the pizza from sticking to it, and place the dough on it. Brush the pizza dough lightly with olive oil.

ADD THE TOPPING. Drain off any liquid in the rapini mixture using a slotted spoon and distribute half of the mixture on the dough. Scatter half the olives evenly over the pizza, and top with half the cheese.

BAKE THE FIRST PIZZA. Bake the pizza in the pan or if you're using a pizza peel slide the pizza directly onto the stone. Bake for 5 to 7 minutes, rotating the pizza halfway through baking, or until the cheese melts and the edges appear crisp and lightly browned.

BUILD AND BAKE THE SECOND PIZZA. While the first pizza is baking, roll out the dough for the second one, and add the topping. Bake it when the first pizza comes out of the oven.

TIP

When you have this much garlic to chop, you can make quick work of removing the skins by smashing each clove with the flat side of a large knife.

Roasted Potato and Artichoke Pizza with Kalamata Olives

This hearty and filling pizza has been off and on our menu for several years, and is especially good with Cafe Flora Caesar Salad (see page 71).

Makes 2 (10-inch) pizzas; each serves 3 to 4

Herbed Pizza Dough (see page 144)

4 medium red potatoes (1 pound)

2 tablespoons olive oil

2 tablespoons chopped garlic (about 6 cloves)

½ teaspoon red pepper flakes

Cornmeal for the pan or peel

½ cup Basil Pesto (see page 233)

2 (14-ounce) cans quartered artichoke hearts, drained and roughly chopped (about 2 cups)

1 cup kalamata olives, pitted and chopped

6 ounces goat cheese, chilled, or feta

MAKE THE DOUGH, AND PREPARE THE OVEN. Make the pizza dough and set it aside to rise. If you're using a pizza stone, preheat it on a lower rack in the oven at least 30 minutes before you bake the pizza.

PREPARE THE POTATOES. Preheat the oven to 400 degrees. Slice the potatoes into ⅛-inch slices (as for au gratin), and toss them in a bowl with the olive oil, garlic, and red pepper flakes.

ROAST THE POTATOES. Spread the potato slices on a rimmed baking sheet large enough to accommodate all of them in a single layer without crowding. (If you crowd them, you will steam rather than roast them.) Roast until tender but not mushy, until a sharp knife easily pierces the potatoes, about 20 minutes.

ROLL OUT THE DOUGH. Turn up the oven to 500 degrees. On a floured surface, roll half of the pizza dough into a 10-inch circle. Sprinkle a baking sheet or pizza peel with cornmeal to keep the pizza from sticking to it, and place the dough on it.

ADD THE TOPPING. Gently spread ¼ cup of Basil Pesto over the dough, leaving a ¼-inch border. Arrange half the potato slices evenly to cover the dough. Scatter with half of the artichoke hearts, ½ cup of the olives, and half of the cheese over all.

BAKE THE FIRST PIZZA. Bake the pizza in the pan, or if you're using a pizza peel slide the pizza directly onto the stone. Bake for 7 to 10 minutes, rotating the pizza halfway through baking, or until the cheese melts and the edges appear crisp and lightly browned.

BUILD AND BAKE THE SECOND PIZZA. While the first pizza is baking, roll out the dough for the second one, and add the topping. Bake it when the first pizza comes out of the oven.

Roasted Chanterelle and Leek Pizza with Roasted Garlic Pecan Pesto

In the Pacific Northwest, we're lucky to have a "chanterelle season," but it's sometimes hard to define. It has a lot to do with the rain, and depending on the weather, we may have a pricey, limited harvest or an inexpensive bumper crop. Keep an eye on the price of chanterelles at farmer's markets where mushroom foragers often sell their harvest, and typically charge lower prices than grocers. And if you're lucky, you'll get to meet the man or woman who picked the chanterelles.

Make this luxurious pizza to celebrate a bumper crop of chanterelles and the arrival of fall.

Makes 2 (10-inch) pizzas; each serves 1 to 2

TIMING

- If the mushrooms are dirty enough that you have to clean them with water, they could take several hours to dry.

- In addition, You'll need about an hour to prepare this pizza. While the pizza dough is rising, roast the chanterelles and the garlic for the pesto at the same time. Both require a little time to cool.

Herbed Pizza Dough (see page 144)

6 cups chanterelle mushrooms (about 1 pound)

1 large leek

1 tablespoon olive oil

Salt and freshly ground pepper

Cornmeal for the pan or peel

Roasted Garlic Pecan Pesto, brought to room temperature (recipe follows)

1 cup grated smoked mozzarella cheese (4 ounces)

1 cup grated Jarlsberg cheese (4 ounces)

MAKE THE DOUGH, AND PREPARE THE OVEN. Make the pizza dough and set it aside to rise. Preheat the oven to 350 degrees. If you're using a pizza stone, preheat it on a lower rack in the oven at least 30 minutes before you bake the pizza.

CLEAN THE MUSHROOMS by brushing off any excess dirt with a towel or pastry brush. If the mushrooms are especially dirty, quickly rinse them under running water, and let dry for several hours on paper towels.

Cut the chanterelles into pieces that are of equal size, trying to keep some of the original trumpet shape.

PREPARE THE LEEK. Cut the leek in half lengthwise and wash it carefully under running water. Slice the white and green part only in ¼-inch crescents.

ROAST THE CHANTERELLES AND LEEKS. In a bowl, toss the chanterelles and leek with the olive oil and a pinch of salt and pepper.

Spread them on a rimmed baking sheet large enough to accommodate the chanterelles and leek in a single layer without crowding. (If you crowd them, you will steam rather than roast them.) Roast for 20 minutes, remove from the oven, and set aside to cool a bit.

ROLL OUT THE DOUGH. Turn up the oven to 500 degrees. On a floured surface, roll out half of the pizza dough into a 10-inch circle. Sprinkle a baking sheet or pizza peel with cornmeal to keep the pizza from sticking to it, and place the dough on it.

ADD THE TOPPING. Leaving a ¼-inch border, gently spread the dough with half of the Roasted Garlic Pecan Pesto, leaving a ¼-inch border, being careful not to tear the dough. Distribute half of the chanterelle and leek mixture evenly on the dough, and scatter ½ cup of each of the cheeses over the top.

BAKE THE FIRST PIZZA. Bake the pizza in the pan, or, if you're using a pizza peel, slide the pizza directly onto the stone. Bake for 5 to 7 minutes, rotating the pizza halfway through baking, or until the cheese melts and the edges appear crisp and lightly browned.

BUILD AND BAKE THE SECOND PIZZA. While the first pizza is baking, roll out the dough for the second one, and add the topping. Bake it when the first pizza comes out of the oven.

Roasted Garlic Pecan Pesto [v]

This recipe is based on a garlic confit, which you make by simply cooking garlic cloves very slowly in oil until they're soft and creamy. This spread is very thick when cold and best brought to room temperature before spreading on the pizza dough; otherwise it may tear the dough.

Makes about 1 cup

GET A HEAD START

You can make the pesto ahead if you want. It keeps refrigerated for up to 1 week.

½ cup garlic cloves, unpeeled
½ cup olive oil
½ teaspoon salt
Pinch freshly ground pepper
1 cup pecan pieces, toasted (see page 150)

ROAST THE GARLIC. Preheat the oven to 350 degrees. Toss the garlic cloves with 1 tablespoon of the olive oil and put them in a small baking dish. Cover with foil and roast until soft, about 30 minutes. Set aside to cool.

PROCESS THE PECANS AND GARLIC. When the garlic is cool enough to handle, squeeze the soft garlic out of its skin into a blender or food processor. Add the

salt and pepper, and with the machine running, drizzle in the remaining olive oil.

Turn the machine off, and add the pecans. Process just until the pecans are well combined, about 10 seconds. (Pecans get gummy when processed too long, and you want a little nut texture.)

Roasted Grape Pizza with Herbed Ricotta

We roast many different fruits throughout the year for pizzas and sandwiches. We've made this pizza successfully with plums and figs, but I think grapes are unique, since most of us seem to eat grapes only as a snack. It's also a terrific way to use up grapes that have fallen off the cluster. You can easily adapt this pizza for vegans by substituting Herbed Tofu Ricotta (see page 160) for the Herbed Ricotta given and omitting the Parmesan cheese.

Makes 2 (10-inch) pizzas; each serves 1 to 2

TIMING

While the grapes are roasting—this takes about 20 minutes—make the Herbed Ricotta.

Herbed Pizza Dough (see page 144)
3 cups grapes, removed from stem
2 tablespoons olive oil
2 teaspoons balsamic vinegar
2 teaspoons chopped fresh rosemary
Salt and freshly ground pepper
Cornmeal for the pan or peel
½ cup Herbed Ricotta (recipe follows)
½ cup grated Asiago or Parmesan cheese (about 5 ounces)
½ cup chopped pistachios, pecans, or sliced almonds, toasted (see page 150)

MAKE THE DOUGH, AND PREPARE THE OVEN. Make the pizza dough and set it aside to rise. Preheat the oven to 400 degrees. If you're using a pizza stone, preheat it on a lower rack in the oven for at least 30 minutes before you bake the pizza.

TOSS THE GRAPES WITH OIL AND VINEGAR. In a bowl, toss the grapes with the olive oil, balsamic vinegar, rosemary, and a good pinch of salt and pepper.

ROAST THE GRAPES. Spread them on a rimmed baking sheet large enough to accommodate them in a single layer without crowding. (If you crowd them, you will steam rather than roast them.) Roast until the grapes start to deflate and shrivel, about 25 minutes. Remove from the oven, and set aside until they're cool enough to handle.

ROLL OUT THE DOUGH. Turn up the oven to 500 degrees. On a floured surface, roll out half of the pizza dough into a 10-inch circle. Sprinkle a baking sheet or pizza peel with cornmeal to keep the pizza from sticking to it, and place the dough on it.

ADD THE TOPPING. Spread ¼ cup Herbed Ricotta evenly over the dough, leaving a ¼-inch border. Drain any liquid from the roasted grapes, and scatter half of them evenly over the ricotta. Sprinkle with half the grated cheese and nuts.

BAKE THE FIRST PIZZA. Bake the pizza in the pan, or, if you're using a pizza peel, slide the pizza directly onto the stone. Bake for 7 to 10 minutes, rotating the pizza halfway through baking, or until the cheese melts and the edges appear crisp and lightly browned.

Let this pizza sit a few minutes before cutting and eating because the roasted grapes are very hot.

BUILD AND BAKE THE SECOND PIZZA. While the first pizza is baking, roll out the dough for the second one, and add the topping. Bake it when the first pizza comes out of the oven.

Herbed Ricotta

This ricotta spread is very versatile. Beyond pizza, spread it on sandwiches, toss it with pasta, or slather it on whole-grain toast for an easy, nutritious breakfast. It keeps a couple of days in the refrigerator. For a delicious vegan variation, use Herbed Tofu Ricotta (see page 160) instead. Try making this recipe with different herbs and nuts: substitute toasted pine nuts for the almonds, and basil for the thyme. Beware, however of adding more garlic. It can really upset the balance of flavors.

Makes about 1 cup

¼ cup sliced almonds, toasted (see page 150)

1 cup ricotta cheese

1 teaspoon chopped garlic

1 teaspoon chopped fresh thyme, or ½ teaspoon dried thyme

2 tablespoons chopped fresh parsley

½ teaspoon salt

¼ teaspoon freshly ground pepper

1 tablespoon olive oil

Put the almonds in a food processor, and pulse until finely chopped. (Be careful not to turn them into almond butter!) Add all the remaining ingredients except the olive oil. With the machine running, drizzle in the olive oil, and process to a smooth paste.

Pear Pizza with Gorgonzola, Four-Herb Pesto, and Toasted Walnuts

By now the combination of pears and Gorgonzola on a pizza may seem old hat, but this continues to be one of our most popular. You can change the pesto based on what you have growing in your garden, but we always use parsley. In fact, a pesto made with parsley alone is quite good on this pizza.

Makes 2 (10-inch) pizzas; each serves 1 to 2

Herbed Pizza Dough (see page 144)
Cornmeal for the pan or peel
½ cup Four-Herb Pesto (recipe follows)
2 large ripe Bosc pears, unpeeled, cored, and cut in thin slices
1 cup crumbled Gorgonzola cheese (4 ounces)
½ cup walnuts, toasted (see page 150) and roughly chopped

MAKE THE DOUGH, AND PREPARE THE OVEN. Make the pizza dough and set it aside to rise. Preheat the oven to 500 degrees. If you're using a pizza stone, preheat it on a lower rack in the oven for at least 30 minutes before you bake the pizza.

ROLL OUT THE DOUGH. On a floured surface, roll out half of the pizza dough into a 10-inch circle. Sprinkle a baking sheet or pizza peel with cornmeal to keep the pizza from sticking to it, and place the dough on it.

ADD THE TOPPING. Spread ¼ cup of the Four-Herb Pesto evenly on the dough, leaving a ¼-inch border. Arrange half the pear slices in a circular pattern covering most of the pizza. Sprinkle with half the Gorgonzola, and scatter with ¼ cup of the walnuts.

BAKE THE FIRST PIZZA. Bake the pizza in the pan, or, if you're using a pizza peel, slide the pizza directly onto the stone. Bake for 5 to 7 minutes, rotating the pizza halfway through baking, or until the cheese melts and the edges appear crisp and lightly browned.

BUILD AND BAKE THE SECOND PIZZA. While the first pizza is baking, roll out the dough for the second one, and add the topping. Bake it when the first pizza comes out of the oven.

Four-Herb Pesto [v]

It may go without saying, but this pesto—any pesto, for that matter—will only work with fresh herbs. If you have only one other herb to combine with the parsley, increase the quantity of sage or thyme to ¼ cup. Be careful when you increase the amount of rosemary, however, as it can overpower the other flavors, so limit it to 2 tablespoons. If parsley is the only herb you're using, increase the quantity to 1¼ cups.

Makes about ⅔ cup

1 cup lightly packed fresh Italian parsley sprigs, roughly chopped
2 tablespoons chopped fresh sage
2 tablespoons fresh thyme
1 tablespoon chopped fresh rosemary
1 clove garlic
½ cup olive oil
Salt and freshly ground pepper

Put all the ingredients except the oil, salt, and pepper in a blender or food processor. With the motor running, add the oil until the pesto is completely blended. Season with salt and pepper to taste.

Roasted Pear, Arugula Walnut Pesto, and Goat Gouda Pizza

This rich and elegant pizza will get rave reviews. The sweet roasted pear, peppery pesto, and flavorful cheese would also make a brilliant topping for canapés or Crostini (see page 224).

Makes 2 (10-inch) pizzas; each serves 1 to 2

TIMING

- While the pizza dough is rising, roast the pears and start on the Arugula Walnut Pesto.

- The Fig Balsamic Reduction takes an hour or so to make, but you can make it the day before or even a week in advance. If you don't have the time (or inclination) to make it, you can drizzle a good balsamic vinegar over the pizza just before you serve it instead.

Herbed Pizza Dough (see page 144)

2 large, ripe but firm pears, such as Bosc or Anjou, unpeeled

Cornmeal for the pan or peel

½ cup Arugula Walnut Pesto (see page 232)

Salt and freshly ground pepper

1 cup grated goat Gouda (4 ounces), or other firm goat cheese

Fig Balsamic Reduction (see page 234), warmed until pourable

MAKE THE DOUGH, AND PREPARE THE OVEN. Make the pizza dough and set it aside to rise. Preheat the oven to 350 degrees. If you're using a pizza stone, preheat it on a lower rack in the oven for at least 30 minutes before you bake the pizza.

ROAST THE PEARS. Halve the pears, and remove the stems and cores. Put the pears on a lightly oiled baking sheet, cut side down. Roast until tender, about 15 minutes. A thin-bladed knife should easily pierce the pears. When done, remove from the oven to cool.

ROLL OUT THE DOUGH. Turn up the oven to 500 degrees. On a floured surface, roll half the pizza dough into a 10-inch circle. Sprinkle a baking sheet or pizza peel with cornmeal to keep the pizza from sticking to it, and place the dough on it.

ADD THE PESTO. Spread ¼ cup of the Arugula Walnut Pesto evenly over the dough, leaving a ¼-inch border.

ADD THE PEARS AND CHEESE. Cut the cooled pear halves lengthwise into slices about ¼ inch thick, and arrange half of them, without overlapping, in a circular pattern to cover the dough. Sprinkle the pear slices with salt and pepper, and then top with ½ cup of the goat cheese.

BAKE THE PIZZA. Bake the pizza in the pan, or, if you're using a pizza peel, slide the pizza directly onto the stone. Bake for 5 to 7 minutes, rotating the pizza halfway through baking, or until the cheese melts and the edges appear crisp and lightly browned.

FINISH THE PIZZA. Remove the pizza from the oven, and drizzle with warmed Fig Balsamic Reduction using a squeeze bottle or dribbling it from a spoon in a sweeping motion. Let this pizza sit a few minutes before cutting and eating, because the roasted pears can be hot enough to burn.

BUILD AND BAKE THE SECOND PIZZA. While the first pizza is baking, roll out the dough for the second one, and add the topping. Bake it when the first pizza comes out of the oven, and finish it as described above.

Stone Fruit Pizza with Brie and Toasted Almonds

There's a wonderful time of year in the Northwest, starting in mid-July, when all the fabulous stone fruits—nectarines, peaches, apricots, plums—start coming in fast and furiously from eastern Washington. We feature stone fruit throughout the menu at this time of year, and a pizza topped with melted Brie is one tasty way to showcase a variety of these fruits. Choose fragrant, ripe but firm fruits; mix them up, or use one favorite.

Makes 2 (10-inch) pizzas; each serves 1 to 2

Herbed Pizza Dough (see page 144)

Cornmeal for the pan or peel

½ cup Tarragon Parsley Pesto (see page 233)

3 cups stone fruits (nectarine, plum, apricot, or peach), unpeeled, cut in thin wedges

Salt and freshly ground pepper

6 ounces Brie, cut into 10 or 12 thin slices

3 tablespoons sliced almonds, lightly toasted (see page 150)

MAKE THE DOUGH, AND PREPARE THE OVEN. Make the pizza dough and set it aside to rise. Preheat the oven to 500 degrees. If you're using a pizza stone, preheat it on a lower rack in the oven for at least 30 minutes before you bake the pizza.

ROLL OUT THE DOUGH. On a floured surface, roll out half of the pizza dough into a 10-inch circle. Sprinkle a baking sheet or pizza peel with cornmeal to keep the pizza from sticking to it, and place the dough on it.

ADD THE PESTO AND FRUIT. Spread ¼ cup of the Tarragon Parsley Pesto evenly over the dough, leaving a ¼-inch border. In a bowl, toss the fruit with a pinch or two of salt and pepper, and arrange half the fruit slices in a circular pattern on the dough. If you're using more than one type of fruit, make sure to distribute the slices evenly so each wedge of pizza will get a bit of each.

ADD THE BRIE. Arrange half of the Brie slices over the fruit, leaving a ½-inch border. (Brie liquefies and spreads when hot and may drip off the pizza and onto the pan or pizza stone.)

BAKE THE FIRST PIZZA. Bake the pizza in the pan, or, if you're using a pizza peel, slide the pizza directly onto the stone. Bake for 5 to 7 minutes, rotating the pizza halfway through baking, until the edges of the dough begin to brown and the cheese melts.

FINISH THE PIZZA. Remove from the oven, sprinkle with half of the toasted almond slices, which will stick to the melted Brie. Cool this pizza for a few minutes before eating because the hot fruit can burn your mouth.

BUILD AND BAKE THE SECOND PIZZA. While the first pizza is baking, roll out the dough for the second one, and add the topping. Bake it when the first pizza comes out of the oven.

> **TIP**
>
> If you can find fresh chervil, a delicious alternative is to drizzle the finished pizza with Chervil Pesto (see page 233)—you'll enjoy its delicate anise flavor.
>
> To make this variation, do not spread the dough with Tarragon Parsley Pesto. Instead brush it with one tablespoon of olive oil. Then add the other ingredients and bake as instructed. When you finish baking the pizza, drizzle the Chervil Pesto over it after you add the toasted almonds. Use a squeeze bottle or dribble it off a spoon in a sweeping motion.

Tropical Pizza [v]

Rich and flavorful vegan pizzas are often hard to create, especially if you limit your thinking to the traditional pizza with Italian-style toppings and cheese. So when we want to put an interesting pizza on the menu for our vegan guests, we look to other cultures for flavor inspiration.

Shiitake mushrooms seasoned with ginger and tamari are baked with pineapple atop a rich Macadamia Roasted Garlic Spread. The hot, crisp pizza is then topped with fresh cilantro and scallions, and drizzled with teriyaki sauce. To add a little zip, serve Sriracha chile sauce on the side. (This hot sauce takes its name from a city on Thailand's eastern seaboard.) You'll find it in Asian markets with other chile sauces.

Makes 2 (10-inch) pizzas; each serves 1 to 2

GET A HEAD START

You can make the Macadamia Roasted Garlic Spread ahead, even a couple of days beforehand, if you want to reduce your time in the kitchen on the day you make this pizza. Or make it while the pizza dough is rising.

Herbed Pizza Dough (see page 144)

1 pound fresh shiitake mushrooms, stems removed (see tip)

2 teaspoons vegetable oil

4 cloves garlic, chopped

2 tablespoons peeled, minced ginger

2 tablespoons tamari (see page 240)

2 tablespoons mirin (seasoned rice wine [see page 239])

2 tablespoons prepared teriyaki sauce

Cornmeal for the pan or peel

½ cup Macadamia Roasted Garlic Spread (see page 234)

1 cup pineapple chunks, cut into ¼-inch pieces

4 scallions, thinly sliced at a sharp angle

8 to 10 sprigs of cilantro

2 tablespoons sweet soy sauce (see page 240)

MAKE THE DOUGH AND PREPARE THE OVEN. Make the pizza dough and set it aside to rise. Preheat the oven to 500 degrees. If you're using a pizza stone, preheat it on a lower rack in the oven for at least 30 minutes before you bake the pizza.

SAUTÉ THE SHIITAKE. Cut the shiitake into ¼-inch-wide pieces. Heat the oil in a wide skillet over medium-high heat. When the pan is hot, add the shiitake, garlic, and ginger. Sauté until the mushrooms are tender and have begun to brown, 4 to 5 minutes.

Add the tamari and mirin, and cook until most of the liquid has evaporated, about 1 minute. Remove from the heat, mix in the teriyaki sauce, and set aside.

ROLL OUT THE DOUGH. On a floured surface, roll out half of the pizza dough into a 10-inch circle. Sprinkle a baking sheet or pizza peel with cornmeal to keep the pizza from sticking to it, and place the dough on it.

ADD THE TOPPING. Gently spread the dough with ¼ cup of the Macadamia Roasted Garlic Spread, leaving a ¼-inch border, being careful not to tear the dough. Scatter half the sautéed shiitake and pineapple evenly over the dough.

BAKE THE FIRST PIZZA. Bake the pizza in the pan, or, if you're using a pizza peel, slide the pizza directly onto the stone. Bake for 5 to 7 minutes, rotating the pizza halfway through baking, until the edges appear crisp and lightly browned.

BUILD AND BAKE THE SECOND PIZZA. While the first pizza is baking, roll out the dough for the second one, and add the topping. Bake it when the first pizza comes out of the oven, and finish it as described above.

FINISH THE FIRST PIZZA. Remove the pizza from the oven, and scatter half the scallions and cilantro sprigs evenly over it. Drizzle the entire pizza with 1 tablespoon of sweet soy sauce. Cut and serve immediately with a bottle of Sriracha chile sauce or your favorite hot sauce on the side to drizzle on each slice as you eat it.

TIP

Don't substitute dried shiitake on this pizza because the results will be disappointing. Freeze the mushroom stems until you're ready to make Mushroom Essence (see page 172).

Herbed Tofu Ricotta [v]

This tasty vegan spread is available for any pizza at Cafe Flora, but it's particularly appetizing with the Roasted Grape Pizza with Herbed Ricotta (see page 154) and other fruit pizzas. You can drop dollops of it on top of the pizza, or spread it on the pizza dough, add other toppings, and then bake as usual.

Although you could consider it a cheese substitute, don't relegate it to vegan dishes. Its great flavor and creamy but grainy texture (like the milk ricotta for which it's named), make it a perfect filling for lasagna and calzones, or to toss with hot pasta.

Makes 1 cup, enough for 2 pizzas

TIMING

The tofu will take about an hour to get cold after you blanch it.

½ pound extrafirm tofu, or pressed firm tofu (see page 22)

1 tablespoon olive oil

⅓ cup finely diced onion

2 cloves garlic, minced

1 teaspoon dried basil

1 teaspoon dried oregano

2 tablespoons red wine

Salt and freshly ground pepper

BLANCH THE TOFU. In a medium saucepan, bring 1 quart water to a boil. Gently set the block of tofu in the boiling water, and blanch for 3 minutes. Remove the tofu from the water. When it's cool enough to handle, pat it dry, and refrigerate until it is cold.

SAUTÉ THE ONION, HERBS, AND GARLIC. Heat the olive oil in a skillet over medium-high heat. Add the onion, garlic, basil, and oregano, and sauté until the onion is soft and translucent, about 10 minutes, stirring often. Add the wine, and cook until it evaporates. Set aside to cool.

BLEND THE TOFU AND ONION MIXTURE. Put the tofu and onion mixture in a food processor. Pulse a few times to break up the tofu, and then process the mixture until thoroughly combined. Add salt and pepper to taste.

SANDWICHES

FOR MANY OF US, LUNCH means a sandwich. But, at least for me, creating delicious vegetarian sandwiches was a real challenge. The vegetarian offerings on other lunch menus all seemed to be variations on the same theme—salad bar items stuffed into a pita pocket; hummus, sprouts, and things on heavy, dense bread; peanut butter and honey or jam; and the all-time favorite, grilled cheese. Coming up with interesting dinner entrees and satisfying brunch dishes was a snap in comparison.

Perhaps that is why, when Cafe Flora first opened, our lunch menu was almost the same as our dinner menu, with the addition of one heartier composed salad and perhaps a single cold sandwich. As time went on, however, our neighborhood changed, with many retail businesses and professional offices opening. Thankfully, Cafe Flora was one of only a few restaurants in the area open for lunch, and our lunch business took off. But many of our lunch clients had only about an hour to eat. We had to reexamine our menu to see how we could continue to offer interesting vegetarian fare and also meet the time constraints of our guests. So we started experimenting with sandwiches.

One of our first, the Roasted Eggplant and Tomato Sandwich, was not only quick to prepare (most of the cooking is done ahead of time, and it is just finished in the oven), but it flew out the door. Around this time, Lisa Lewis and Marie Holtz joined our kitchen staff. They really had a flair for creating interesting sandwiches and burgers—in fact most of the sandwiches in this chapter are their creations. They are still with Cafe Flora, and still coming up with great lunch ideas every week.

An important thing to remember when making these sandwiches or creating your own vegetarian sandwich is the importance of bread. Generally, if the sandwich filling is really soft, like the Artichoke Poorboy with Green Peppercorn Aïoli, then the crust of the bread should be tender. Sandwiches with moist toppings like roasted fruit, eggplant, or tomato that are finished in the oven require a sturdier rustic bread or focaccia. Most vegetarian burgers tend to be on the soft side as well, so try to find a flavorful, whole-grain bun with a tender texture and crust so that all the guts don't mush out when you bite into it.

Our sandwich breads come from several of the wonderful artisanal bakers in Seattle. Luckily, many communities have local bakers making rustic breads and rolls; look for them at the bakery, specialty-food or natural-food store, farmer's markets or even at your local chain grocery.

Pear Sandwich with Pecan Parsley Pesto

In this sandwich, we use Rosemary Diamante, a rustic bread infused with rosemary, from Seattle's Essential Baking Company. Although an herbed rustic bread is best with this sandwich, it would also be good on crusty sourdough or even walnut or pecan bread that's not sweet.

Makes 4 open-face sandwiches with 2 slices per person

TIMING

While the pears are roasting, make the Pecan Parsley Pesto.

2 large firm yet ripe pears, such as Bosc, unpeeled

1 tablespoon olive oil

1 large white onion, cut in half, and sliced thinly lengthwise

8 (½-inch) slices crusty bread

Pecan Parsley Pesto (recipe follows)

Cambozola, Brie, Gorgonzola, sharp white cheddar, or Sage Derby cheese (see "About the Cheese" for amounts)

ROAST THE PEARS. Preheat the oven to 350 degrees. Halve the pears lengthwise, and remove the stems and cores. Put the pears on a lightly oiled baking sheet, cut sides down. Roast until tender, about 15 minutes. A thin-bladed knife should easily pierce the pears.

SLICE THE PEARS. When done, remove from the oven to cool. (Leave the oven on.) Cut the pear halves lengthwise in ¼-inch-thick slices.

SAUTÉ THE ONION. Heat the olive oil in a pan over medium heat. Add the onion, and cook for 5 minutes, stirring once or twice, until it has reduced in volume and begun to soften.

Turn down the heat to low, and cook the onion for 15 to 20 minutes, stirring occasionally. If the onion starts to stick, add 1 to 2 tablespoons water (or cooking sherry, if you have it), and stir to remove any bits of onion from the bottom of the pan. When done, the onion should be various shades of brown, soft, and sweet. Remove from the heat, and set aside.

TOAST THE BREAD. Lay the bread slices directly on the oven rack, and bake until lightly toasted, 2 or 3 minutes.

BUILD THE SANDWICH. Spread about 1 tablespoon Pecan Parsley Pesto (or more if you want) to cover the bread right to the edges. Arrange one-quarter of a roasted pear on top, and then add about 1½ tablespoons of the sautéed onion and one-eighth of the cheese. Repeat this for the remaining 7 slices of bread.

TOAST THE SANDWICH. Put the sandwiches on a baking sheet, and bake until the cheese is melted and the pears are hot, 5 to 7 minutes. Serve open faced.

TIP

If you have *perfectly* ripe pears on hand, give this sandwich a try without roasting the pears. In that case, begin the recipe by sautéing the onion.

Pecan Parsley Pesto [v]

This keeps up to one week in the refrigerator.

Makes ½ cup

2 cups lightly packed fresh parsley, roughly chopped

3 scallions, thinly sliced

3 cloves garlic, chopped

½ cup olive oil

1 cup pecans, toasted (see page 150)

Salt and freshly ground pepper

BLEND THE PARSLEY, SCALLIONS, AND GARLIC. Put the parsley and garlic in a blender or food processor. With the machine running, drizzle in the oil. Turn the machine off, and scrape down the sides of the container.

ADD THE PECANS and process just until they are well combined, about 10 seconds. (You don't want to turn the nuts into nut butter, and you want a little texture.) Add salt and pepper to taste.

About the Cheese

The amount of cheese varies with the type you put on this sandwich:
- Cambozola or Brie: 12 ounces, very thinly sliced
- Gorgonzola: 8 ounces, crumbled
- Sharp white cheddar: 8 ounces, grated (2 cups)
- Sage Derby: 8 ounces, grated (2 cups) This mild cheddar-type cheese is made using leaf sage for its subtle flavor and chlorophyll for a green marbled finish. Sage Derby was developed in the 17th century when it was believed that sage was good for the digestion.

To speed cheesy cleanup, spread a sheet of parchment paper on the baking sheet before you toast the sandwich.

Roasted Plum Sandwich with Crispy Fried Onions

I think the seasonal fruit sandwich started with our wildly popular pizzas topped with fruit and flavorful cheeses. This got us to thinking: why not try roasting fruit for a sandwich? From there we just kept experimenting with different fruit, pestos and spreads, and all the world's wonderful cheeses. This sandwich is one we serve every summer and early fall when plums are abundant; the oval-shaped Italian prune is a natural for roasting as well.

Makes 4 open-face sandwiches with 1 slice per person

GET A HEAD START

To reduce your time in the kitchen the day you plan to make this sandwich, make the Arugula Walnut Pesto ahead. You can also roast the plums the day before.

3 large plums or 8 Italian prunes, ripe but firm

3 tablespoons balsamic or sherry vinegar

Salt and freshly ground pepper

½ medium yellow or white onion, cut from stem to root end

½ cup unbleached all-purpose flour

½ teaspoon salt

Vegetable oil for frying

4 slices rustic bread, about ½ inch thick (see "About the Bread")

¼ to ½ cup Arugula Walnut Pesto (see page 232)

6 ounces Brie or Cambozola cheese, cut into ¼-inch slices

PREPARE THE PLUMS. Preheat the oven to 350 degrees. Cut the unpeeled plums in half, and remove the pits. Slice the plum halves in ½-inch wedges, and toss with the vinegar to coat.

ROAST THE PLUMS. Lightly oil a rimmed baking sheet large enough to accommodate all the plums in a single layer without crowding. (If you crowd the plums, you will steam rather than roast them.) Spread the plums on the baking sheet, and sprinkle with a few pinches of salt and pepper. Roast for 20 minutes, and set aside to cool. (Leave the oven on.)

PREPARE THE ONION. While the plums are roasting, cut the onion into crescents as thin as you can possibly slice them. (If you have a mandoline, here's the time to use it.) Put the onion crescents in a bowl of cold water, and stir to separate the pieces.

In another bowl, mix the flour and ½ teaspoon salt. Drain the onion crescents, and toss with the flour-salt mixture until they are completely coated. (There will be excess flour at the bottom of the bowl.)

FRY THE ONION SLICES. Pour oil into a heavy pot to a depth of 2 inches. (Make sure the pot is at least 4 inches tall to reduce spattering.) When the oil reaches 350 to 360 degrees, gently drop one-third of the onion pieces into the hot oil. Be careful not to add too many at one time, or the temperature of the oil will drop. (If you don't have a thermometer, see page 199 for alternative instructions.)

Fry the onion slices until light brown, about 3 minutes, turning them every minute or so. Remove with a slotted spoon, and drain in a single layer on paper towels. Fry the remaining batches of onion, and set aside.

TOAST THE BREAD. Lay the bread slices directly on the oven rack. Bake until lightly toasted, 2 or 3 minutes.

BUILD THE SANDWICH. Spread 1 to 2 tablespoons of pesto on a slice of bread right to the edges. Arrange plum wedges on the bread in a single layer, and top with 3 or 4 slices of cheese. (Both Brie and Cambozola spread when heated so the cheese slices do not have to cover the entire surface.) Repeat with the remaining 3 slices of bread.

BAKE AND SERVE THE SANDWICH. Put the open-face sandwiches on a lightly oiled baking sheet. (To speed cheesy cleanup, spread a sheet of parchment paper on the baking sheet, or lightly oil it before you bake the sandwich.) Bake until the cheese melts, about 10 minutes. Remove from the oven.

SERVE THE SANDWICH. Top each with one-fourth of the fried onion, and serve. Let the sandwiches cool a few minutes before you serve them, as the hot fruit can really burn your mouth. (To see how we serve this dish at Cafe Flora, see the photo on page 000.)

About the Bread

For this sandwich we use a round rustic rosemary loaf sprinkled with coarse salt made by one of the many great artisanal bread bakers in Seattle. If you're using a round loaf as well, cut the bread for this sandwich from the center of the loaf to get four slices of bread all approximately six inches wide. Save the uncut portion of bread to serve with another meal. If you're not going to use it right away, wrap it carefully and freeze. (My freezer is always full of bread because I'm a notorious bread saver, obsessed with using every crumb of bread I buy.)

Fried Green Tomato Sandwich

Using fried green tomatoes on a sandwich is a mouthwatering way to use up end-of-the-season tomatoes that are not going to ripen on the vine. When you panfry the tomatoes, however, make sure not to overcook them or your sandwich filling will be mushy.

Creamy fresh or smoked mozzarella makes a great counterpoint to the crunchy tart tomatoes. But do try thinly sliced, sharp white cheddar, some paper-thin slices shaved from a block of Pecorino Romano, or a sharp, tangy Italian sheep's milk cheese.

Makes 4 sandwiches

2 tablespoons Basil Pesto (see page 233) or purchased basil pesto

¼ cup mayonnaise

4 medium green (unripe) tomatoes (about 1 pound)

½ cup all-purpose flour

¼ teaspoon cayenne pepper

Salt and freshly ground black pepper

½ cup buttermilk or milk

1 cup panko (Japanese bread crumbs (see page 239), or unseasoned bread crumbs, toasted (see page 129)

¼ cup cornmeal

1 tablespoon onion powder

Vegetable oil for frying

8 (⅜-inch) slices sourdough, or sandwich-size French bread

2 (4-ounce) balls fresh mozzarella or smoked mozzarella, thinly sliced

2 cups mixed salad greens or arugula

GET READY. Mix the pesto and mayonnaise in a small bowl until well combined. Preheat the oven to 350 degrees.

SLICE AND DRY THE TOMATOES. Slice the tomatoes about ⅜ inch thick, and pat dry.

GET THE BREADING READY. Mix the flour, cayenne, ¼ teaspoon salt, and a pinch of black pepper in a shallow bowl. Put the buttermilk in another shallow bowl. In a third bowl, stir together the panko, cornmeal, onion powder, ¼ teaspoon salt, and another pinch of black pepper.

DREDGE EACH TOMATO SLICE in the flour mixture and then in the buttermilk to coat. Finally put in the panko mixture, pressing the breading onto the tomato slice to coat it fully.

Spread the breaded tomato slices on an ungreased baking sheet until you're ready to fry them.

PANFRY THE TOMATOES. Heat about ¼ inch of oil in a heavy skillet over medium heat. When the oil is hot, put 3 or 4 tomato slices in the skillet, leaving enough room to flip them. When the tomato slices are golden brown on one side, flip them and brown the other side, 2 to 2½ minutes per side.

Skim the oil occasionally to remove any burned bits of breading. Drain the fried tomato slices on paper towels, and keep them warm in a 200-degree oven until ready to serve.

TOAST THE BREAD. Lay the bread slices directly on the oven rack. Bake until lightly toasted, 2 or 3 minutes.

PUT THE SANDWICHES TOGETHER. Spread each slice of toasted bread with basil mayonnaise. Divide the slices of fried green tomatoes among 4 slices of bread, and cover with cheese slices. Pile some salad greens on top. Top with the other 4 slices of toasted bread. Cut each sandwich in half, and serve immediately.

Artichoke Poorboy with Green Peppercorn Aïoli

Our lunch chef, Lisa Lewis, is always thinking about the next great sandwich. She tells me this one came to her while having lunch with her uncle, who was enjoying a classic New Orleans favorite, the fried oyster po'boy. But don't stop with sandwiches. These artichoke hearts would also make a terrific appetizer served with the tart Spicy Remoulade (see page 231).

Makes 4 sandwiches

½ cup unbleached all-purpose flour

1 teaspoon pimenton (Spanish smoked paprika [see page 240])

1 teaspoon onion powder

½ teaspoon salt

¼ teaspoon pepper

⅛ cup cornmeal

½ cup panko (Japanese bread crumbs [see page 239]), or unseasoned bread crumbs, toasted (see page 129)

1 egg

1 (14-ounce) can whole artichoke hearts packed in water, drained

Canola, peanut, or olive oil for frying

4 (6-inch) French rolls, or French baguettes, cut into 6-inch lengths and split

Green Peppercorn Aïoli (see page 231)

Shredded Romaine, thinly sliced tomatoes, and red onion

GET READY. Preheat the oven to 350 degrees. Mix the flour with the pimenton, onion powder, salt, and pepper in a shallow bowl. Mix the cornmeal and panko in another shallow bowl. Lightly beat the egg in a third shallow bowl.

CUT THE ARTICHOKES IN HALF. The size of canned artichokes seems to vary wildly, so if you get a particularly small one, don't bother to halve it. You need about 16 artichoke halves, or pieces of about the same size.

DREDGE THE ARTICHOKES. Dip each artichoke half in the flour mixture first, then in the egg, and finally in the cornmeal-panko mix, shaking off the excess after each dipping. Coat all the artichokes at once, laying them on an ungreased baking sheet until you're ready to fry them.

FRY THE ARTICHOKES. Pour oil into a heavy pot to a depth of 2 inches. (Make sure the pot is at least 4 inches tall to reduce spattering.) When the oil reaches 350 to 360 degrees, gently drop the artichoke halves into the hot oil. Be careful not to add too many at one time, or the temperature of the oil will drop. (If you don't have a thermometer, see page 199 for alternative instructions.) Skim the oil between batches to remove any bits of breading before it burns.

Fry until golden brown, 3 to 4 minutes, and drain on paper towels. You can hold them in a 200-degree oven while you finish frying them.

PREPARE THE ROLLS. Split each roll, but don't cut it completely in half. Lay the rolls on a baking sheet, cut side up. Bake until lightly toasted, 2 or 3 minutes.

PUT THE SANDWICH TOGETHER. Slather half of each bun with Green Peppercorn Aïoli. Into the split roll, tuck a layer of shredded lettuce and a few slices of tomato and onion. Top with 3 or 4 fried artichoke hearts, and serve at once.

> **TIP**
>
> For suggestions about how to save oil for later use, read "Saving Oil," on page 199.

Falafel Sandwich with Bulgur Wheat Salad [v]

Falafel makes one of the most satisfying and universally enjoyed sandwiches on earth. If you're serving nonvegans, try our tangy Lemon Oregano Yogurt Sauce (see page 230) or your favorite tzatziki (Trader Joe's makes a good one) along with the Tahini Sauce.

These fritters can also be the centerpiece of a meze-style supper of small dishes. Serve a platter of falafel with bowls of Tahini Sauce, Bulgur Wheat Salad, olives, and pepperoncini. Set out a plate of Grilled Eggplant (see page 29) and Laban (a cheese you can make from yogurt described on page 31) or chunks of feta cheese.

Makes about 24 patties, about 8 servings of 3 patties each

In this dish

- Falafel
- Tahini Sauce (see page 232)
- Bulgur Wheat Salad
- Dijon Curry Vinaigrette (see page 87)

Falafel

1½ cups dried chickpeas (garbanzos), soaked for 3 to 8 hours, or 2 (15-ounce) cans (3¼ cups cooked)

1 medium yellow onion, coarsely chopped

2 stalks celery, coarsely chopped

6 cloves garlic, coarsely chopped

2 tablespoons freshly squeezed lemon juice

2 teaspoons ground turmeric

2 teaspoons cumin seeds, toasted and ground (see page 52)

¼ teaspoon cayenne pepper

1 tablespoon salt

½ cup chopped fresh parsley

½ cup unseasoned bread crumbs, toasted (see page 129)

⅓ cup whole wheat or all-purpose white flour

8 pitas, flat or pocket style

Vegetable oil for frying falafel

Shredded lettuce, tomato slices, alfalfa sprouts, and cucumber slices

Tahini Sauce (see page 232)

COOK THE CHICKPEAS. If you're using dried chickpeas, drain them, and cover with fresh water in a pot. Bring to a boil, lower the heat, and cook, covered, at a gentle simmer until the chickpeas are very tender, 1 hour or more (depending on how dry (and old) the beans were). A chickpea should smash easily between your thumb and index finger. (Careful! They're hot!) Drain the chickpeas, and cool completely.

If you're using canned chickpeas, rinse them under cold water, and drain well.

CHOP THE VEGETABLES. Put the onion, celery, and garlic in a food processor, and pulse several times, until they are very finely chopped. (Pulsing minces the vegetables but prevents them from becoming puréed.) Put them into a large mixing bowl.

CHOP THE CHICKPEAS. Put the cooled chickpeas in the food processor, and pulse several times, until they're broken up. Then, run the food processor until the chickpeas are very finely chopped. (You use this two-step process to get an even consistency.) Put the chickpeas in the large bowl with the vegetables, and mix well. Preheat the oven to 300 degrees.

ADD THE REMAINING INGREDIENTS. Put the chickpeas in the large bowl with the vegetables. Mix in the lemon juice, turmeric, cumin, cayenne, salt, and parsley. Sprinkle the bread crumbs and flour over all, and mix thoroughly with your hands.

WARM THE PITAS. Wrap them in foil and warm them in the oven until they're flexible and soft.

SHAPE THE FALAFEL. Using 2 tablespoons of the chickpea mixture, shape it into balls. It should hold together easily. (If not, see tips.) Gently flatten the balls with your fingertips into patties about 1½ inches in diameter. Smooth out the jagged edges so they don't break off when you cook them. Lay them on an ungreased baking sheet until you're ready to fry them.

TEST FRY A FALAFEL FIRST. Pour oil into a heavy pot to a depth of 2 inches. (Make sure the pot is at least 4 inches tall to reduce spattering.) When the oil reaches 350 to 360 degrees, gently drop sample falafel into the hot oil. (If you don't have a ther-

mometer, see page 199 for alternative instructions.) Cook on each side for 2 to 3 minutes.

FRY THE FALAFEL. If the test falafel held together, fry the rest of the patties a few at a time so the temperature of the oil doesn't drop. Drain on paper towels.

SERVE THE FALAFEL. Let everyone build their own sandwiches. Serve the Bulgur Wheat Salad and the falafel in separate bowls, and put out a platter with the shredded lettuce, thinly sliced tomatoes, alfalfa sprouts, and thinly sliced cucumbers. Put the warm pitas in a basket and the Tahini Sauce in a small bowl on the side.

TIPS

- If the falafel falls apart easily when you form it into a ball or test fry it, you may need to tweak it as described in "Tips for Making Sturdy Patties and Burgers," on page 177.

- If you're using small pocket pitas, cut off the top. Nine- or ten-inch pocket pitas cut in half, may serve two people.

- For suggestions about how to save oil for later use, read "Saving Oil," on page 199.

Bulgur Wheat Salad [v]

Use a colorful combination of dried fruits. If you can't find raw pistachios, slivered almonds or cashews taste good, too. For another variation on this salad using different grains, see the Curried Grain Salad (see page 83).

Makes 3 cups

GET A HEAD START

This salad is especially good made ahead. It really tastes better the next day, when the curry dressing has had a chance to soak into the bulgar wheat.

1 cup bulgur wheat
½ cup Dijon Curry Vinaigrette (see page 87)

½ cup dried fruit (cranberries, cherries, apricots cut into tiny pieces, currants, or golden raisins)

½ cup pistachio nuts, toasted (see page 150) and roughly chopped

3 scallions, white and green parts, thinly sliced at a very sharp angle

Salt and freshly ground pepper

SOAK THE BULGUR WHEAT. In a bowl, pour 1 cup boiling water over the bulgur wheat, and let it sit for an hour. Drain it, and press the water out of it.

MIX THE SALAD. Pour the dressing over the bulgur wheat and mix thoroughly. Add the dried fruit, pistachios, and scallions, and mix well. Add salt and pepper to taste.

Cafe Flora French Dip Sandwich [v]

I am not kidding: we've had guests call Cafe Flora to find out the name of "that roast-beef sandwich on your lunch menu." I always wonder if they're calling because they're worried that they were actually served meat at a vegetarian restaurant, or just because they love our most-requested sandwich so much.

To truly duplicate this popular sandwich, a dense, chewy baguette is essential.

Makes 4 sandwiches

GET A HEAD START

You can make all the parts of the sandwich ahead so that when you're ready to serve it, it's just a matter of minutes before you can dig in. The Mushroom Essence and the French Dip Spread can both be made days, or even weeks, ahead and stored frozen. You can also roast the mushrooms and sauté the onion a day in advance.

In this dish

- French Dip Sandwich
- French Dip Spread
- Mushroom Essence

---

3 tablespoons olive oil

2 teaspoons minced garlic

3 portobello mushrooms, reserving the stems for Mushroom Essence

Salt and freshly ground pepper

1 large yellow onion, halved and sliced in thin crescents

1 rustic baguette

French Dip Spread (recipe follows)

Optional: 4 slices Swiss, mozzarella, or provolone cheese

About 1⅓ cups Mushroom Essence (see page 172) warmed

PREPARE THE MUSHROOMS. Preheat the oven to 350 degrees. Mix 2 tablespoons of the olive oil and the garlic in a small bowl. Brush the portobello caps on both sides with this mixture, and sprinkle each side with salt and pepper.

ROAST THE PORTOBELLOS. Place them gill sides down (the very dark side) on a baking sheet, and roast for 25 minutes. (Leave the oven on.)

When the mushrooms are cool enough to handle, slice each cap thinly at an angle, trying to get at least 8 to 10 slices per cap. Set the mushroom slices aside.

SAUTÉ THE ONION. While the portobello caps are in the oven, heat the remaining 1 tablespoon olive oil in a pan over medium heat. Add the onion, and cook for 5 minutes, stirring once or twice, until it has begun to soften.

Turn down the heat to low, and cook the onion for 15 to 20 minutes, stirring occasionally. If the onion starts to stick, add 1 to 2 tablespoons water (or cooking sherry, if you have it), and stir to remove any bits of onion from the bottom of the pan. When done, the onion should be various shades of brown, soft, and sweet. Remove from the heat, and set aside.

CUT THE BAGUETTE into 4 equal portions 5 or 6 inches long from the middle of the loaf. (Don't use the ends.) Slice each hunk in half lengthwise.

GRIDDLE THE BREAD. Spread each of the 8 halves with 1 tablespoon of French Dip Spread.

Heat a large skillet over medium heat. Place as many baguette pieces as can fit in the pan spread-side down, and griddle the bread for 3 minutes. Repeat this process for the remaining bread.

PUT THE SANDWICH TOGETHER. Place 4 baguette pieces, griddled side up, on a lightly oiled baking sheet. Top them with ¼ of the portobello slices and sautéed onions. Top with a slice of cheese, if you're using it.

BAKE THE SANDWICH. Put these 4 bottom halves in the 350 degree oven, and bake until the cheese melts and the sandwich is heated through, about 10 minutes. Top with the remaining buttered halves of baguette, and bake for 3 minutes longer.

SERVE THE SANDWICH. Slice each sandwich in half at an angle and serve with a side dish of Mushroom Essence as a dipping sauce, about ⅓ cup for each person.

TIP

• To speed cheesy cleanup, spread a sheet of parchment paper on the baking sheet or lightly oil it before you toast the sandwich.

French Dip Spread [v]

The herbed spread is made with soybean margarine because this dish is offered as vegan on our menu, but you may substitute butter. Most margarine tends to be salty, so I find that I don't need additional salt when using margarine. You can freeze any leftover spread lightly wrapped in plastic wrap for up to a month.

Makes about ½ cup

½ teaspoon olive oil
½ shallot, minced
½ teaspoon minced garlic
1 tablespoon chopped fresh herbs (parsley, thyme, chives, or basil), or 1 teaspoon dried
2 tablespoons white wine
¼ pound (1 stick) soybean margarine, or unsalted butter, softened to room temperature
Salt and freshly ground pepper

SAUTÉ THE SHALLOT AND GARLIC. Heat the olive oil in a small skillet over medium heat. Add the shallot, garlic, and herbs, and cook for 2 minutes, stirring constantly. Add the wine, and cook until most of it has evaporated, but the mixture is still moist. Remove from the heat, and cool completely.

COMBINE THE MARGARINE AND SHALLOT MIXTURE. Add the cooled shallot mixture to the softened margarine, and mix well. Add salt and pepper to taste.

Mushroom Pecan Pâté Sandwich with Green Peppercorn Aïoli

When you make our Portobello Wellington (see page 135), you'll have some of the Mushroom Pecan Pâté left over, which will be enough to make four of these incredibly delicious sandwiches. But even if you make this meatloaflike pâté from scratch for this sandwich, you'll love having it in your fridge. Dish it up hot with mashed potatoes and green beans for a classic American supper, vegetarian style. Or serve it with crackers, mustard, and gherkins as an appetizer just as you would any pâté.

Although this sandwich can be served cold, the warmed pâté is much more flavorful. We use the wonderful, soft potato bread from Macrina Bakery for this sandwich, but any bread or roll with a tender crust will do. At Cafe Flora, we serve a little green salad tossed in a balsamic vinaigrette on the side.

Try substituting Red Onion Confit (see page 33) for the sliced red onion; you'll need ¼ to ½ cup for four sandwiches. (Because the confit is sweet, you might want to use a mustard that's not.) Or top the pâté side of the sandwich with sliced Gruyère or Jarlsberg cheese before you put it into the oven.

Makes 4 sandwiches

GET A HEAD START

The pâté requires 45 minutes baking time and another hour or more to chill. If you're the sort of person who plans ahead, you could make it a day or two ahead. You can also make the aïoli several days ahead.

Mushroom Essence [v]

Use this reduced mushroom stock or "essence" in recipes where you want an intense mushroom flavor: risottos, stews, sauces, and the like. Save up your mushroom stems and pieces. Just stick them in the freezer until you're ready to make this. Like any broth, this freezes well, so while you're at it, make a double recipe and freeze small portions, including some in an ice cube tray.

Makes 2 cups

½ pound whole crimini or domestic mushrooms, including stems

6 cloves garlic, lightly crushed

2 tablespoons tamari

MAKE THE BROTH. Combine the mushrooms, garlic, and 6 cups of water in a 3-quart saucepan. Bring to a boil, lower the heat, and cook at a low boil—that is, lots of small bubbles are just about to break the surface. Cook for about 1 hour, or until the liquid has been reduced to 2 cups. If you want an even more intense mushroom flavor, keep the saucepan on the stove for several hours at a very low simmer, until the liquid has been reduced to 1 cup or less.

STRAIN THE LIQUID, and add the tamari. Keep warm until ready to use, or refrigerate or freeze for use later.

8 slices potato bread, or other soft-crusted bread or rolls

4 tablespoons sweet hot mustard, or a good honey or Dijon mustard

8 to 12 (½-inch) slices Mushroom Pecan Pâté (see page 137)

Thinly sliced red onion and tomatoes, and lettuce leaves

¼ cup Green Peppercorn Aïoli (see page 231), or mayonnaise

TOAST THE BREAD. Preheat the oven to 350 degrees. Lay the bread slices directly on the oven rack. Bake until lightly toasted, 2 or 3 minutes.

START THE SANDWICH. Lay 4 slices of bread on your work surface. Spread each with 1 tablespoon of the mustard, and then lay 2 or 3 slices of pâté on top, overlapping slightly if necessary.

WARM THE PÂTÉ. Put the pâté-covered bread on the baking sheet, and bake until the pâté is warmed through, about 10 minutes.

FINISH THE SANDWICHES. Top the pâté with some slices of red onion and tomatoes and layer on lettuce. Spread 1 tablespoon of the Green Peppercorn Aïoli on each of the remaining slices of bread. Put the sandwich together, cut in half at an angle, and serve at once.

Nutburger with Tomato Jam [v]

This rich, nutty burger was the first on our menu. It owes its unique flavor in part to the use of a bottled condiment, Pickapeppa Sauce, which is made in Jamaica. Similar to Worcestershire sauce, Pickapeppa is a little fruitier in taste but is completely vegetarian, unlike Worcestershire sauce which contains anchovies. The Tomato Jam is a tart and fresh complement to these burgers, but they're also good spread with a spicy mayonnaise, like Cayenne Aïoli (see page 209). And of course, you can always add a slice of your favorite cheese.

Makes 6 to 8 patties

> **GET A HEAD START**
>
> Make the Tomato Jam and cook the wild rice and millet ahead of time. The Tomato Jam holds for a week, and you could cook the wild rice and millet a day, or even two, before you plan to make and serve the burgers. You can also make the nutburger mixture a day or two in advance.

¼ cup sesame seeds

½ cup hulled sunflower seeds

½ cup wild rice

⅓ cup millet

2 teaspoons olive oil

1 small yellow onion, finely diced (about 1 cup)

½ cup celery, finely diced (about 2 stalks)

1 small bell pepper, seeds removed and finely diced (about 1 cup)

4 cloves garlic, minced

½ cup rolled oats (not instant)

2 teaspoons cumin seeds, toasted and ground (see page 52)

5 tablespoons peanut butter

1 tablespoon tamari (see page 240)

2 tablespoons Pickapeppa Sauce

4 ounces firm tofu, drained and crumbled

½ teaspoon salt
½ teaspoon pepper
Vegetable oil for cooking
6 to 8 soft buns, cut in half
Tomato Jam (recipe follows)
Lettuce, tomato and onion slices, and pickles

TOAST THE SESAME SEEDS by tossing them in a dry skillet over medium heat just until fragrant and starting to color, 2 to 3 minutes. As soon as they're done, take them out of the pan to cool.

TOAST THE SUNFLOWER SEEDS by tossing them in a dry skillet over medium heat just until light brown, 3 to 4 minutes. As soon as they're done, take them out of the pan to cool.

COOK THE WILD RICE. Rinse the wild rice in a strainer under cold water. Put it in a small saucepan with 2 cups water, and bring to a boil. Lower the heat to a simmer, and cook, uncovered, stirring occasionally, until tender, about 40 minutes.

Add more water if most of it evaporates before the rice is tender. Drain off any remaining liquid, and set aside to cool completely.

COOK THE MILLET. Bring 1 cup water to a boil in a small saucepan. Stir in the millet, lower the heat, and simmer, covered, until tender, about 25 minutes. Drain off any remaining liquid, and set aside to cool. (Millet has a tendency to get really mushy and waterlogged, so you probably won't need to add more water.)

SAUTÉ THE VEGETABLES. While the grains are cooking, heat the olive oil in a skillet over medium heat. Sauté the onion, celery, and bell pepper until the onion is soft and translucent and the celery tender, about 10 minutes. Add the garlic, and cook 1 minute more. Set aside to cool completely.

GRIND THE OATS. While you're sautéing the vegetables, put the oats in a food processor or blender.

Grind until all the flakes are broken up, but not as fine as a flour. Set the oats aside.

MIX THE GRAINS, VEGETABLES, AND OTHER INGREDIENTS. Combine the cooked and cooled grains and vegetables in a large bowl. Add cumin seeds, peanut butter, tamari, Pickapeppa Sauce, tofu, salt, and pepper. Mix well, using your hands to fully combine all ingredients.

ADD THE OATS. Sprinkle the ground oats over the mixture and mix well with your hands until it holds together when you shape a portion into a patty.

SHAPE THE BURGERS. Using ½ cup mixture per burger, gently shape each portion into a patty about 3½ inches in diameter. Gently flatten the burgers, and smooth out the jagged edges so they don't break off when you cook them. Preheat the oven to 350 degrees (for toasting the buns).

PANFRY THE BURGERS. Heat 1 tablespoon oil in a large nonstick skillet over medium-high heat. (If you don't have a nonstick pan, any heavy skillet works well.) When it's hot, put several burgers in the pan, leaving enough room to flip them easily.

Cook on each side until browned and heated through, 3 to 4 minutes per side. Add 1 tablespoon of oil to the skillet for each pan of burgers you fry.

TOAST THE BREAD. Lay the buns on a baking sheet, cut side up. Bake until lightly toasted, 2 or 3 minutes.

SERVE THE NUTBURGERS. Spread Tomato Jam on the cut side of each bun, add a nutburger, and top with your favorite burger fixin's: lettuce, tomato, onion slices, and a pickle.

- Look for Pickapeppa Sauce in a market that caters to a Caribbean community. Or hunt for it in a large grocery store in the natural-food aisle or in the specialty condiment section along with other "exotic" sauces like chipotle and hot pepper. If you can't find it, there are other brands of vegetarian Worcestershire-like sauce that would make a good substitute.

- If you're serving people who are allergic to peanuts, almond or cashew butter works fine.

- If the burgers fall apart as you shape or fry them, see "Tips for Making Sturdy Patties and Burgers," on page 177.

Tomato Jam [v]

This saucy accompaniment to our nutburger is not thick like ketchup, but more like a smooth fresh salsa that is at once sweet and tart.

Makes about 1⅓ cups

1 medium shallot, peeled

3 cloves garlic

1 tablespoon olive oil

1 (14.5-ounce) can diced tomatoes in juice, drained

1 tablespoon balsamic vinegar

2 teaspoons tamari (see page 240)

2 tablespoons finely chopped chives, or scallion

Salt and freshly ground pepper

ROAST THE GARLIC AND SHALLOT. Preheat the oven to 375 degrees. Cut the shallot so it is about the same size as a garlic clove. Toss the garlic and shallot with the olive oil, and put in a small covered baking dish with foil. Roast until soft, about 20 minutes. Give them a stir, remove the foil, and continue roasting until they start to brown, another 5 to 10 minutes.

BLEND ALL THE INGREDIENTS. Put all the ingredients, except salt and pepper, in a blender or food processor, and blend until thoroughly combined. Add salt and pepper to taste.

Curried Lentil and Quinoa Burger with Tomato Chutney [v]

This burger, called the Curry Burger on our menu, is so popular it even has an out-of-town following. One guest who frequently travels to Seattle would call ahead and ask us to freeze a dozen or so for him to take home. But he lives in the Bay area with numerous vegetarian restaurants and health food stores within easy striking distance of home. I asked him what it was about these burgers that he couldn't find there. He explained their appeal: they don't try to mimic a hamburger, but have a flavor and texture uniquely their own.

The Tomato Chutney makes a spicy and chunky alternative to ketchup. And if you're serving nonvegans, try our Lemon Oregano Yogurt Sauce (see page 230). Drizzle it on half a bun before you put the burger on it.

Makes 10 burgers

You can cook the lentils and the quinoa or mix up the entire batch of burgers in advance, even a day or two ahead.

¾ cup red lentils

1 bay leaf

½ cup quinoa (see page 239)

1 teaspoon vegetable oil

1 cup diced yellow onion

1 cup diced celery

2 tablespoons chopped garlic

2 teaspoons salt

¼ cup chopped fresh parsley

1 teaspoon paprika

1 teaspoon curry powder

1 teaspoon cumin seeds, toasted and ground (see page 52)

1 teaspoon chili powder

¼ cup rolled oats (not instant)

2 tablespoons all-purpose or whole wheat flour

½ cup unseasoned bread crumbs, toasted (see page 129)

Vegetable oil for cooking the burgers

10 soft rolls or burger buns

Lettuce and thinly sliced onion

Tomato Chutney (recipe follows)

COOK THE LENTILS. Rinse the lentils, and put them in a small pot with 2 cups cold water and the bay leaf. Bring to a boil and then lower the heat. Simmer, covered, until tender, 15 to 20 minutes, adding more water if necessary. (It's OK if they're mushy.) Drain and set aside.

PREPARE THE QUINOA. Thoroughly rinse the quinoa in a mesh strainer under running water until the water runs clear. This will remove the bitter powdery residue that coats each grain.

COOK THE QUINOA. In a medium saucepan, bring 1 cup of water to a boil. Add the rinsed quinoa, lower the heat to a simmer, and cook, covered, until all the water is absorbed, about 15 minutes. Remove the pan from the heat, leaving the lid on, and let the quinoa steam for 5 minutes. Then fluff the grains with a fork.

COOK THE VEGETABLES AND SPICES. Heat the oil in a skillet over medium heat. Add the onion, celery, garlic, and salt. Cook, stirring often, until the onion

is soft and translucent and the celery is tender, about 10 minutes.

Stir in the parsley, paprika, curry powder, cumin, and chili powder until thoroughly combined. Set the mixture aside to cool.

GRIND THE OATS. While you're sautéing the vegetables, put the oats in a food processor or blender. Grind until all the flakes are broken up, but not as fine as flour. Set the oats aside.

MIX UP THE PATTIES. When all the cooked ingredients are cool enough to handle, put them in a large bowl, and stir until well combined. Sprinkle the oats, flour, and bread crumbs over this mixture, and mix thoroughly using your hands.

SHAPE THE BURGERS. Using ½ cup mixture per burger, gently shape each portion into a patty about 3½ inches in diameter. Gently flatten the burgers, and smooth out the jagged edges so they don't break off when you cook them. Preheat the oven to 350 degrees (for toasting the buns).

PANFRY THE BURGERS. Heat 1 tablespoon oil in a large nonstick skillet over medium-high heat. (If you don't have a nonstick pan, any heavy skillet works well.) When it's hot, put several burgers in the pan, leaving enough room to flip them easily. Cook on each side until browned and heated through, 3 to 4 minutes per side. Add 1 tablespoon of oil to the skillet for each pan of burgers you fry.

SERVE THE BURGERS. Split each bun and lay the halves cut side up on a baking sheet. Bake until lightly toasted, 2 or 3 minutes. Put a burger on one half of a bun, lay on lettuce and onions, and top with Tomato Chutney.

Tips for Making Sturdy Patties and Burgers

It can be a challenge to make patties and burgers (fritters and croquettes, too) from vegetables, beans, and grains that hold together while you cook them. But it's a bit like making bread dough: after some practice you'll become familiar with the look and feel of the mixture, and you'll know what it needs to hold its shape.

NOTE: If you plan to broil the burgers, brush each side with vegetable oil before broiling so they don't stick.

Making Patties

Patties should stick together when you put some of the mixture in your hand and press it. If the patties aren't holding together, the following tips are your first line of defense. If these don't work, try adding ingredients as described in "If the Patty Doesn't Hold Together."

REMOVE AS MUCH LIQUID AS POSSIBLE FROM THE PATTY MIXTURE. Make sure that sautéed vegetables or other wet ingredients, like tofu or soaked TVP (textured vegetable protein) are as dry as possible before you mix them with the rest of the ingredients. The patty should be moist, but not wet or soggy.

REFRIGERATE PATTIES BEFORE YOU FRY THEM because cold patties hold together better during cooking. Refrigerate either the mixture or the already formed patties or burgers until cold and firm, about an hour.

MAKE PATTIES AND BURGERS ON THE SMALLER SIDE, especially those that are deep-fried. They'll hold together better during cooking.
- Use 2 to 3 tablespoons of mix (about the size of a golf ball) for patties, fritters, and croquettes, and make them $1\frac{1}{2}$ to 2 inches in diameter.
- Use $\frac{1}{2}$ cup mixture per burger, and shape them into patties about $3\frac{1}{2}$ inches in diameter.

TEST FRY A PATTY BEFORE YOU PLUNGE IN. Make a sample patty and test it by cooking it according to the method suggested in the recipe. If it falls apart easily when you put it in the frying pan, you may need to tweak it (as described below). When you think you've got it right, test fry another to make sure.

If the Patty Doesn't Hold Together

IF THE PATTY FALLS APART BECAUSE IT'S TOO WET, add more of the binding ingredient 1 tablespoon at a time, and stir until the mixture holds together easily. In our recipes, these include panko (Japanese bread crumbs), all-purpose flour, whole wheat flour, ground oatmeal, or cornstarch. It's very important to add binders a tablespoon at a time, or you may end up with something that will be dry and pasty once cooked, and taste too much of the binder.

IF THE PATTY MIXTURE CRUMBLES BECAUSE IT'S TOO DRY, use more of the wet ingredients in the recipe. These include lightly beaten egg, Egg Replacer reconstituted with water, mayonnaise (either vegan or nonvegan), or tahini. Again, add these ingredients 1 tablespoon at a time, testing after each addition until the mixture holds together.

Tomato Chutney [v]

Makes 1½ cups

2 teaspoons vegetable oil

2 teaspoons dark mustard seeds

1 teaspoon fennel seeds

1 (14.5-ounce) can diced tomatoes, or 1½ cups chopped, fresh tomatoes

2 teaspoons light brown sugar or brown rice syrup

½ teaspoon crushed red pepper flakes

½ teaspoon salt

SAUTÉ THE SPICES. In a skillet, heat the oil over medium heat. Add the mustard and fennel seeds. Stir until the mustard seeds begin to pop.

ADD THE REMAINING INGREDIENTS. Lower the heat and simmer for 10 minutes, until the liquid is reduced a bit and the chutney thickens to a saucy consistency. Remove from the heat, and set aside to cool.

Southwestern Yam and Bean Burger [v]

These burgers don't need to be served as burgers at all. For a great dinner, cook them up and serve two per person, dolloped with guacamole and salsa. On the side, serve corn on the cob and a big salad of chopped romaine lettuce, cherry tomatoes, cucumber, and jicama dressed with lime juice, olive oil, salt, and pepper. When corn on the cob is not in season, try serving them with Basil Corn Relish (see page 212), which can be made with frozen corn, and Smoky Collard Greens (see page 211).

If you love cheese, melt a slice of pepper jack on top a minute or two before you're finished cooking them. If you're not serving these burgers to vegans, spread them with our zippy Cayenne Aïoli (see page 209) as you would mayonnaise.

Makes 8 patties

GET A HEAD START

You can roast the yams and cook the millet even a day or two in advance. You can also make the burger mixture a day or two ahead.

TIMING

Yams have varying levels of moisture in them and that may affect the way the patties hold together. Refrigerate the mixture for an hour before forming into patties to help them hold together better for cooking.

1½ pounds yams (see page 241), unpeeled and cut in half

⅓ cup millet (see page 239)

1 cup rolled oats (not instant)

½ small red onion, diced

½ cup lightly packed fresh cilantro, chopped

1 teaspoon chili powder

Portobello Wellington with Madeira Sauce

Roasted Delicata Apple Pizza with Sage Walnut
Pesto and Smoked Mozzarella

Roasted Plum Sandwich with Crispy Fried Onions

Omelet-wrapped Quesadilla Stuffed with
Roasted Potatoes and Corn

Hibiscus Sunrise

1 tablespoon cumin seeds, toasted and ground (see page 52)

1 (15-ounce) can kidney beans, drained and rinsed

½ teaspoon salt

Vegetable oil for cooking burgers

8 soft buns or hamburger buns cut in half

Guacamole (see page 226)

Pico de Gallo (see page 226), or purchased salsa

Lettuce, sliced tomatoes and onions, pickles, and your favorite hot sauce

GET READY. Preheat the oven to 400 degrees.

ROAST THE YAMS. Put the yams, cut sides down, on a rimmed baking sheet. Roast in the oven until they're soft to the touch, for 30 to 40 minutes. (If the yams are very large, this could take longer.)

When they're cool enough to handle, remove the skin and roughly chop the flesh. Set aside to cool completely. (Lower the oven temperature to 350 degrees.)

COOK THE MILLET. Bring 1 cup of water to a boil in a small saucepan. Stir in the millet, lower the heat, and simmer covered, until tender, about 25 minutes. Drain off any remaining liquid, and set aside to cool. (Millet has a tendency to get really mushy and waterlogged, so you probably won't need to add more water.)

GRIND THE OATS. While the millet cooks, put the oats in a food processor or blender. Grind until all the flakes are broken up, but not as fine as a flour. Set aside the oats.

MIX THE BURGERS. When the yams and millet are cool, combine them with the onion, cilantro, chili powder, cumin, beans, and salt in a mixer using the paddle attachment (or by hand if you have no paddle attachment). Mix really well; it's OK if the beans get partially broken and squished.

ADD THE OATS. Sprinkle the ground oats over the mixture and mix well with your hands until it holds together when you shape a portion into a patty.

SHAPE THE BURGERS. Using ½ cup mixture per burger, gently shape each portion into a patty about 3½ inches in diameter. Gently flatten the burgers, and smooth out the jagged edges so they don't break off when you cook them. Preheat the oven to 350 degrees (for toasting the buns).

PANFRY THE BURGERS. Heat 1 tablespoon oil in a large nonstick skillet over medium-high heat. (If you don't have a nonstick pan, any heavy skillet works well.) When it's hot, put several burgers in the pan, leaving enough room to flip them easily.

Cook on each side until browned and heated through, 3 to 4 minutes per side. Add 1 tablespoon of oil to the skillet for each pan of burgers you fry.

TOAST THE BREAD. Lay the buns on a baking sheet, cut sides up. Bake until lightly toasted, 2 or 3 minutes.

SERVE THE BURGERS family style with lettuce, tomato and onion slices, pickles, and your favorite hot sauce.

TIP

- **If the burgers fall apart as you shape or fry them, see "Tips for Making Sturdy Patties and Burgers," on page 177.**

Roasted Eggplant and Tomato on Focaccia

I'm still surprised when I think about the popularity of this sandwich—a cross between a pizza and bruschetta—because the ingredients are so simple. Squares of focaccia are split in half as the base for the roasted eggplant and tomato mixture and then cheese is melted over all. You can substitute other bread, like a French baguette or Italian ciabatta, but the crust can be a little tough.

Makes 4 open-face sandwiches with 2 slices per person

GET A HEAD START

To make fixing the sandwich faster, you can roast the eggplant and tomatoes ahead of time.

3 tablespoons olive oil

2 tablespoons balsamic vinegar

1 tablespoon minced garlic

1 medium eggplant (about 1 pound), cut in ½-inch dice

4 Roma tomatoes, cut in ½-inch dice

Salt and freshly ground pepper

½ cup shredded mozzarella cheese (2 ounces)

¼ cup shredded Parmesan, Asiago, or Romano cheese (or a mix of all 3)

4 (4-inch) squares focaccia

½ cup Basil Pesto (see page 233)

GET READY. Preheat the oven to 400 degrees. In a small bowl, whisk together the olive oil, balsamic vinegar, and garlic.

DRESS THE EGGPLANT AND TOMATOES. Put the eggplant and tomatoes in 2 separate bowls. Drizzle three-quarters of the dressing on the eggplant, add a pinch of salt and pepper, and toss to coat.

Drizzle the remainder of the dressing on the tomatoes, add a pinch of salt and pepper, and toss to coat.

ROAST THE EGGPLANT AND TOMATOES. Keeping the tomatoes and eggplant separate, spread them on 2 separate baking sheets large enough to accommodate everything in a single layer without crowding. (If you crowd the vegetables, you will steam rather than roast them.)

Roast the eggplant and tomatoes for 15 minutes, and then remove the tomatoes from the oven. Give the eggplant a stir, and continue roasting until it's quite tender and soft, for 15 to 20 more minutes. (Lower the oven temperature to 350 degrees.)

Combine the roasted eggplant and tomatoes, and set aside.

MIX THE MOZZARELLA AND PARMESAN CHEESES, and set aside.

BUILD THE SANDWICH. Split the focaccia squares as you would an English muffin or bagel, and thinly spread the cut side of each of 8 halves with 1 tablespoon Basil Pesto all the way to the edges.

Spread the eggplant and tomato mixture over each square, and sprinkle each with one-eighth of the cheese mixture.

BAKE THE SANDWICH. Put the sandwiches on a lightly oiled baking sheet, and bake until the cheese melts and the eggplant mixture is hot, about 5 minutes.

TIP

To speed cheesy cleanup, spread a sheet of parchment paper on the baking sheet or lightly oil it before you toast the sandwich.

Yam and Cheese Sandwich with Pumpkin Seed Pesto

This Cafe Flora variation on a classic grilled cheese sandwich with roasted yam, pumpkin seeds, and sage is weirdly good, the perfect fall sandwich. We make it with a wonderful sticcola roll from La Panzanella Bakery in Seattle. The roll is flavorful, dense, and chewy, but the crust is tender enough that all the insides of the sandwich don't squish out when you bite into it. You can use any kind of sandwich roll with a chewy texture like that: a ciabatta, a kaiser, or even a French-style hoagie roll.

Makes 4 sandwiches

GET A HEAD START

You can make the Pumpkin Seed Pesto as much as several days ahead, and roast the yams the day before. If you're going to make this all at once, you can make the pesto while the yam is roasting.

1 large yam (see page 241) (about 1 pound), peeled and sliced in rounds, about ⅛ inch thick

2 tablespoons olive oil

1 teaspoon pimenton (Spanish smoked paprika [see page 240])

Salt and freshly ground pepper

1 medium onion, sliced in rounds about ¼ inch thick

4 sticcola rolls, or other chewy rolls or buns with a tender crust

Pumpkin Seed Pesto (recipe follows)

4 slices fontina or provolone cheese

Sweet hot mustard, Dijon, or your favorite mustard

A couple handfuls spinach leaves

GET READY. Preheat the oven to 400 degrees. Toss the yam in a bowl with 1 tablespoon of the olive oil and the pimenton. Sprinkle with salt and pepper, and toss again.

ROAST THE YAM. Spread the yam slices on a rimmed baking sheet large enough to accommodate them in a single layer without crowding. (If you crowd the yams, you will steam rather than roast them.) Roast until tender, but not mushy, so that a sharp knife easily pierces the yam slices, about 15 minutes. Remove from the oven, and set aside. Lower the oven temperature to 350 degrees.

BROWN THE ONION. Heat the remaining 1 tablespoon olive oil in a wide, heavy-bottomed skillet over medium-high heat. When the skillet is hot, add the onion in a single layer, trying to keep the slices intact. Cook undisturbed until one side is browned, about 5 minutes.

Flip the onion rounds over—it's OK if they fall apart at this point—and continue to cook. Flip the onion occasionally until it's tender and browned evenly all over, about 5 more minutes.

TOAST THE BREAD. Slice the rolls in half, and lay them, cut sides up, on a baking sheet. Bake until lightly toasted, 2 or 3 minutes.

MAKE THE SANDWICHES. Spread each of the 8 halves right to the edges with 1 or 2 tablespoons of Pumpkin Seed Pesto. Layer 4 halves (the bottom halves) with 5 or 6 slices of roasted yam, one-fourth of the onion, and finish with a slice of cheese.

BAKE THE SANDWICH HALVES. Put all 8 sandwich halves on a lightly oiled baking sheet (or on a sheet of parchment paper), and bake until the cheese melts, about 5 minutes.

SERVE THE SANDWICHES. Remove the sandwich halves from the oven. Spread the top halves with sweet hot mustard. Top the bottom halves with spinach leaves, put the sandwich together, and eat!

You can grill the onion on your barbecue instead of cooking it on the top of the stove.

Pumpkin Seed Pesto [v]

Makes about 1 cup

½ cup raw green pumpkin seeds, hulled

Salt

6 to 8 large fresh sage leaves, roughly chopped (about 3 tablespoons)

½ cup fresh parsley sprigs, roughly chopped

1 teaspoon chopped garlic

¼ cup olive oil

Freshly ground pepper

TOAST THE PUMPKIN SEEDS by tossing them in a dry sauté pan over high heat until they start to pop. Add salt to taste, and set aside to cool.

MIX ALL THE INGREDIENTS. Put the pumpkin seeds, sage, parsley, and garlic in a food processor. Pulse several times until the mixture resembles coarse meal. With the machine running, add the olive oil through the feed tube, processing until the mixture is chunky (like chunky peanut butter). Season with salt and pepper to taste.

TIP

If you can find toasted pumpkin seeds (or pepitas), use those and skip the toasting instructions.

Chickpea and Roasted Yam Wrap with Tahini Sauce [v]

This substantial wrap sandwich, so popular at Cafe Flora, puts a new twist on the standard hummus sandwich. Mashing the chickpeas gives this wrap a chunky texture that goes well with the tender cubes of roasted yam and its embellishment of crunchy vegetables.

Makes 4 hearty wraps

GET A HEAD START

You can make the Tahini Sauce as much as several days ahead, and cook the chickpeas and roast the yam the day before. If you're going to make this all at once, you can make the Tahini Sauce while the yam is roasting.

1 teaspoon fenugreek seeds

1 teaspoon cumin seeds

1 cup dried chickpeas (garbanzos), soaked for 3 to 8 hours, or 1 (15-ounce) can chickpeas

2 bay leaves

1 large (12- to 14-ounce) yam (see page 241), peeled and cut into ½-inch dice

1 tablespoon olive oil

1 teaspoon chili powder

⅛ teaspoon cayenne pepper

Salt

1 tablespoon tamari (see page 240)

1 tablespoon mirin (see page 239)

4 (12-inch or wrapsize) spinach or sun-dried tomato flour tortillas (see "About the Tortillas," page 183)

½ cup Tahini Sauce (see page 232)

2 cups mixed salad greens, or chopped romaine lettuce

Additional chopped raw vegetables (see "About the Vegetables," page 184)

Sweet Chili Dipping Sauce (page 235)

GET READY. Preheat the oven to 400 degrees. Toast the fenugreek and cumin seeds together in a hot skillet until fragrant, stirring a few times.

COOK THE CHICKPEAS. If you're using dried chickpeas, drain them, and put them in a pot along with the bay leaves, cumin seed, and fenugreek. Cover with cold water. Bring to a boil, lower the heat, cover the pot, and simmer until the chickpeas are very tender, about 1 hour.

If you're using canned chickpeas, rinse them under cold water, and drain well. Add the toasted cumin, fenugreek seeds, bay leaves, and two cups of water. Simmer for 20 minutes to infuse the canned chickpeas with flavor.

PREPARE THE YAM. While the chickpeas are cooking, toss the yam pieces in a mixing bowl with the olive oil to coat. Toss again with the chili powder, cayenne, and a pinch or two of salt.

ROAST THE YAM. Spread the yam pieces on a rimmed baking sheet large enough to accommodate them in a single layer without crowding. (If you crowd the pieces, you will steam rather than roast them.) Roast until the yam is very tender but not mushy, about 30 minutes. Set aside.

DRAIN THE CHICKPEAS. Discard the bay leaves (if you're using them). Drain the chickpeas in a mesh strainer (keeping the cumin and fenugreek seed with the chickpeas), reserving about ½ cup of the cooking liquid.

MASH THE CHICKPEAS. Put the cooked chickpeas, tamari, mirin, and 2 tablespoons of cooking liquid in a food processor. Pulse several times until the chickpeas are coarsely broken, and the mixture holds together slightly in a crumbly mash. If the mixture doesn't hold together, add 1 tablespoon of cooking liquid or water at a time until it does.

ADD THE YAM TO THE CHICKPEAS. Gently fold the roasted yam into the chickpeas; you don't want to turn the yam to mush. Add salt to taste.

WARM A TORTILLA in a large skillet over medium-high heat for 10 to 15 seconds. Flip it over, and warm the other side for 5 to 10 seconds. Repeat for the remaining tortillas as you build the wraps.

BUILD THE WRAP. Lay the tortilla flat on a work surface, and spread with 2 tablespoons of Tahini Sauce, leaving a 2-inch border all around.

Put ⅔ cup of the chickpea-yam mixture in the center of the wrap, and spread it over the sauce. (If you're planning to add a lot of chopped vegetables, cut this mixture back so you can still roll the wrap.)

Top this with ½ cup salad greens, spreading them to cover the chickpea-yam mixture. (If you're adding veggie chunks, this would be the time to do it.)

ROLL THE WRAP. Fold the sides of the wrap in towards the filling. Roll the tortilla starting with the end closest to you, keeping the sides folded in. Build the 3 remaining tortillas, and roll them as described here.

SERVE THE WRAPS. Using a very sharp knife, cut each wrap in half at an angle. Serve the Sweet Chili Dipping Sauce in 4 small bowls for dipping.

About the Tortillas

The wrap for this sandwich is an extralarge flour tortilla, sometimes labeled as "wrapsize," flavored with sun-dried tomatoes or spinach. Look for these wraps with the other tortillas in your grocery store. At Cafe Flora, we use flavored tortillas for their attractive color. There's really no appreciable difference in flavor compared with the plain tortillas, so substitute those if the flavored ones aren't available.

About the Vegetables

For an even more nutritious sandwich, scatter veggie chunks on top of the salad greens before you roll up the wrap. You can use bell pepper strips, diced cucumber and tomato, and roughly chopped pitted kalamata olives, or any other vegetable that appeals to you. Those who aren't vegan can add feta cheese.

You'll need about ½ cup of any ingredient you want to add—1 or 2 tablespoons for each wrap. And depending how much you add, you'll probably need less of the yam mixture so the wrap isn't too chubby to roll up. That way, you might end up with five (or more) wraps instead of four.

Teriyaki Tofu Wrap with Macadamia Roasted Garlic Spread [v]

This just would not be a vegetarian cookbook without at least one recipe that calls for sprouts! For this sandwich you need the spicy crunchiness you get from sprouts—the likes of sunflower, buckwheat, radish, or clover sprouts. You can most often find them in the produce section of natural food stores or at Asian grocers. If you live on the West coast, look for a mix of colorful bean sprouts called Salad Munchies. These aren't very spicy but will add a nutty quality. Serve this wrap with chunks of ripe juicy melon.

Makes 4 wraps.

GET A HEAD START

Press the tofu and prepare the Macadamia Roasted Garlic Spread ahead, even a day or two before.

TIMING

Start making the seasoned rice while you bake the tofu so it has time to cool. The baked tofu will need to cool as well before you can use it.

In this dish

- Teriyaki Wrap
- Macadamia Roasted Garlic Spread (see page 234)
- Seasoned Rice

Teriyaki Wrap

1 (14- to 16-ounce) block firm tofu, pressed (see page 22), or extrafirm tofu

About 1 cup prepared teriyaki sauce

4 (12-inch or wrap size) spinach flour tortillas (see "About the Tortillas," page 183)

½ cup Macadamia Roasted Garlic Spread (see page 234)

Seasoned Rice (recipe follows)

1 cup shredded carrots (about 2 medium)

3 scallions, thinly sliced

1 cup spicy or crunchy sprouts, or shredded cabbage or daikon radish

GET READY. Preheat oven to 350 degrees. Pat dry the pressed tofu blocks, and cut them across the shorter side into ½-inch slabs. Lay them in a baking dish in a single layer.

BAKE THE TOFU. Pour ½ cup teriyaki sauce over the tofu slices. Bake until the teriyaki sauce forms a thick glaze, 25 to 35 minutes. Check occasionally to make sure that it doesn't burn, and gently turn the tofu several times as it cooks.

COOL THE TOFU. Remove the tofu from the pan while it's still hot, and pour the thickened sauce over the slices. Set aside to cool. When it's cool, cut each slice into 4 thick sticks.

WARM A TORTILLA in a large skillet over medium-high heat for 10 to 15 seconds. Flip it over and warm on the other side for 5 to 10 seconds. Repeat for the remaining tortillas as you build the wraps.

BUILD THE WRAP. Lay the tortilla flat on a work surface, and spread with 2 tablespoons of the Macadamia Roasted Garlic Spread, leaving a 2-inch border all around.

Drop ½ cup of the Seasoned Rice in the center of the wrap and spread it out. Top this with one-fourth of the baked teriyaki tofu sticks.

Scatter ¼ cup of the carrots, 2 tablespoons of the scallions, and ¼ cup of the sprouts over the tofu. Drizzle 1 teaspoon of the teriyaki sauce over all.

ROLL UP THE WRAP. Fold the sides of the tortilla in towards the filling. Roll the tortilla starting with the end closest to you, keeping the sides folded in.

Build the 3 remaining wraps, and roll them up as described above.

SERVE THE WRAPS. Using a very sharp knife, cut each wrap in half at an angle. Serve the remaining teriyaki sauce in 4 small bowls on the side for dipping.

About Pineapple Teriyaki Sauce

Pineapple teriyaki sauce is ideal for marinating the tofu in this wrap if you can find it. Soy Vay makes a particularly good one called Island Teriyaki. It's a commercially prepared product that is about as natural as you can make at home—real ginger, garlic, lots of sesame seeds, organic oil, etc. Look for it at large supermarkets, specialty markets like Trader Joe's, or Asian food markets.

Seasoned Rice [v]

Jasmine rice is a long-grained, aromatic rice from Thailand with a flavor comparable to basmati rice. It's much less expensive than basmati, and when cooked, it's a bit stickier.

¾ cup jasmine rice

1 cup packed cilantro sprigs

1 tablespoon chopped, peeled, fresh ginger

2 cloves garlic

½ cup mirin (rice wine [see page 239])

1 tablespoon rice vinegar

½ jalapeño chile, ribs and seeds removed, minced

WASH AND COOK THE RICE. Rinse the rice several times until the water runs clear. Put the rice in a saucepan with 1¼ cups water, and cover the pot. Bring the pot to a boil, cover, and turn down the heat to the lowest possible setting. Cook until the rice is tender and all the water has been absorbed, about 15 minutes.

MIX THE SEASONING. While the rice cooks, put all the remaining ingredients in a blender or food processor. Process until smooth and set aside.

SEASON THE RICE. Remove the rice from the heat, and gently fold the seasoning into the still-hot rice until they're fully combined. Cool to room temperature.

Zesty Tofu Reuben

This sandwich takes some time to put together, but it hits the spot when you want a spicy-hot deli sandwich.

For this meatless variation on a classic, we slather rye bread with our jazzed-up version of Thousand Island dressing. We stuff it with spicy marinated and baked tofu, smoky sauerkraut, and oven-roasted zucchini and onion. And last, we melt Jarlsberg cheese over it.

I suggest a hearty, dense rye bread so it won't fall apart under the moist filling. If the loaf is on the small side, this might make more than six sandwiches.

Makes 6 substantial sandwiches

GET A HEAD START

You can make almost all the components of this sandwich in advance.

- Make the sauerkraut and the Russian Dressing even a few days in advance.
- Smoke the mushrooms, roast the vegetables, and marinate and bake the tofu the day before.
- But leave roasting the zucchini and onion to the end, when you're ready to put the sandwich together.

In this dish

- Zesty Tofu and Roasted Vegetables
- Smokey Sauerkraut
- Russian Dressing

Zesty Tofu and Roasted Vegetables

¼ cup sambal oelek (chile garlic sauce [see "About Sambal Oelek" page 187)

3 tablespoons minced garlic

½ cup olive oil, plus 2 to 3 tablespoons

¼ cup Dijon mustard

2 tablespoons pimenton (Spanish smoked paprika [see page 240])

2 (14- to 16-ounce) blocks firm tofu, pressed (see page 22), or extrafirm tofu

2 medium zucchini (about ⅔ pound)

1 large red onion

Makes a lot

MAKE THE MARINADE. In a small bowl, stir the sambal, garlic, ½ cup of the olive oil, mustard, and pimenton until mixed well, and set aside.

MARINATE THE TOFU. Pat dry the tofu blocks, and cut them along the longer side into ¼-inch slabs. Lay them in a baking dish in a single layer, and pour the marinade over them. Marinate the tofu for 1 hour, turning the pieces 2 or 3 times.

GET READY TO BAKE THE TOFU. Preheat the oven to 350 degrees. Grease a rimmed baking sheet with olive oil.

BAKE THE TOFU. Reserving any remaining marinade, lay the tofu slabs in a single layer on the baking sheet, and bake for 30 minutes. Remove from the oven, and generously brush both sides of each slice with the reserved marinade. Set aside to cool, but leave the oven on.

SLICE THE ZUCCHINI AND ONION. Slice the zucchini lengthwise in ¼-inch slices, discarding the slices that are mostly skin. Slice the onion in thick rounds about ¼ inch thick, trying to keep the rings intact.

ROAST THE ZUCCHINI AND ONION. Brush the long zucchini slices and onion rounds all over with the remaining olive oil. Keeping the zucchini and onion separate, arrange them on the baking sheet in a single layer. Roast the zucchini and onions until tender, about 20 minutes.

About Sambal Oelek

This fiery red sauce is made from ground fresh chilies, salt and vinegar. Like other sambals, it's used as a condiment and can often be found on the table at Vietnamese, Thai, and other southeast Asian restaurants. Look for it at Asian markets where you may recognize a popular brand, Huey Fong, in glass or plastic jars with a distinctive rooster on the label.

Smoky Sauerkraut[v]

If you want a quicker fix and don't want to bother smoking the mushrooms, just omit the mushrooms entirely. It's still pretty good!

Makes about 3 cups

1½ teaspoons olive oil

1 rib celery, finely diced

1 small onion, finely diced

½ cup smoked mushrooms (see page 79), chopped

1½ tablespoons caraway seeds

2 cups (16 ounces) sauerkraut, drained and rinsed

½ cup white wine

SAUTÉ THE VEGETABLES AND SMOKED MUSHROOMS. In a large heavy skillet, heat the olive oil over medium heat. Add the celery, onion, and mushrooms, and cook until the onion is soft and translucent and the celery is tender, about 10 minutes. Add the caraway seeds, and sauté for 2 more minutes.

ADD THE SAUERKRAUT AND WHITE WINE and sauté, stirring often, until most of the liquid has evaporated and the sauerkraut turns light brown. Remove from the heat, and cool.

Russian Dressing

Makes about ¾ cup

½ cup mayonnaise

1 tablespoon ketchup

2 tablespoons sweet hot mustard

3 tablespoons minced red onion

1½ teaspoons pimenton (Spanish smoked paprika [see page 240])

1½ teaspoons onion powder

½ teaspoon minced garlic

½ teaspoon freshly ground pepper

Put all the ingredients in a bowl, and mix well.

Put the Sandwich Together

12 (½-inch) slices sturdy rye bread

6 tablespoons Dijon, or other good (not yellow) mustard

Roasted Vegetables (recipe above)

1½ cups Smokey Sauerkraut (recipe above)

8 ounces thinly sliced Jarlsberg or Swiss cheese

½ cup Russian Dressing (recipe above)

Zesty Tofu (recipe above)

Kosher dill pickles

GET READY. Make sure the oven is heated to 350 degrees. Lightly oil a baking sheet.

TOAST THE BREAD. Lay the bread slices directly on the oven rack. Bake until lightly toasted, for 2 or 3 minutes.

BUILD THE SANDWICHES. For each sandwich lay 2 slices of rye toast on a work surface. Spread mustard on 1 slice of bread, and top with one-sixth of the roasted onion, ¼ cup of the sauerkraut, and 1 or 2 slices of the cheese.

Spread some of the Russian Dressing on the other slice of the rye toast, and top with 2 or 3 slices of Zesty Tofu, and 2 or 3 slices of zucchini. Repeat this process to make 5 more sandwiches.

BAKE THE SANDWICHES. Put all the sandwich halves on the baking sheet, and bake for 5 to 10 minutes, or until the ingredients are warmed through and the cheese melts.

PUT THE SANDWICHES TOGETHER AND SERVE. Carefully put the 2 halves of each sandwich together, and cut them in half. Serve with kosher dill pickles.

> **TIPS**
>
> - If you're using really big pieces of bread, you may need more cheese to cover the Reuben filling.
>
> - To speed cheesy cleanup, spread a sheet of parchment paper on the baking sheet or lightly oil it before you toast the sandwich.

BRUNCH

BRUNCH INSPIRES STRONG FEELINGS AMONG people. Most professional cooks I know detest brunch, but everyone I know who is not a cook loves to go out to brunch. Although I am not one to stand in a line without coffee for over an hour to wait for a table, I can certainly see its appeal. For some it's a ritual; it's what they *do* on Sunday mornings. For others, it's a good way to get together with friends or family when there's a definite end. Once the dishes are cleared, the coffee drained, and the bill paid, then you have the rest of the day.

Within weeks of starting at Cafe Flora, I was put in charge of brunch. Most cooks do not consider that a promotion. "Dinner is where it's at; you don't want to get stuck doing brunch," they would say. But I love breakfast food and I love the morning. I also love the way a restaurant feels when no one is there yet, but will be soon: turning on the lights and the ovens in complete silence, walking out into the dark dining room, and going to the espresso machine and pulling my triple shot. (*That* gets me going!) I watch the random jogger who returns my gaze with the recognition of a fellow early riser. I see the yawning driver of the only car on our deserted street, and I wonder where he's going to or coming from. I wait until I absolutely must turn on the noisy hood fans because then the spell will be broken.

Lemon Rice Pancakes with Blueberry Coulis

These delicate lemony pancakes are the perfect solution for rice left over from dinner the night before. The blueberry sauce is such a perfect complement that some have been known to lick their plate!

Makes about 12 (4-inch) pancakes, about 4 servings

GET A HEAD START

You can make the Blueberry Coulis a day or more ahead, and then reheat it gently while you make the pancakes.

1 egg
1 cup buttermilk
2 teaspoons vegetable oil, plus oil for the griddle
1 cup unbleached all-purpose flour
1 teaspoon baking powder
1 teaspoon baking soda
2 teaspoons sugar
½ teaspoon salt
1 cup cooked rice, preferably basmati
2 teaspoons lemon zest, finely chopped
Blueberry Coulis (recipe follows)

MIX THE PANCAKE BATTER. Whisk the egg, buttermilk, and oil together. Sift the dry ingredients together and add to the buttermilk mixture. Stir just until all the dry ingredients are incorporated, being careful not to overbeat. Fold in the rice and lemon zest.

COOK THE PANCAKES. Heat a lightly greased griddle or nonstick skillet over medium heat. When it is hot, drop ¼ cup of the batter per pancake onto the hot skillet. Cook until bubbles form, about 3 minutes, and then flip to brown the other side, about 1 minute. (You may need to grease the griddle between pancakes.)

Stack the pancakes on a plate, cover with a damp towel, and keep warm in a 200-degree oven until all the pancakes are done.

SERVE THE PANCAKES. Overlap 3 pancakes in a circle on a plate, and douse with Blueberry Coulis.

Blueberry Coulis [v]

This slightly thickened berry sauce is wonderful with waffles and pancakes and is also tasty over ice cream. Lemon juice and the hint of cinnamon bring out the natural flavor of the fruit. If you're a hiker or know where to find tiny wild blueberries, this sauce will be even better.

Makes 2½ cups

3 cups fresh or frozen blueberries
⅓ cup sugar
½ cup water
2 teaspoons freshly squeezed lemon juice
Pinch of ground cinnamon
2 teaspoons cornstarch mixed with 1 tablespoon water

COOK THE SAUCE. Put all the ingredients except cornstarch in a small saucepan, and cook over medium-high heat for 15 minutes, stirring occasionally.

ADD THE CORNSTARCH. Stir the cornstarch mixture into the berries, and cook over medium-high heat until thickened, about 3 minutes.

SERVE IMMEDIATELY, or refrigerate covered. Reheat over low heat.

Coconut Macadamia Pancakes with Tropical Fruit Compote

OK, this dish may sound a little like a dessert, but these pancakes are really not very sweet. The pancakes are light and fluffy and studded with crunchy, nutty bits; the freshness of the Tropical Fruit Compote is a perfect foil for the rich pancakes. Of course, if you like your pancakes sweet, douse them with maple syrup.

Makes about 12 (4-inch) pancakes, about 4 servings

TIMING

Make the Tropical Fruit Compote first so you can chill it in the fridge while you mix up and cook the pancakes.

2 tablespoons unsalted butter

½ cup unsweetened shredded coconut

½ cup unsalted macadamia nuts

1 cup unbleached all-purpose flour

1½ teaspoons baking powder

2 teaspoons sugar

½ teaspoon salt

1 cup milk

1 egg

Vegetable oil for the griddle

Tropical Fruit Compote (see page 217)

Maple syrup

GET READY. Preheat the oven to 300 degrees. Melt the butter, and set it aside to cool.

TOAST THE COCONUT AND NUTS. Spread the coconut and macadamia nuts in a single layer on a baking sheet, keeping them separate (in case they toast at different rates). Toast for 6 to 8 minutes, or until both are golden brown, stirring 2 or 3 times to make sure they don't burn.

Remove the baking sheet from the oven, and take the coconut and nuts off the baking sheet to cool. When cool, chop both roughly.

MIX THE PANCAKE BATTER. Sift all the dry ingredients together. Mix the milk and egg, stir in the melted butter, and add the dry ingredients. Stir just until all the dry ingredients are incorporated, being careful not to overmix. Fold in the coconut and nuts.

COOK THE PANCAKES. Heat a lightly greased griddle or nonstick skillet over medium heat. When it is hot, drop about ¼ cup of the batter per pancake onto the hot skillet. Cook until bubbles form, about 3 minutes, and then flip to brown the other side, about 1 minute. (You may need to grease the griddle between pancakes.)

Stack the pancakes on a plate, cover with a damp towel, and keep warm in the already warm oven until you're ready to serve them.

SERVE THE PANCAKES. Overlap 3 pancakes in a circle on a plate, and top with a quarter of the Tropical Fruit Compote. Serve maple syrup on the side.

TIPS

- Look for shredded, not finely ground, unsweetened coconut at natural-food stores and ethnic grocers. If you can't find unsweetened coconut, substitute sweetened; it'll just make the pancakes a bit sweeter. But be careful when you toast sweetened coconut. It only takes 2 or 3 minutes to brown and burns easily, so watch it carefully.

- If you can't find unsalted macadamia nuts, get the salted variety and wash off the salt. You may need to toast them a little longer to restore their crispness.

Vanilla Lavender Waffle [V]

Eggs are a critical component in traditional waffle recipes, but Egg Replacer is an easy substitute if you beat it until it's frothy and fold it in right before baking. The resulting waffle will be a little chewier than one made with eggs.

One of my favorite flavor combinations is blackberry and lavender, so try these waffles with fresh blackberries or a blackberry syrup.

Makes 6 to 8 waffles, depending on the size of your waffle iron

⅓ cup vegetable oil, plus extra oil for the waffle iron, or oil spray

2 cups plain or vanilla rice or soy milk

1 teaspoon vanilla extract

2 cups unbleached all-purpose flour

1½ teaspoons baking soda

1 tablespoon baking powder

½ teaspoon salt

2 tablespoons sugar

2 teaspoons dried lavender blossoms (see tip)

1 tablespoon Egg Replacer (see page 239), or other egg substitute equal to 2 eggs

GET READY. These waffles tend to stick to the waffle iron more than regular waffles, so make sure to spray the grid generously with a cooking spray or brush it thoroughly with vegetable oil. (You may need to do this after each waffle.) Preheat the waffle iron.

MIX THE WAFFLE BATTER. In a small bowl, mix ⅓ cup oil, milk, and vanilla. Sift all the dry ingredients into a large bowl. Add the milk mixture to the dry ingredients, and stir just until combined. Be careful not to overbeat. The batter will be quite thick and gloppy.

ADD THE LAVENDER. Crush the lavender blossoms with your fingers to release their oils. Fold the crushed lavender into the batter.

ADD THE EGG REPLACER. In a small bowl, whisk the Egg Replacer with ½ cup water until frothy, as if you were whisking egg whites. Fold it into the batter.

BAKE THE WAFFLES. When the waffle iron is hot, add the batter, using ½ to ¾ cup for a single round waffle iron, and up to 1½ cups batter for a square 4-waffle iron. Bake until the waffle stops steaming.

Jim's Crunchy French Toast with Brown Sugar Sour Cream

This French toast was on our menu when I first started at Cafe Flora. I'm thinking, what kind of crazy, hippie French toast is this, dipped in wheat germ? But it's pretty darned good: thick slabs of raisin bread are soaked in a luscious batter spiked with orange zest and cinnamon, then coated with the toasty, nutty wheat germ and griddled. We use raisin challah (which can be difficult to find), but really any sturdy raisin bread will work; just try to get a loaf you can cut into ½-inch slices yourself.

Serves 4

3 eggs, beaten

1 cup heavy cream, half-and-half, or light cream

1 tablespoon brown sugar

½ teaspoon ground cinnamon

1 tablespoon grated orange zest

Pinch of salt

8 (½-inch) slices raisin bread

⅔ cup toasted wheat germ (see Tip)

3 to 4 tablespoons clarified butter (see page 201)

Brown Sugar Sour Cream (recipe follows)

Maple syrup

MIX THE FRENCH TOAST BATTER. Whisk the eggs, cream, brown sugar, cinnamon, orange zest, and salt until the sugar has dissolved. Pour the batter into a shallow bowl, wide enough to dip the slices of bread.

COAT THE BREAD. Soak each slice of bread in the batter for 1 to 2 minutes on each side, giving the egg mixture a stir in between slices to prevent the orange zest from sinking to the bottom of the bowl.

Pour the wheat germ into a shallow bowl, and coat each side of the dipped bread with the wheat germ.

PANFRY THE FRENCH TOAST. Melt 1 tablespoon of the clarified butter in a large skillet over medium heat. Put 2 or 3 slices of bread in the pan, and cook for 3 to 4 minutes on each side. Wipe the skillet between batches to prevent wheat germ bits from burning.

Add 1 tablespoon of clarified butter to the pan for each batch of 2 or 3 slices. Keep the French toast warm in a 200-degree oven while you fry the remaining slices of bread.

SERVE THE FRENCH TOAST. Serve 2 slices of French toast with a dollop of Brown Sugar Sour Cream, and drizzled with maple syrup.

> **TIP**
> Kretschmer wheat germ (found in the cereal aisle of most grocery stores) is already toasted. The wheat germ found in most natural-food stores is raw, so if you buy that, you'll need to toast it before you use it. (Toasting the wheat germ heightens its nutty flavor.)

Brown Sugar Sour Cream

When I dollop this velvety topping on pancakes, French toast, or waffles, my guests are always surprised to find that it's simply sour cream and brown sugar. This creamy, tart, and sweet topping is also a knockout with sliced peaches, nectarines, or fresh berries. For a less caloric, but equally delicious topping, substitute yogurt, using low-fat yogurt if you want.

Makes 1 cup

8 ounces sour cream or 2 cups plain yogurt, drained (see page 11) to 1 cup
2 tablespoons brown sugar

Mix the brown sugar into the sour cream, stirring until the sugar crystals are dissolved. Cover and refrigerate until ready to serve.

Guava y Queso French Toast Sandwich with Tropical Fruit Compote

This easy-to-make breakfast sandwich is crisp and toasty on the outside, and luscious on the inside, and the bright juicy compote is a good foil for the rich French toast. First you make a guava–cream cheese sandwich, dip both sides in the batter, and then fry it as you would single slices of French toast.

Makes 4 sandwiches

TIMING

Get out the cream cheese first so it can come to room temperature. After you make the cream cheese sandwiches, they'll need about 30 minutes in the fridge before you dip them into the egg-cream mixture. (Chilling keeps the sandwiches from falling apart when you cook them.) While the sandwiches are getting cold, make the compote so it can chill while you finish the French toast.

4 ounces (½ cup) cream cheese, at room temperature

½ cup guava jam (see Tips)

8 (½-inch) slices day-old bread

3 large eggs, beaten

1 cup heavy cream, half-and-half, or light cream

1½ teaspoons vanilla extract

½ teaspoon grated nutmeg

1 teaspoon ground cinnamon

¼ cup light brown sugar

Pinch of salt

4 teaspoons vegetable oil for the griddle

Tropical Fruit Compote (see page 217)

MAKE THE SANDWICHES. Mix the cream cheese and guava jam until smooth and well blended. Spread one-quarter of the cream cheese mixture evenly on each of 4 slices of bread, and top with the remaining slices to make 4 sandwiches.

REFRIGERATE THE SANDWICHES until the cream cheese is solid, about 30 minutes.

MIX THE FRENCH TOAST BATTER. Whisk the eggs with the cream, vanilla, nutmeg, cinnamon, brown sugar, and salt, mixing well. Pour the batter into a shallow bowl wide enough to dip the sandwiches.

COAT THE SANDWICHES. Soak each sandwich in the batter for 1 to 2 minutes on each side, giving the egg mixture a stir in between sandwiches if it separates.

PANFRY THE SANDWICHES. Heat 1 teaspoon oil in a large skillet over medium heat. Put 2 sandwiches in the pan, and cook for about 4 minutes on each side. Add 1 teaspoon oil to the pan for each batch of sandwiches.

Keep the finished sandwiches covered and warm in a 200-degree oven while you fry the remaining sandwiches.

SERVE THE FRENCH TOAST. Cut each sandwich in half, diagonally. Put a triangle on each plate, and prop the second half against the first at an opposing angle so you can see that it's a sandwich. Top each serving with one-fourth of the Tropical Fruit Compote, and serve.

TIPS

- French toast works best with a sturdy older bread. We use brioche or challah because it soaks up batter better, doesn't fall apart as easily, and results in a more luscious texture. (Plus it uses up all that old bread!)

- Guava jelly doesn't work as well as guava jam or guava paste, which you can often find in Latino markets. Guava is also a popular ingredient in Hawaiian foods, which some larger Asian grocers carry. Look for the Hawaiian Sun brand of guava jam. If you can't find guava jam or paste, then replace it with your favorite jam.

Beignets

Beignets take some time to make, but there is nothing that says love better than hot baby doughnuts. At Cafe Flora, we serve hot-out-of-the-fryer beignets on a puddle of Crème Anglaise drizzled with Raspberry Purée—something like a deconstructed cream and jelly doughnut. (You could always use your favorite preserves or fruit sauce in place of the purée.) But they're just as delicious served New Orleans style, simply dusted with powdered sugar. For the true New Orleans experience, brew up a pot of extrastrong coffee with chicory, and add hot milk.

Makes about 2 dozen beignets

GET A HEAD START

If you want to treat the special people in your life with beignets for breakfast, but don't want to get up at daybreak to do it, make the dough through the step, "Cut the beignets." Set them out on the baking sheet covered well with plastic wrap, and refrigerate overnight. Bring them to room temperature until they're puffy and soft before frying in the morning. This takes less than half an hour.

You can make the Raspberry Purée up to 3 days ahead and the Crème Anglaise the day before.

TIMING

If you're going to make beignets in one day, make the Raspberry Purée and the Crème Anglaise while the doughnuts are rising the first time.

In this dish
- Beignets
- Crème Anglaise
- Raspberry Purée

Beignets

½ cup milk

¼ cup unsalted butter

½ cup sugar plus a pinch

¼ cup warm water (a tiny bit warmer than body temperature, 100 to 110 degrees)

1 package active dry yeast (1 scant tablespoon)

1 egg, beaten

2 cups all-purpose unbleached flour, plus some for rolling out dough

1 teaspoon mace or ground nutmeg

1 teaspoon salt

Vegetable oil for frying

Thermometer for deep-frying

Powdered sugar for dusting

SCALD THE MILK. Put the milk, butter, and ½ cup sugar in a small saucepan over medium heat, and stir to dissolve the sugar and melt the butter. Cook until tiny bubbles form around the edge of the pan, watching carefully to make sure it doesn't boil.

Remove the pan from the heat, and set aside to cool until a bit warmer than body temperature. (Speed the cooling process by putting the pan in the refrigerator.)

ACTIVATE THE YEAST. While the milk cools, pour the water into a small bowl. Sprinkle in the yeast and a pinch of sugar, stir, and let stand until foamy, about 10 minutes.

MIX THE LIQUID INGREDIENTS. Combine the egg, the milk mixture, and the yeast mixture.

MIX THE DOUGH. In a large mixing bowl, combine the flour, mace, and salt, and add the liquids. Mix until a soft, sticky ball forms. (Yes, it's sticky and that's OK.) Gather up all the dough, including any clinging to the mixing bowl, and set onto a lightly floured surface.

LET THE DOUGH RISE. Grease the bowl—you don't need to wash it first—with oil or soft butter. Put the dough ball back into the bowl, and cover with plastic wrap.

Set the dough in a warm spot in the kitchen, and let it rise until it has doubled in bulk, about 1 hour.

ROLL OUT THE DOUGH. Turn the dough onto a lightly floured surface. Knead 8 to 10 times, and then pat it into a small rectangle. Roll it into a rounded rectangle that's about 10 × 13 inches and ¼ inch thick. If you would like perfectly square beignets, trim the rounded corners of the rectangle.

CUT THE BEIGNETS. Cut the dough into 2- to 2½-inch squares using a very sharp knife. Put the squares on a lightly floured baking sheet, about 1 inch apart. Cover with plastic wrap, and set out on a counter at room temperature until they're slightly puffy and very soft, about 30 minutes.

FRY THE BEIGNETS. Heat oil in a heavy pot to a depth of 2 inches. (Make sure the pot is at least 4 inches tall to reduce spattering.) When the oil reaches between 360 and 370 degrees on your thermometer, gently drop 3 or 4 beignets into the hot oil. Be careful not to add too many at one time, or the temperature of the oil will drop.

Keep the oil temperature steady between 360 and 370. Any higher and the beignets will brown before they're done in the center; any lower and the beignets will be greasy. You'll probably need to tinker with the setting on your stove.

Fry the beignets on one side until they are puffy and deep golden brown, about 45 seconds to 1 minute. Flip them over, and fry until the other side is the same color, another 45 seconds to 1 minute. Drain on paper towels, and dust generously with powdered sugar as you make them.

TIP

Unlike all the other recipes in this book that call for deep-frying, keeping the temperature between 360 and 370 degrees is so important that you must use a thermometer. See p. 199 for a tip about saving oil after frying.

Crème Anglaise

Crème anglaise is simply a thin, pourable vanilla custard and can be served as a sauce with many desserts. Try it with a dense chocolate torte or poured over sweetened berries. You can keep this one day in the fridge.

Makes about 2 cups

4 egg yolks
¼ cup sugar
2 cups half-and-half
2 teaspoons vanilla extract

GET READY. Fit a fine mesh strainer over a bowl sitting in another bowl of ice water. (You'll use this to strain the sauce and you need to have it ready to use as soon as the custard is done.) In a medium bowl, whisk together the egg yolks and sugar until thick and pale yellow, about 4 minutes.

SCALD THE HALF-AND-HALF in a heavy-bottomed saucepan over medium heat until tiny bubbles form around the edge of the pan. Watch carefully to make sure it doesn't boil. Take the pot off the heat.

MIX THE EGGS AND HALF-AND-HALF. Slowly pour ½ cup of the half-and-half into the egg mixture, stirring constantly. Then slowly pour this egg mixture back into the remaining half-and-half in the pot, stirring constantly.

HEAT THE EGG MIXTURE. Return the pot to the stove over medium-low heat, stirring constantly with a wooden spoon. (Do not let the mixture boil.) Cook until the mixture coats the back of the spoon and is the consistency of heavy cream. (When you can draw a line with your finger along the back of the spoon and it leaves a distinct path, the custard is finished.)

STRAIN THE CUSTARD. Pour it through the strainer into the bowl sitting in ice water, and stir in the vanilla extract. Give the mixture a stir once or twice while it cools. Once the mixture is cool, it's ready to serve.

If you're not using the custard right away, remove the bowl from the ice bath, press plastic wrap onto the surface of the custard (to keep a skin from forming), and refrigerate.

Raspberry Purée (v)

This uncooked berry sauce is great with many desserts (like ice cream) or drizzled on waffles or pancakes. We generally save our whole, fresh berries for eating or garnishing desserts and use frozen berries for purée, but if you're lucky enough to have lots of raspberries, use them. You can keep this sauce for three days in the refrigerator. You can serve it at room temperature or chilled.

Makes 1 cup

2 cups (10-ounce bag) unsweetened frozen raspberries, thawed, or fresh raspberries
3 tablespoons sugar

Put the berries and sugar in a blender or food processor. Blend until smooth and then strain into a bowl, pressing as much purée as possible through the strainer with a spoon or rubber spatula.

Serve the Beignets

Crème Anglaise (see page 197)
Beignets (see page 196)
Raspberry Purée (recipe above)

TO SERVE THIS ON INDIVIDUAL PLATES, pool ¼ cup of the Crème Anglaise in the center of a small plate. Pile 3 or 4 piping hot beignets on the sauce, and drizzle with some of the Raspberry Purée.

TO SERVE FAMILY STYLE, put the powdered-sugar-covered beignets on a platter and serve the Crème Anglaise and Raspberry Purée on the side in small pitchers or bowls with spoons.

Omelet-Wrapped Quesadilla Stuffed with Roasted Potatoes and Corn

This is by far our most popular brunch dish because it has something for everyone in it. We spread a tortilla with chile-hot roasted potatoes and sweet corn. We throw on a small handful of cheese and fold it in half. We heat the almost done quesadilla to melt the cheese and then cloak it with a thin layer of omelet. We serve it with a small green salad and Pico de Gallo Salsa (see page 226).

Serves 6

TIMING

This is brunch, so you should have time to make this for a late-morning breakfast. While you roast the vegetables, make the Pico de Gallo Salsa and the Lime Crème Fraîche.

½ pound Yukon Gold or Yellow Finn potatoes, cut in ¼-inch dice

1 ear corn, kernels removed from the cob, or 1 cup frozen whole-kernel corn, thawed

2 teaspoons cumin seeds, toasted and ground (see page 52)

1 teaspoon chili powder

1 teaspoon salt

3 tablespoons vegetable oil

1 poblano chile (see page 238), roasted (see page 212) and roughly chopped

6 (8-inch) flour tortillas

1½ cups grated pepper jack cheese (6 ounces)

12 large eggs

Pico de Gallo Salsa (see page 226)

Lime Crème Fraîche (see page 230)

BOIL THE POTATOES. Preheat the oven to 375 degrees. Put the potatoes in a saucepan and cover with water. Bring to a boil, cook for 4 minutes, and drain.

ROAST THE POTATOES AND CORN. Mix the potatoes with the corn, cumin, chili powder, and salt. Toss with 1 tablespoon oil until fully coated. Spread the potato mixture on a baking sheet with a rim large enough to accommodate everything in a single layer without crowding. (If you crowd the potatoes, you will steam rather than roast them.)

Roast until tender but not mushy, so that a sharp knife easily pierces the potatoes, about 15 minutes. Check after 10 minutes to make sure they're cooking evenly, giving them a stir if needed.

MIX THE POTATOES AND THE POBLANO. Transfer the potato-corn mixture to a bowl and combine with the poblano chile. Lower the oven temperature to 200 degrees (to keep the quesadillas warm as you make them).

ASSEMBLE THE QUESADILLAS. Put ½ cup of the potato mixture on one half of a tortilla, and sprinkle with ¼ cup of the grated cheese. Fold it in half.

COOK THE QUESADILLAS. Heat a nonstick 8- or 9-inch skillet over medium-high heat. When the pan is hot, put 1 or 2 quesadillas in the pan, and cook for 3 minutes.

Turn the quesadillas over carefully to prevent any filling from falling out, and cook until the cheese begins to melt, 2 more minutes. (Peek inside to see if the cheese is getting melty; it will melt further during the following steps.)

Put quesadillas on a baking sheet, and keep them warm in the oven, uncovered, while you repeat these steps for the remaining quesadillas.

GET READY TO MAKE THE OMELET. Wipe out any quesadilla filling that may have fallen into the skillet. Swirl 1 teaspoon oil in the skillet, and lower the heat to medium.

MAKE THE OMELET. Beat 2 of the eggs in a small bowl, and pour them into the hot skillet. Swirl the egg around the hot skillet once or twice so it covers the bottom. Using a spatula, gently lift the edges to allow the uncooked egg to run underneath so it will cook faster. The egg should be set with a thin uncooked layer on top.

WRAP THE QUESADILLA IN THE EGG. Put 1 quesadilla on top of the omelet with the open side of the quesadilla flush with the outer edge of the pan. Cook about 20 seconds, and then slip a spatula under the egg on the quesadilla's open side, and gently turn the quesadilla over. (The quesadilla is now completely encased in the omelet.) Cook for 10 seconds on this side.

Gently remove from the pan to a platter or serving dish and place in the warm oven while you cloak the remaining 5 quesadillas with egg.

SERVE THE QUESADILLA, 1 per person, with Pico de Gallo Salsa and Lime Crème Fraîche drizzled on the top.

> **TIP**
> Coating the quesadillas with egg only works in a nonstick pan.

Asparagus Tarragon Scramble with Sun-Dried Tomato Aïoli

Luckily we can get asparagus from our friend Merv Dykstra in eastern Washington for two months starting in late spring. During that time we try to feature asparagus as often as we can. It's fun thinking up new asparagus dishes each year, but guests clamor for this tried-and-true favorite. Roasted Rosemary Potatoes (see page 213) make a terrific accompaniment.

Serves 2 (generously) to 3

> **GET A HEAD START.**
> Make the Sun-Dried Tomato Aïoli 2 or 3 days ahead and store it in the refrigerator. If you're making this in a day, note that the sun-dried tomatoes soak for 30 minutes before you can blend them. Finish the aïoli before you start the scramble.

½ pound asparagus, trimmed
1 tablespoon clarified butter (see "Clarifying Butter"), or a mixture of olive oil and butter
Salt and freshly ground pepper
1 teaspoon finely chopped fresh tarragon
1 teaspoon finely chopped fresh parsley
6 eggs, beaten
Sun-Dried Tomato Aïoli (recipe follows)

BLANCH THE ASPARAGUS. Fill a medium pot with 1 quart of water, and bring to a boil. Slice the asparagus thinly at a sharp angle in 1-inch pieces. When the water is boiling, drop the asparagus into the water, and cook for 1 minute. Dump into a colander, and cool under cold running water. Drain thoroughly, and set aside.

COOK THE ASPARAGUS AND HERBS. Heat the butter in a nonstick skillet over medium heat until the butter begins to foam. Add the asparagus, a pinch or 2 of salt, and a grind of pepper, and sauté for 1

Clarifying Butter

We use clarified butter—butter with the milk solids removed—to cook many of our egg dishes at Cafe Flora. We love its pleasant, nutty flavor, but, even more important, we like being able to use butter without worrying about burning it. (It is the milk solids that burn, so removing them lets you use butter at a much higher heat than regular butter.) Store clarified butter in the refrigerator.

If you don't want to go to the trouble of making clarified butter, you can get similar advantages by combining olive oil and butter in equal parts. Simply heat the olive oil and butter together in a skillet until the butter melts and begins to foam, and proceed with the recipe.

Makes about ⅓ cup clarified butter

¼ pound (1 stick) unsalted butter

Melt the butter over low heat. When it is completely melted, remove it from the heat, and let it stand until the milk solids settle to the bottom, a few minutes. Skim (or drain) the clear (clarified) butter from the top, discarding the milky residue.

---

minute. Add the tarragon and parsley, and sauté for 30 more seconds.

SCRAMBLE THE EGGS. Pour the eggs into the skillet. Gently stir and fold the eggs with a heatproof spatula or spoon until large curds form, distributing the asparagus pieces evenly throughout the eggs. Just before the eggs reach the consistency you like, remove the pan from the heat; the eggs will continue to cook off the heat.

SERVE THE SCRAMBLE. Divide the eggs among 2 or 3 warm plates, and top each portion with a dollop of Sun-Dried Tomato Aïoli.

Sun-Dried Tomato Aïoli

This "cheater" version of aïoli makes short work of a delicious accompaniment to this scramble. If you have aïoli left over, spread it on any sandwich, particularly the Artichoke Poorboy (see page 167), any of our burgers, or the Artichoke Croquettes (see page 121).

Makes ½ cup

1 ounce sun-dried tomatoes (8 to 10 tomato halves)
2 cloves garlic, minced
2 teaspoons freshly squeezed lemon juice
¼ cup mayonnaise
Salt and freshly ground pepper

SOAK AND CHOP THE TOMATOES. In a small bowl, cover the sun-dried tomatoes with 1 cup hot water, and soak them for about 30 minutes. Remove the tomatoes from the water, and squeeze out excess water, reserving the soaking liquid. Finely chop the tomatoes.

MIX ALL THE INGREDIENTS. Put the tomatoes in a blender with all the remaining ingredients except the salt and pepper. Purée, adding the reserved tomato water a little at a time to get a smooth texture. Scrape down the sides of the jar, and blend again until smooth. Add salt and pepper to taste.

Southwest Scramble

I love scrambles that have more "stuff" than eggs and a lot of flavor, like this one, loaded with vegetables, it can easily serve four. For a big, special breakfast, dish it up with your favorite hot sauce or salsa (like our Pico de Gallo Salsa [see page 226]), and our Roasted Rosemary Potatoes (see page 213) or warm corn or flour tortillas.

Serves 2 (generously) to 4

3 tablespoons raw green pumpkin seeds, hulled

Salt

3 tablespoons vegetable oil

2 cups sliced crimini mushrooms

1 cup fresh or frozen corn kernels

½ red bell pepper (about ¼ pound), seeds removed and julienned

½ green bell pepper (about ¼ pound), seeds removed and julienned

1 clove garlic, minced

3 scallions, sliced

1 chipotle chile in adobo (see page 238), finely chopped, seeds removed

Pepper

6 eggs, beaten

½ cup crumbled queso fresco (see Tips)

TOAST THE PUMPKIN SEEDS by tossing them in a dry sauté pan over high heat until they start to pop. Add salt to taste, and set aside.

SAUTÉ THE MUSHROOMS. Heat 1 tablespoon of the oil in a large nonstick skillet over medium-high

heat. Add the mushrooms, and sauté for 2 minutes.

SAUTÉ THE REMAINING VEGETABLES. Add the remaining 2 tablespoons oil along with the corn, bell peppers, garlic, scallions, and chipotle chile, and cook for 4 minutes. Season with a pinch or two of salt and pepper.

SCRAMBLE THE EGGS. Lower the heat to medium, and add the eggs. Gently stir and fold the eggs with a heatproof spatula or spoon until large curds form, distributing the vegetables evenly throughout the eggs. Just before the eggs reach the consistency you like, remove the pan from the heat, and fold in the queso fresco. (The eggs will continue to cook off the heat.)

SERVE THE SCRAMBLE. Divide the eggs among 2 or 3 plates, and sprinkle each serving with the pumpkin seeds.

TIPS

- If you find toasted pumpkin seeds (or pepitas), use those and skip the toasting instructions.

- QUESO FRESCO is a fresh (not aged), soft, moist yet crumbly cheese with a mild flavor. It does not melt when cooked and is typically sprinkled on enchiladas, salads, and beans. Look for it at larger grocers that carry Mexican food products, near the refrigerated tortillas. It's often sold as Ranchero by Cacique, a major producer of Mexican-style cheeses.

Wild Mushroom Scramble

There is nothing more pleasing than sautéed wild mushrooms with softly scrambled eggs. My favorite mushroom in spring is the morel and, in the fall, chanterelle. But you can also substitute hedgehog, oyster, or porcini mushrooms, or whatever wild mushrooms you can get.

You may be tempted to cook some elaborate dish to fully realize the full, earthy flavor of wild mushrooms, but I say the simpler the better. A nonstick pan is ideal for making scrambles, but sautéing mushrooms in a little fat sears them and intensifies the flavor.

A wild mushroom scramble is a special brunch dish, especially with our Roasted Rosemary Potatoes (see page 213). But it also makes a simple and elegant supper served with crusty bread and a fruit salad like the Fresh Pear, Stilton, and Walnut Salad with Scallion Cream Dressing (see page 61) or Strawberry Salad with Walnut Vinaigrette (see page 59). The embellishments, particularly the white truffle oil, are nice, but not necessary.

Serves 2 generously

TIMING

If the mushrooms are really dirty, and you have to clean them with water, they could take several hours to dry.

6 ounces wild mushrooms

2 tablespoons clarified butter (see page 201), or olive oil

Salt and freshly ground pepper

6 eggs, beaten

Optional: 1 teaspoon chopped fresh thyme, ½ teaspoon white truffle oil, or ¼ cup freshly grated Parmigiano-Reggiano cheese

CLEAN THE MUSHROOMS by brushing off any excess dirt with a towel or pastry brush. If the mushrooms are especially dirty, quickly rinse them under running water, and let dry for several hours on paper towels.

CUT UP THE MUSHROOMS in small pieces, about 1 to 2 inches long, trying to maintain the natural shape of the mushroom. Trumpet-shaped chanterelles and hedgehogs do not really have stems, so we use the entire mushroom. Cut off the base of the oyster mushrooms. A large porcini cap and stem can be sliced and the morel's conical shape can be cut in half or quartered.

SAUTÉ THE MUSHROOMS. Melt 1 tablespoon of the butter in a large skillet over medium-high heat. Add the mushrooms, and sauté until tender and fragrant, 3 to 5 minutes. Add salt and pepper to taste.

SCRAMBLE THE EGGS. Add the remaining butter to the mushrooms in the pan and let it melt. (If you're using a nonstick pan, you may not need this additional fat.) Lower the heat to medium, and add the eggs. Gently stir and fold the eggs with a heatproof rubber spatula or spoon until large curds form.

Remove the pan from the heat to stop the cooking. Fold in the herbs, truffle oil, or cheese if you're using them, and serve at once.

About White Truffle Oil

White truffle oil is olive oil infused with white truffles (actually more a beige color). Look for this aromatic oil at specialty-food stores that carry imported Italian foods.

Provençal Tofu Scramble [v]

This tofu scramble was on our brunch menu for years and remains one of my favorites. It's especially good on those mornings when you are craving some protein but want something light and fresh. With some Roasted Rosemary Potatoes (see page 213) on the side, this is a healthy start for an active day.

Serves 2

TIMING

Pressing tofu takes an hour.

1 tablespoon olive oil

1 (14- to 16-ounce) firm tofu, pressed (see page 22), or extrafirm tofu, patted dry

1 medium red onion, diced

2 cloves garlic, minced

1 tablespoon chopped fresh basil

2 tablespoons chopped fresh parsley

1 teaspoon chopped fresh thyme

1 teaspoon chopped fresh rosemary

1 tomato, diced

8 to 10 kalamata olives, pits removed and cut in half

Salt and freshly ground pepper

1 to 2 tablespoons balsamic vinegar

Scrambling Tofu

It's a shame that tofu scrambles often end up being wet and mushy. We find that if we sear the crumbled tofu at high heat, it begins to brown and develop a bit of crispy crust (something like hash browns). Searing tofu by grilling, roasting, or frying elevates it above the "I know I should eat this because it's good for me" level. The tofu tastes better, and searing gives it a nice caramel color and a more appealing texture, slightly crispy on the outside and soft inside.

Three things are key to searing tofu for flavorful scrambles.

*   First, use pressed tofu that has been patted dry. (You'll find instructions for pressing tofu on page 22.)
*   Second, use a skillet or wok with a surface area that's large enough to give the tofu plenty of room to brown. I find searing tofu works best in a nonstick pan, with little or no oil; you could also use a pan spray. (It's a bonus, too, for those trying to limit fat intake!)
*   And third, use high heat, as you would for a stir-fry.

Here's how to put this advice into practice.

BROWN THE TOFU. Crumble the tofu into a hot pan, and spread it out to cover the bottom. Over high heat, stir and shake the pan to brown the tofu on all sides.

COOK THE TOFU WITH THE VEGETABLES. Once you've seared the tofu, you can lower the heat, and add onions, garlic, and any other vegetables that need to be cooked.

After the vegetables are crisp tender, and the tofu is browned and crispy, you can add the ingredients that just need to be heated, like fresh herbs or chopped tomatoes.

BROWN THE TOFU. Heat the olive oil in a large non-stick skillet or wok over high heat. When it is hot, crumble the tofu into the pan, and spread it out to cover the bottom. Cook, stirring and shaking the pan, until the tofu has begun to brown and has some crispy edges, about 5 minutes.

COOK ALL BUT THE LAST 2 INGREDIENTS WITH THE TOFU. Lower the heat to medium, add the onion and garlic, and sauté for 3 or 4 minutes. Add the herbs, tomato, and olives, and cook just until the tomato is warm, about 1 minute.

SERVE THE SCRAMBLE. Season to taste with salt and pepper, drizzle with balsamic vinegar, and serve immediately.

Roasted Tomatillo and Pepita Tofu Scramble [v]

This scramble takes its name in part from a common ingredient in Mexican cooking, pumpkin seed, or *pepita* in Spanish. We serve it, like all of our egg and tofu scrambles, with a side of Roasted Rosemary Potatoes (see page 213). But this would be equally good served with Black Bean Stew (see page 133), Pico de Gallo Salsa (see page 226), and warm tortillas for a very substantial brunch, or even supper.

Serves 2 generously

¼ cup raw green pumpkin seeds, hulled

6 tomatillos, husks removed, washed, left whole

1 jalapeño chile, cut in half lengthwise, ribs and seeds removed (for less heat)

3 tablespoons vegetable oil

2 tablespoons chopped garlic

1½ teaspoons salt

½ teaspoon black pepper

1 (14- to 16-ounce) block firm tofu, pressed (see page 22), or extrafirm tofu, patted dry

¼ pound crimini mushrooms, sliced (about 1½ cups)

¼ cup white wine

2 scallions, green and white parts, sliced

TOAST THE PUMPKIN SEEDS by tossing them in a dry sauté pan over high heat until they start to pop. Add salt to taste, and set aside.

PREPARE THE TOMATILLOS AND JALAPEÑO. Preheat the oven to 350 degrees. Toss the tomatillos and jalapeño chile with 1 tablespoon of the oil to coat.

ROAST THE TOMATILLOS AND JALAPEÑO. Put them in a baking pan, and roast, uncovered, for 20 minutes. The tomatillos will collapse and be browned and soft.

BLEND THE TOMATILLOS AND JALAPEÑO in a food processor or blender. Add the pumpkin seeds, garlic, salt, and pepper, and process until smooth. Set this mixture aside.

BROWN THE TOFU. Heat the remaining 2 tablespoons of oil in a large nonstick skillet or wok over high heat. Crumble the tofu into the pan, and spread it out to cover the bottom. Cook, stirring and shaking the pan, until the tofu has begun to brown and has some crispy edges, about 5 minutes.

COOK THE REMAINING INGREDIENTS WITH THE TOFU. Lower the heat to medium, add the mushrooms, and cook until they're browned, about 5 minutes.

Add the wine and cook, scraping the bottom of the pan to loosen the browned bits of tofu. Add the tomatillo mixture and scallions. Sauté until the mixture is very hot, another 2 minutes. Season with salt and pepper to taste, and serve immediately.

TIP

- If you find toasted pumpkin seeds (or pepitas), use those and skip the toasting instructions.

Roasted Vegetable Tofu Scramble [v] with Cafe Flora Fu Sauce

We roast the vegetables in this scramble ahead of time to make cooking this dish faster and easier during our very busy brunches. We usually use five or six different vegetables for color and contrast, varying them with the season. At one time or another, we've used delicata or butternut squash, turnips, beets, green beans, fennel, bell peppers, and mushrooms. Roasting intensifies the flavor of the vegetables and makes them sturdier for this scramble, but you could use any type of cooked vegetables or even start with raw vegetables. If you use raw vegetables, allow enough cooking time for them to become tender before you add the tofu.

As with scrambled eggs, Roasted Rosemary Potatoes (see page 213) make a satisfying accompaniment.

Serves 3 to 4

GET A HEAD START

If you're making this for brunch and want a little more sleep in the morning, a day or two beforehand press the tofu (that takes about an hour), roast the vegetables, and make the Fu Sauce while they are roasting.

1 carrot, peeled and sliced at an angle

1 onion, halved and sliced in ¼-inch crescents

1 cup broccoli florets

1 cup cauliflower florets

1 cup ½-inch dice zucchini

1 cup ½-inch dice yam (see page 241)

2 tablespoons vegetable oil

1 (14- to 16-ounce) block firm tofu, pressed (see page 22), or extrafirm tofu, patted dry

1 teaspoon chopped garlic

¼ cup Cafe Flora Fu Sauce (recipe follows)

Optional: Pinch of red pepper flakes

PREPARE THE VEGETABLES. Preheat the oven to 400 degrees. Combine the vegetables in a big mixing bowl and drizzle with 1 tablespoon of the oil. Toss well to fully coat the vegetables.

ROAST THE VEGETABLES. Spread the vegetables on a rimmed baking sheet large enough to accommodate all the vegetables in a single layer without crowding. (If you crowd them, you will steam rather than roast them.) Roast until the vegetables are tender but not mushy, so that a sharp knife easily pierces the carrots, 25 to 30 minutes. Remove from the baking sheet and set aside.

BROWN THE TOFU. In a large nonstick skillet or wok, heat the remaining 1 tablespoon vegetable oil over high heat. Crumble the tofu into the pan, and spread it out to cover the bottom. Cook, stirring and shaking the pan, until the tofu has begun to brown and has some crispy edges, about 5 minutes.

FINISH THE SCRAMBLE. Lower the heat to medium, add the garlic and vegetables, and continue to sauté until the entire mixture is hot.

Give the Fu Sauce one last whisk, and add it along with the red pepper flakes if you want the extra heat. Cook for 1 more minute, and serve immediately.

TIPS

Perfectly scrambled tofu is an art; see page 204 for instructions.

Cafe Flora Fu Sauce [v]

We often use this spicy sauce to spark up bland "to-fu," hence its name. It's also a flavorful marinade for tofu when you plan to grill it.

Makes about 1 cup

1 teaspoon white sesame seeds

1 teaspoon black sesame seeds

¼ cup tamari (see page 240)

½ cup mirin (seasoned rice wine [see page 239])

¼ cup rice vinegar

¼ cup minced or grated peeled fresh ginger

1 tablespoon Dijon mustard

⅛ teaspoon red pepper flakes

¼ cup finely chopped garlic

1 tablespoon sesame oil

TOAST THE SESAME SEEDS by tossing them in a dry sauté pan over medium heat just until they're fragrant and the light seeds are starting to color, 2 to 3 minutes.

MIX ALL INGREDIENTS together in a bowl, and refrigerate until ready to use. If the solids settle, make sure to shake the sauce up before you use it.

Hoppin' John Fritters [V] with Cayenne Aïoli

Typically, hoppin' John is a stewlike bean and rice dish. There are many stories about the origins of the name *hoppin' John*, but the combination of rice and beans was a well-known staple of African slaves in the Americas. (In fact, variations, mostly involving different varieties of peas or beans, are found all over the American South and the Caribbean.) Tradition has it that eating hoppin' John on New Year's Day guarantees a year's worth of good luck.

We've built on this delicious Southern tradition by making hoppin' John into fritters. We serve two fritters per person with a dollop of Cayenne Aïoli for a peppery kick. For a more elaborate brunch, serve these fritters with Cafe Flora Cheesy Grits (see page 213), Smoky Collard Greens (see page 211), and Basil Corn Relish (see page 212).

Makes 15 to 18 fritters

TIMING

If you're using dried black-eyed peas, start them soaking at least 2 hours ahead. (It's also OK to start them the night before.) After you make the fritter mix, it needs to chill for 30 minutes. That would be a good time to make the aïoli.

2 cups dried black-eyed peas, soaked for at least 2 hours or up to 8, or 4 (14.5-ounce) cans

1 tablespoon olive oil

1 large carrot, peeled and finely diced

2 stalks celery, finely diced

1 small red onion, finely diced

1 teaspoon minced garlic

¼ cup white wine

1 cup cooked white rice, cooled

1 tablespoon chopped fresh sage, or 1 teaspoon dried

3 tablespoons chopped fresh Italian parsley

2 to 3 sprigs thyme, leaves picked

½ bunch scallions, white and green parts, chopped

1 smoked chipotle chile in adobo, minced (see Tips)

1 teaspoon salt

1 tablespoon cornstarch

Vegetable oil for frying

Cayenne Aïoli (recipe follows)

PREPARE THE BLACK-EYED PEAS. If you're using dried peas, drain them, put them in a pot, and cover with about an inch of fresh water. Bring to a boil, lower the heat, and simmer, uncovered, until tender, 45 minutes to 1 hour. Check the pot during cooking to see if it needs more water. Drain, and set aside to cool.

If you're using canned black-eyed peas, rinse them under cold water, and drain well.

SAUTÉ THE VEGETABLES. Heat the olive oil in a skillet over medium heat. Add the carrot, celery, red onion, and dried sage (if you're using it). Sauté until the onion is soft and translucent, about 10 minutes. Add the garlic, and cook for 1 more minute.

Add the wine, and stir to remove any bits of vegetable from the bottom of the skillet. Cook until all the wine has evaporated and the mixture is dry. Set aside to cool.

MASH THE BLACK-EYED PEAS. Reserve 2 cups of black-eyed peas to add at the end. Put the remaining peas into the bowl of a mixer. Using a mixer with a paddle attachment, mash the peas until they begin to stick together. (You can also do this by hand using a potato masher.)

MAKE THE FRITTER MIX. To the black-eyed peas in the mixer, add the vegetables, rice, herbs (including the fresh sage if you're using it), scallions, chipotle chile, and salt. Mix well.

Sprinkle the cornstarch over the fritter mix, and stir for 1 minute. Gently fold in the reserved 2 cups peas, trying to keep some peas whole. Chill the mixture for half an hour before forming into patties.

SHAPE THE FRITTERS. Using 3 tablespoons of the mixture for each fritter, shape it into balls. Gently flatten each ball with your fingertips into a patty about 2½ inches in diameter. Smooth out the jagged edges so they don't break off when you cook them. Lay the patties on an ungreased baking sheet until you're ready to fry them.

PANFRY THE PATTIES. Heat 2 tablespoons oil in a large, heavy skillet over medium-high heat. Put several patties in the pan, leaving enough room to flip them easily.

Cook on each side until browned and crispy, 4 to 5 minutes per side. Cook the remaining fritters in the same way.

Drain the fritters on paper towels, keeping them warm in a 200-degree oven until ready to serve.

SERVE THE FRITTERS. Serve 2 or 3 fritters with a dollop of Cayenne Aïoli, page 209.

> **TIPS**
>
> - If you're using canned black-eyed peas, read the label carefully to make sure they're vegetarian. Because black-eyed peas are such a staple in Southern cooking, they often contain lard.
>
> - You can get chipotle chiles as smoked chipotles in adobo in a four-ounce can (Embasa brand).
>
> - If the fritters fall apart as you shape or fry them, see "Tips for Making Sturdy Patties and Burgers," on page 177.

Cayenne Aïoli

Makes about ½ cup

½ cup mayonnaise
2 teaspoons freshly squeezed lemon juice
¼ teaspoon cayenne pepper
2 teaspoons Dijon mustard
2 cloves garlic, minced

Whisk all the ingredients in a small bowl, and refrigerate until ready to serve.

Southern Brunch Platter

We like to offer some dishes on our brunch menu that are not the usual breakfast foods, like this dish, which makes a perfectly delicious dinner as well. We started doing this plate with a Southern flair when we came upon some green tomatoes that we thought would be tasty cornmeal battered, fried, and topped with our Spicy Rémoulade (see page 231). So with the tomatoes as the centerpiece, we served such sides as Black-Eyed Pea Salad, also known as Texas Caviar, and Smoky Collard Greens with fresh Basil Corn Relish alongside.

The availability of green tomatoes is usually limited to the very beginning and the very end of the summer growing season, so when we can no longer get them, we keep the Southern spirit of the platter. We take out the Fried Green Tomatoes and the Basil Corn Relish and replace them with crispy Hoppin' John Fritters (see page 207) and rich Cafe Flora Cheesy Grits (see page 213). But feel free to experiment, mixing and matching these dishes however you like.

serves 6 to 8

GET A HEAD START

This is a platter you probably won't want to make in a day. (Plus it's for brunch. You don't want to get up that early!)

- BLACK-EYED PEA SALAD: If you're using dried black-eyed peas, start them soaking at least 2 hours ahead. (It's also OK to start them the night before.) You can also cook and dress them a day or two before to give the flavor time to develop.

- SMOKY COLLARD GREENS: Smoke the mushrooms ahead of time (even a week in advance). You can also cook the collards a day or two before you plan to serve them. Heat them up slowly, stirring occasionally, in a covered saucepan with ¼ cup water, just until hot.

- FRIED GREEN TOMATOES: Make these the morning you plan to serve them, but make the Spicy Rémoulade ahead, even several days in advance.

- BASIL CORN RELISH: You can't make this in advance, but make it first so the flavors can mellow while you heat up the other dishes and fry the tomatoes.

Fried Green Tomatoes (recipe follows)
Spicy Rémoulade (see page 231)
Black-Eyed Pea Salad (recipe follows)
Smoky Collard Greens (recipe follows)
Basil Corn Relish (recipe follows)

TO SERVE THIS ON INDIVIDUAL PLATES, arrange 2 tomato slices on one side of each plate. Top with a dollop of rémoulade sauce, and then place scoops of each of the other dishes next to the tomatoes.

TO SERVE THIS FAMILY STYLE, put the Fried Green Tomatoes on a platter. (The rémoulade is a topping for these.) Put the rest of the components in separate bowls, and invite your guests to help themselves.

Black-Eyed Pea Salad (Texas Caviar) (v)

We were looking for an easy, flavorful side dish with some protein to complement the other parts of our Southern Brunch Platter and to replace the usual breakfast eggs (or tofu scramble). Black-eyed peas seemed to go well with the Southern theme, and our brunch sous-chef, Sarah Wong, was enthusiastic about this particular dish, which she'd had at a party. Texas Caviar is a lot like salsa and would make a relatively nutritious snack served with tortilla chips.

Makes about 3 cups

¾ cup dried black-eyed peas, soaked for 2 hours or up to 8 hours, or 2 (15-ounce) cans (about 2¼ cups cooked)

1 small red bell pepper, roasted (see page 212) and chopped

1 small green bell pepper, seeds removed and cut into small dice

1 small tomato, cut into small dice

2 scallions, trimmed and sliced (use white and most of green part)

¼ cup finely chopped fresh Italian parsley

1 jalapeño chile, ribs and seeds removed and minced

1 tablespoon finely chopped fresh oregano, or 1 teaspoon dried

1 tablespoon finely chopped fresh thyme, or 1 teaspoon dried

2 large cloves garlic, minced

½ teaspoon Dijon mustard

1 tablespoon white wine vinegar

3 tablespoons olive oil

Salt and freshly ground pepper

PREPARE THE BLACK-EYED PEAS. If you're using dried peas, drain them, and cover with about an inch of fresh water in a pot. Bring to a boil, lower the heat, and simmer, uncovered, until tender, 45 minutes to 1 hour. Check the pot during cooking to see if it needs more water. Drain and set aside to cool.

If you're using canned black-eyed peas, rinse them under cold water, and drain well.

MIX THE PEAS, VEGETABLES, AND HERBS. Put the black-eyed peas in a large mixing bowl. Add the bell peppers, tomato, scallions, parsley, and jalapeño chile. If you're using fresh herbs, add them now, and toss lightly to combine. (If you're using dried herbs, add them when you make the dressing.)

MAKE THE DRESSING. In a small bowl, whisk together the garlic, mustard, vinegar, and the dried herbs (if you're using them). Slowly whisk in the olive oil until the mixture is creamy. Add salt and pepper to taste.

DRESS THE SALAD. Pour the dressing over the black-eyed pea mixture, and mix well. Refrigerate the salad for at least 1 hour to let the flavors develop. Bring to room temperature before serving.

TIP
If you're using canned black-eyed peas, read the label carefully to make sure they're vegetarian. Because black-eyed peas are such a staple in Southern cooking, they often contain lard.

Fried Green Tomatoes

Fried Green Tomatoes also make a flavorful first course or appetizer topped with a dollop of our Spicy Rémoulade (see page 231), Sun-Dried Tomato Aïoli (see page 231), or other garlicky mayonnaise, or drizzled with a pesto, such as Basil Pesto (see page 233).

Serves 6 to 8

2 pounds green (unripe) tomatoes, unpeeled

½ cup unbleached all-purpose flour

¼ teaspoon cayenne pepper

Salt and freshly ground black pepper

½ cup buttermilk

1 cup panko (Japanese bread crumbs [see page 239]), or unseasoned dried bread crumbs

¼ cup coarsely ground cornmeal (polenta)

1 tablespoon onion powder

Vegetable oil for frying

SLICE AND DRY THE TOMATOES. Slice the tomatoes about ⅜ inch thick, and pat dry.

GET THE BREADING READY. Mix the flour with the cayenne, ½ teaspoon salt, and a pinch black pepper in a shallow bowl. Put the buttermilk in another shallow bowl. In a third bowl, mix the panko, cornmeal, onion powder, ½ teaspoon salt, and another pinch of black pepper.

DREDGE EACH TOMATO SLICE first in the flour mixture, and then in the buttermilk to coat. Finally dredge in the panko mixture, pressing the breading onto the tomato slice to coat it fully.

Spread the breaded tomato slices on an ungreased baking sheet until you're ready to fry them.

FRY THE TOMATOES. Heat about ¼ inch of oil in a heavy skillet over medium-high heat. When the oil is hot, put 3 or 4 tomato slices in the skillet, leaving enough room to flip them.

When the tomato slices are golden brown on one side, flip them and brown on the other side, frying them for 5 to 6 minutes total. Skim the oil occasionally to remove any burned bits of breading.

Drain the fried tomato slices on paper towels and keep them warm in a 200-degree oven until ready to serve.

Smoky Collard Greens (v)

If you don't have time to smoke the mushrooms, don't let that stop you from making this dish. It will still taste great, just not as smoky. Also, we recommend cooking the collards for about 30 minutes. Traditionally, however, particularly in the South, greens are cooked for hours; if you like them like that, you'll have to keep adding water to keep them from drying out and burning.

Serves 6 to 8

2 tablespoons olive oil

½ pound domestic or crimini mushrooms, smoked (see page 79) and sliced

1 onion, thinly sliced

3 cloves garlic, minced

2 bunches collard greens

1 cup water

½ teaspoon Tabasco sauce

2 tablespoons apple cider vinegar

1 teaspoon salt

SAUTÉ THE MUSHROOMS AND ONION. Heat the olive oil in a large heavy-bottomed, lidded soup pot or Dutch oven over medium-high heat. Add the smoked mushrooms, and cook for 5 minutes. Lower the heat to medium, and add the onion and garlic. Sauté until the onion is soft and translucent, about 10 minutes.

PREPARE THE COLLARDS. While the onion and mushrooms are cooking, remove most of the stems, and tear the leaves. You'll have about 4 quarts of collards.

COOK THE COLLARDS. Add the water to the mushroom-onion mixture, fill the pot to the top with greens, and put the lid on the pan. Lower the heat to medium.

In about 5 minutes, when the greens are wilted, add any remaining collards. Stir the contents of the pan, cover, and cook until the greens are tender, 25 to 30 minutes. Stir occasionally, and add more water as needed, a little at a time. Cook longer if you like your greens very tender.

FINISH THE DISH. Take the pot off the heat. Add the Tabasco sauce, vinegar, and salt to the collards, and mix well. Adjust these seasonings to taste.

Basil Corn Relish (v)

2 large ears corn, kernels cut from the cob, or about 2 cups frozen whole-kernel corn

4 large basil leaves

3 tablespoons apple cider vinegar

2 teaspoons light brown sugar

1 red bell pepper, seeds removed, roasted (see "Roasting Peppers"), and finely diced

4 scallions, white and green part, thinly sliced

Salt and freshly ground pepper

BLANCH THE CORN. Prepare a bowl of ice water big enough to hold the corn. Bring 2 quarts of water to a boil in a medium pot. Drop the corn kernels in, and cook for 2 minutes. Drain, as for pasta, into a

Roasting Peppers

When you buy peppers for roasting, look for ones with few crevices so it's easier to peel off the skin after roasting. There are three methods for roasting peppers: over a gas burner, under a broiler, or on a grill.

GET READY. If you're going to grill over coals, get them going; if you're using a broiler, preheat it. Brush the peppers with a small amount of vegetable oil.

ROAST THE PEPPER

- Over the flame on a gas stove. Pierce the top of the pepper near the stem with a fork, and using the fork as a handle, hold it over the flame on medium-high heat. Turn the pepper over the flame until the skin is completely blistered and charred.

- Under the broiler. Put the pepper on a pan under the broiler three to four inches from the heat. Turn the pepper over every couple of minutes until it's blistered and charred all over.

- On a grill. Follow the instructions for roasting over a gas flame, but without the fork. Just roll the pepper around on the grill until all the surfaces are blistered and charred.

STEAM THE PEPPER. Put the pepper in a bowl, and cover it with plastic wrap to steam the pepper and loosen the skin. You can also steam it in a paper bag or wrapped in a paper towel.

REMOVE THE SKIN AND SEEDS. When the pepper is cool, peel off the charred skin and pull off the stem. If you're handling spicy chiles, do this using a paper towel to protect your fingers. Split the pepper in half lengthwise and scrape away the seeds.

colander or sieve, and then plunge the corn into the ice water. When the corn is cool, drain well.

CUT THE BASIL IN A CHIFFONADE. Stack the basil leaves on top of each other. Roll them up tightly starting at the stem, and slice thinly across the rolled-up leaves. This will give you long thin strips of basil.

MAKE THE DRESSING. In a medium bowl, whisk together the vinegar and brown sugar until the sugar dissolves.

COMBINE ALL THE INGREDIENTS. Add the basil, bell pepper, scallions, and corn to the dressing, and toss to combine well. Season with salt and pepper to taste.

About Peppers

To save time or when red pepper prices are high, use the roasted red peppers that are widely available commercially. (Trader Joe's bottles a couple of varieties that are especially good, and well priced.) Look for those packed in water or brine, rather than oil, and in jars rather than cans (they have a better flavor). Rinse them before you use them.

There is really no good substitute for roasting your own poblano chiles; canned green chiles are milder and less flavorful.

Roasted Rosemary Potatoes [v]

We parboil the potatoes before we roast them so they're crispy on the outside and tender and creamy on the inside. We serve these potatoes at brunch with all of our egg and tofu scrambles, but they are great alongside any of our burgers or the French Dip Sandwich (see page 170).

Serves 4

1½ pounds red potatoes, cut in ½-inch chunks

2 tablespoons olive oil

3 cloves garlic, minced

6-inch sprig rosemary, leaves picked off and chopped

Coarse salt and freshly ground pepper

PARBOIL THE POTATOES. Preheat the oven to 400 degrees. Put the potatoes in a medium saucepan, cover with cold water, and bring to a boil. Cook for 10 minutes, drain, and rinse.

SEASON THE POTATOES. Toss the potatoes with the olive oil, garlic, and rosemary. Sprinkle with a couple of big pinches of salt and several grindings of pepper.

ROAST THE POTATOES. Spread the potatoes on a baking sheet with a rim large enough to accommodate them in a single layer without crowding. (If you crowd the potatoes, you will steam rather than roast them.)

Roast until nut brown, for 25 to 30 minutes, stirring the potatoes occasionally to make sure they brown evenly.

Cafe Flora Cheesy Grits

The requests for cheesy grits every weekend brunch are so overwhelming that we make them a standard accompaniment to our scrambled tofu and egg dishes. Or we top wedges of panfried cheesy grits with poached eggs and serve them with Black Bean Stew (see page 133) and Pico de Gallo Salsa (see page 226) as a brunch special. We also often put cheesy grits on the menu as an accompaniment to dishes with a Southern theme or whenever we serve Hoppin' John Fritters (see page 207).

1 cup heavy cream

2 cups water

1 teaspoon salt

¾ cup quick grits

1 teaspoon hot pepper sauce (like Tabasco sauce)

½ cup (2 ounces) grated smoked mozzarella cheese

COOK THE GRITS. Mix the cream, water, and salt in a medium saucepan over medium-high heat. Bring to a boil, and gradually stir in the grits, stirring or whisking constantly to avoid lumps. Reduce the heat to medium-low, and cook for 5 minutes, stirring occasionally.

ADD THE HOT SAUCE AND GRATED CHEESE, stirring until the cheese is completely melted. (These grits are thick, so if you want a softer consistency, add water or more cream at the very end, after you've finished cooking them.) Serve immediately.

Variation: panfried cheesy grits [v]

TIMING

If you plan to make the Panfried Cheesy Grits, the grits need an hour to chill before you can cut and fry them.

Serves 6 to 8 as a side dish

CHILL THE COOKED GRITS. Pour the finished grits into a greased 8-inch square pan. Chill until set, about 1 hour. Remove the grits from the pan, cut into 6 squares, and then cut each square on a diagonal to make 12 triangles.

PANFRY THE GRITS. Spray or brush a skillet with vegetable oil, or use a nonstick pan. Fry the grits over medium heat until lightly browned on each side. (Be careful! Moisture in the grits can cause the oil to pop and give you tiny burns.)

Cafe Flora Soy Sausage [v]

We always serve these sausage patties on our family breakfast platters of scrambled eggs or tofu, Roasted Rosemary Potatoes (see page 213), Cafe Flora Vegan Coffee Cake (see page 213) and fresh fruit. Seasoned like spicy Italian sausage and cooked up browned and crispy, these satisfy the breakfast cravings of our most carnivorous guests.

Makes about 14 patties

TIMING

Pressing the tofu takes about an hour. At the same time, you can soak the TVP for 15 minutes and then drain it in the fridge until it's cool, about an hour.

5 ounces (about 1½ cups) TVP (unflavored textured vegetable protein [see "About TVP"])

1¼ cups very hot water

2 tablespoons Egg Replacer (see page 239), or other egg substitute equal to 2 eggs

½ cup cold water

½ (14- to 16-ounce) block firm tofu, pressed (see page 22), or extrafirm tofu

2 tablespoons chopped garlic

1 tablespoon chopped fresh rosemary

1½ teaspoons dried thyme

1½ teaspoons dried sage

2 teaspoons fennel seeds, toasted and coarsely ground (see page 52)

1 teaspoon red pepper flakes

2 teaspoons salt

1 teaspoon freshly ground black pepper

2 tablespoons cornstarch

Vegetable oil for frying

PREPARE THE TVP. In a large bowl, cover the TVP with the hot water, stir once, and then cover the bowl with plastic wrap to steam for 15 minutes.

Remove the plastic wrap; put the TVP in a mesh strainer over a bowl to drain. If you're using the chunk form of TVP, chop it finely.

MAKE THE SAUSAGE MIXTURE. In a medium bowl, whisk the Egg Replacer with the cold water until it is slightly foamy like whipped egg white. Pat the tofu dry, and crumble it into the Egg Replacer. Mix with your hands until thoroughly combined.

Add the drained TVP along with all the remaining ingredients, except the oil, and mix well.

SHAPE THE PATTIES. Using 3 tablespoons of the TVP mixture for each patty, shape it into balls. Gently flatten each ball with your fingertips into a patty about 2½ inches in diameter. Smooth out the jagged edges so they don't break off when you cook them. Lay the patties on an ungreased baking sheet until you're ready to fry them.

FRY THE SAUSAGE. Heat about ¼ inch oil in a non-stick skillet over medium-high heat. (If you don't have a nonstick pan, any heavy skillet works well.) When it's hot, put several patties in the pan, leaving enough room to flip them easily. Cook on each side until browned and heated through, about 2 minutes per side.

Drain the patties on paper towels. Keep them warm in a 200-degree oven until ready to serve (no longer than half an hour).

About TVP

TVP (or textured vegetable protein) is a dried, soy-based product that is low in fat and high in protein. It absorbs the flavors of the food it's cooked with and adds a meatlike texture to dishes. It's used in products ranging from soy burgers and hot dogs to breakfast cereals and frozen desserts. Look for TVP in bags or in bulk at natural-food stores, in well-stocked grocery stores in granular or chunk form, or online at www.bobsredmill.com

In its dried state, TVP keeps well, up to six months unrefrigerated. But you must soak it to use it, after which it must be refrigerated and used within a few days.

About Making Sausages That Hold Together

For successful soy sausages, make sure to remove as much water as possible from the soaked TVP and tofu, or the mixture may not hold together. Pressing tofu removes much of the liquid. The more water you remove from these ingredients, the sturdier the patties will be for panfrying. However, if the sausage patties still fall apart as you shape or fry them, see "Tips for Making Sturdy Patties and Burgers," on page 177.

Cafe Flora Vegan Coffee Cake [v]

We make this coffee cake every weekend, changing the fruit with the season or using whatever fruit we have on hand. (We've even been known to substitute orange zest for the fruit or even a scant cup of chocolate chips.)

To make this vegan coffee cake, we adapted the traditional recipe in which you cream butter and sugar before you add the eggs and other ingredients. Because a solid form of fat is necessary for creaming, we use margarine. Fortunately, there are several brands on the market now that are made without hydrogenated or partially hydrogenated oils, so you can make this coffee cake with a clear conscience.

Makes one 9½-inch, round coffee cake

GET A HEAD START

Although this may surprise you, this cake really does taste better the next day. (Wrap it tightly in plastic wrap after it's cooled to keep the moistness in.) And that's good for you because you can sleep a bit longer on a Saturday or Sunday and still have coffee cake for breakfast.

1 cup soy or rice milk

1 tablespoon vinegar

1½ cups berries or diced fruit

2½ cups unbleached all-purpose flour, plus 2 tablespoons for fruit

Optional: 1 tablespoon lemon or orange zest, or ½ teaspoon cinnamon

1½ cups sugar

½ teaspoon ground cinnamon

4 tablespoons (½ stick) cold margarine, plus ¼ pound (1 stick)

1 teaspoon baking powder

1¼ teaspoons baking soda

¼ teaspoon salt

1½ teaspoons Egg Replacer (see page 239) or other egg substitute equal to 1 egg mixed with 2 tablespoons water

GET READY. Preheat the oven to 350 degrees. Grease a 9½-inch springform pan. In a small bowl, mix the milk with the vinegar.

PREPARE THE FRUIT. If you're using a firm fruit like apples, cut into ¼-inch dice. Cut softer fruit like peaches into about ½-inch dice. Toss fruit in a bowl with the 2 tablespoons flour to coat (and cinnamon or zest if you're using it), and set aside.

MAKE THE CRUMBLE TOPPING. Mix together ½ cup of the flour, ½ cup of the sugar, and the cinnamon in a medium bowl. Cut the 4 tablespoons margarine into small chunks, and add to the dry ingredients, mixing with your fingers until the mixture resembles coarsely chopped nuts. Freeze until ready to use. (It's easier to scatter evenly over the batter when it's very cold.)

SIFT THE DRY INGREDIENTS. Sift the remaining 2 cups flour with the baking powder, baking soda, and salt into a small bowl. (If you don't have a sifter or sieve, whisk the dry ingredients to aerate and lighten them.)

If you want, add zest or cinnamon to the flour that you toss the fruit in. If you're using berries or stone fruit (peaches, plums, nectarines, or apricots), add lemon or orange zest; if you're using apples or pears, add the ½ teaspoon cinnamon.

CREAM THE MARGARINE AND SUGAR. In a large bowl, use an electric mixer to cream the remaining stick of margarine with the remaining 1 cup sugar for 1 minute.

MIX THE WET AND DRY INGREDIENTS. Starting with the dry ingredients, add one-third of the dry ingredients to the margarine-sugar mix alternately with the milk-vinegar mixture, ½ cup at a time. Mix just until no floury streaks are showing, ending with the dry ingredients. Do not overbeat. Fold in the Egg Replacer, until fully incorporated. Gently fold in the fruit.

BAKE THE COFFEE CAKE. Spoon the batter into the prepared pan. Sprinkle the crumble topping evenly over the batter. Bake for about 35 minutes, or until a toothpick, inserted in the center, comes out with some crumbs attached. When the cake is done, it will be higher in the center, but it will settle.

COOL AND SERVE THE CAKE. Let the cake cool for an hour or more. Run a knife around the edge, remove the rim, and slide the cake onto a plate.

> **TIP**
>
> Instead of cutting the fruit into chunks and mixing it into the batter, slice the fruit. Then press the slices (or berries if that's what you're using) into the *top* of the batter once it's in the pan, and sprinkle the topping over the fruit.

Tropical Fruit Compote (v)

This fresh compote makes a colorful and juicy accompaniment to any rich brunch dish. Although kiwifruit is not really a tropical fruit, we add it for its brilliant green color. Mango, papaya, and kiwifruit seem to be readily available in most large grocery stores these days, but if you can't find one or the other, substitute fresh pineapple. Sliced banana is good, too, but even bathed in lime juice, it can turn brown quickly, so serve this compote right away if you include it. And if you're lucky enough to come across a ripe passion fruit—it looks like a wrinkled purple egg—cut the fruit in half, scoop out the aromatic flesh, and mix it in with the other diced fruits.

These fruits seem to be available most of the time, but they're generally less expensive and more abundant in the winter. Kiwi is the most difficult to tell when it is ripe because it's not fragrant. But ripe kiwi should not be rock hard and should give a little when you press it (gently!).

Makes about 4 cups

1 mango, peeled
1 papaya, peeled and seeds scooped out
3 kiwifruits, peeled
1 teaspoon finely chopped lime zest (1 lime)
2 tablespoons lime juice

Cut the mango, papaya, and kiwifruits into ¼-inch dice, and combine in a medium bowl. Stir in the lime zest and juice, and refrigerate until ready to serve.

BEVERAGES

WHETHER IT'S A THIRST-QUENCHING glass of Rosemary Lemonade, or a warm mug of Spiced Cider, a flavorful beverage can delight the senses and soothe the soul. Most of these recipes are twists on old favorites and are supremely easy to make.

For a spring or summer garden party, a big punch bowl of Lavender Nectar or Rosemary Lemonade makes a great centerpiece. Make ice cubes with little sprigs of lavender or rosemary frozen inside to float in the bowl.

Hibiscus Sunset [v]

Impress your guests with this beverage at brunch. If you're like me and think a big glass of fruit juice is a little too much sugar first thing in the morning, this is a perfect wake-up tonic.

We offer a large selection of teas at Cafe Flora, and at one time we served a beautiful red-hued herbal tea called Wu Wei from the Blue Willow Tea Company in Seattle. Eventually we created our own hibiscus blend called Garnet Spring, a refreshing combination of hibiscus flowers, rose petals, star anise, lemon verbena, sassafras, and cloves. Celestial Seasonings Red Zinger makes a good substitute. However, Wu Wei and Garnet Spring contain the herb sweetleaf (stevia) making them sweeter than Red Zinger, so if you use Red Zinger, you may want to add sugar or honey to taste.

Although this layered drink looks tricky to make, it's actually quite easy. The secret is to pour the tea slowly over the back of a spoon to regulate the flow of tea into the glass so it floats on top of the orange juice.

Makes 4 (12-ounce) servings

3 cups boiling water
2 tablespoons Wu Wei or 6 tea bags Red Zinger tea
Ice cubes (not crushed ice)
3 cups freshly squeezed orange juice (6 or 7 juicy oranges)

BREW THE TEA. Pour the boiling water over the tea, and steep until it's a dark shade of pink. If you steep it too long, until the tea is deep red, it will be hard to see the layer of orange juice on the bottom of the glass. Refrigerate the tea until it is cold.

FILL GLASSES WITH ICE AND ORANGE JUICE. Fill 4 (12-ounce) glasses with ice, and fill each glass halfway with orange juice.

ADD THE TEA TO THE ORANGE JUICE. Put the tea in a little pitcher or measuring cup (or something with a spout) so you can control the flow of the tea into the glass. Rest a tablespoon or soup spoon on the inside rim of the glass and slowly pour the tea over it filling the glass almost to the top. The tea will "sit" on top of the orange juice. Serve immediately—and gently!—so as not to shake up the orange juice.

> **TIP**
> If your grocery store sells freshly squeezed orange juice, you can use that.

Rosemary Lemonade [v]

Rosemary Lemonade is Cafe Flora's most popular beverage year-round. It's really simple to make: essentially you make rosemary "tea," and use this as part of the water in the lemonade. It's so easy to grow rosemary in a pot or in your yard, and next to impossible to kill it, so you can make Rosemary Lemonade year-round, too.

Makes 2 quarts

1 bunch of rosemary, 8 (6-inch) sprigs (1 ounce)
4 cups water, plus more as needed
1 cup sugar
1 cup freshly squeezed lemon juice (about 6 lemons)

MAKE THE ROSEMARY TEA. In a saucepan, cover the rosemary with the 4 cups water. Bring to a boil, and simmer for 20 minutes. Strain the rosemary water into a 2-quart pitcher, and dissolve the sugar in the hot rosemary water. Set aside to cool.

ADD THE LEMON JUICE. When the rosemary tea is cool, add the lemon juice and enough water to make 2 quarts. Serve chilled.

Ginger Lemonade [v]

A variation on Rosemary Lemonade (see page 220), we make this tea using grated, fresh ginger instead of rosemary.

Makes 2 quarts

1 (4- or 5-inch) piece unpeeled fresh ginger, grated or finely chopped

4 cups water, plus more as needed

1¼ cups sugar

1 cup freshly squeezed lemon juice (about 6 lemons)

MAKE THE GINGER TEA. Put the ginger in a pot with the water. Bring to a boil, lower the heat, and simmer for 20 minutes. Add the sugar and stir thoroughly to dissolve it. Cool the ginger tea in the pot.

STRAIN IN THE TEA. As soon as it is cool, pour through a fine strainer into a 2-quart pitcher, and discard the ginger. (If you let the ginger sit in the tea too long, it could be so spicy as to overpower the lemon flavor.)

ADD THE LEMON JUICE to the ginger tea. Mix in enough cold water to make 2 quarts. Serve chilled.

Lavender Nectar [v]

This punch would look very nice served in a large bowl with ice cubes or a block of ice and edible flowers like pansies or violas floating on the surface. The addition of sugar helps bring out the flavor of the lavender, but you may omit it.

Makes about 1½ quarts

4 tablespoons dried lavender blossoms

1½ cups water

3 tablespoons sugar

2 cups apricot nectar

2 cups pear nectar

2 cups peach nectar

Ice cubes

Sparkling or mineral water

MAKE THE LAVENDER TEA. Put the lavender blossoms in a small pot with the water. Bring to a boil, reduce the heat, and simmer for 20 minutes.

Add the sugar and stir thoroughly to dissolve it. Cool the lavender liquid in the pot, and strain into a pitcher, discarding the lavender blossoms.

ADD THE FRUIT NECTARS, stir, and chill.

SERVE THE NECTAR. Fill a glass with ice, and pour in the Lavender Nectar until the glass is three-fourths full. Top off with sparkling or mineral water.

Crush the cardamom pod once to break the outer shell without crushing the seed. Add all the spices to the cider, and heat in a saucepan until it just boils. Remove from the heat, and let the spices steep in the cider for 3 or 4 hours. Strain and serve either cold over ice or steaming hot.

Spiced Cider [v]

In fall and winter at Cafe Flora, we heat individual servings of spiced cider using the steam wand on our espresso machine to serve it piping hot. If you have an espresso machine at home with a steaming wand, try it. (It also saves cleaning a pot.) Use whole spices, because ground spices make the cider cloudy.

Makes 1 quart

GET A HEAD START

The flavors of this spicy cider mellow over time, so it's best made at least 3 or 4 hours ahead.

1 cardamom pod
1 cinnamon stick
½ teaspoon whole cloves
¼ teaspoon whole allspice
1 quart sweet apple cider

Cranberry Ginger Cider

This drink, affectionately named Cringer by our guests, starts with a ginger tea to which you add cranberry juice. In fall and winter, serve this spiced cider piping hot. If you have an espresso machine at home with a steaming wand, use that to heat it. It makes short work of heating and saves cleaning a pot.

Makes 1½ quarts

1 (4- to 5-inch) piece of unpeeled fresh ginger, grated or finely chopped
2 cups water
1 quart cranberry juice cocktail

BREW THE TEA. Put the ginger in a pot with the water. Bring to a boil, lower the heat, and simmer for 20 minutes. (The longer you simmer the tea, the spicier it will be.)

STRAIN IN THE TEA. Cool the ginger tea in the pot, and then pour it through a fine strainer into a pitcher that will hold at least 6 cups. Discard the ginger.

ADD THE CRANBERRY JUICE to the pitcher of ginger tea and stir. Serve either cold over ice or steaming hot.

SIDE DISHES

CALLING THESE RECIPES SIDE DISHES does not do them justice. I hope these will become staples that you use again and again, not only with the dishes in this book, but with other meals you cook, too.

Crostini [v]

Crostini can be made from any kind of bread. A heavy rustic Italian or peasant loaf will make sturdy, crunchy crostini while bread with a lighter texture, like a typical French baguette, will make a more delicate, crispy crostini. Keep a batch of crostini on hand for emergency snacks. They'll add a homemade touch to cheeses or spreads you bring home from the local deli.

Makes 24

1 good-quality baguette
Olive oil for brushing

SLICE THE BAGUETTE AND BRUSH WITH OIL. Preheat the oven to 400 degrees. Cut the baguette into ¼- to ½-inch-thick diagonal slices. Brush both sides of the bread with olive oil, and put the slices on a baking sheet in a single layer.

OVEN TOAST THE BREAD. Bake in the middle rack of the oven until golden brown and crisp, 10 to 20 minutes. (The length of time depends on how dry the bread is and how thinly it's sliced.) Rotate the baking sheet halfway through the cooking time to brown evenly. Cool on a rack.

> **TIP**
> If you're a garlic lover, a tasty variation is to rub the toasted bread with raw garlic halves.

Chipotle Pinto Purée [v]

You may serve these addictive beans with many Mexican dishes—for example, our Roasted Yam Enchiladas with Smoky Tomato Sauce (see page 111). These beans also make a delicious and nutritious snack served with tortilla chips.

Makes about 5 cups

1 pound pinto beans, washed, picked through, and soaked for 3 to 8 hours, or 3 (15-ounce) cans (4½ cups cooked)
2 tablespoons Chipotle Chile Purée (see Tip)
2 teaspoons cumin seeds, toasted and ground (see page 52)
4 cloves garlic, minced
2 teaspoons hot pepper sauce such as Tabasco or Frank's Red Hot
3 tablespoons tamari (see page 240) or soy sauce

PREPARE THE PINTO BEANS. If you're using dried pintos, rinse the soaked beans, put them in a large heavy-bottomed saucepan or Dutch oven, and cover with about 2 inches of cold water. Bring to a boil, lower the heat to medium, and cook until the beans are mushy and most, but not all, of the water has been absorbed, about 45 minutes.

If you're using canned pinto beans, drain them in a strainer and rinse them under cold water. Put the beans in a saucepan with ½ cup water. Heat the beans, stirring occasionally.

PURÉE THE BEANS. Put the hot beans in a food processor with their liquid, and add all the remaining ingredients. Process until you get the consistency you want. You may have to add water to get a smooth purée.

Return the beans to the pot, and keep them warm over low heat until you're ready to serve them.

> **TIP**
> You can substitute two chipotle chiles for the Chipotle Chile Purée. In that case, soak them in hot water until soft, about 30 minutes, and then chop very finely.

Chipotle Chile Purée [v]

Chipotle peppers are actually dried smoked jalapeños. Canned in adobo, a flavorful red sauce, they are packed with heat and smoky flavor and add a quick spark to a dish. You can find small cans (three ounces) with brand names such as Herdez or Embasa in the Latino foods aisle of most grocery stores or in Latino markets.

If you can't use an entire can within a week, just put the purée in a zippered plastic bag or in ice cube trays. Store it in the refrigerator for up to three weeks, or freeze it.

1 (3-ounce) can chipotle chiles in adobo

Put the entire contents of the can in a food processor or blender, and purée. Refrigerate in a covered container topped with a thin layer of oil to prevent a crust forming on top.

Coconut Raita

This simple yogurt dish is served as a cooling accompaniment to spicy curries. We drain the yogurt to thicken it because we add liquid to the raita in the form of coconut milk to intensify the coconut flavor. If you're a lover of Indian food, either homemade or takeout, a bowl of Coconut Raita will be a welcome addition. Or try it with a simple platter of roasted beets.

Makes about 2½ cups

16 ounces plain yogurt
½ cup unsweetened coconut flakes (not finely ground) (see Tips)
2 teaspoons vegetable oil
1 tablespoon brown mustard seeds
½ cup coconut milk
Pinch cayenne pepper
½ teaspoon salt
¼ cup chopped fresh cilantro

DRAIN THE YOGURT. Put the yogurt in a strainer lined with a paper coffee filter. Set the strainer over a deep container, and let it drain for 1 hour to remove some of the whey.

PREPARE THE COCONUT. Meanwhile, put the coconut flakes in a small bowl, cover with 1 cup hot water, and soak for 20 minutes. Drain the water from the coconut and then roughly chop it by hand.

MAKE THE COCONUT MIXTURE. Heat the oil in a small skillet, add the mustard seeds, and cook until they begin to sputter. Add the coconut and coconut milk, bring to a boil, and then remove from the heat.

ADD THE COCONUT MIXTURE AND YOGURT. In a small bowl, mix the hot coconut mixture and the yogurt, and combine thoroughly. Stir in the cayenne, salt, and cilantro, and refrigerate until ready to use.

TIP

- Unsweetened coconut usually comes in flake or ground form, but you want the flake form. Look for it at natural-food stores and ethnic grocers. Do not substitute sweetened baking coconut. If you're lucky enough to get fresh coconut (or you live in a place where they're readily available), substitute freshly grated coconut. In that case, just skip the step where you soak the coconut in hot water.

Guacamole [v]

We often recommend guacamole in our dishes as a soothing balance for peppery heat, so we don't make it very spicy. If you want a spicier guacamole—for example, as a dip with chips—you could add minced onion and jalapeños, or a few big pinches of cayenne and toasted, ground cumin seeds.

Makes 2½ cups

2 ripe avocados

2 Roma tomatoes, cored, most of the seeds removed and finely diced

Juice of 1 large lime

3 tablespoons chopped fresh cilantro

salt

Cut the avocados in half, remove the pits, and scoop out the flesh into a mixing bowl. Mash with a fork or potato masher, leaving small chunks. Fold in the remaining ingredients, and mix well. Add salt to taste, and serve at once.

Pico de Gallo Salsa [v]

Pico de gallo—"beak of the rooster" in English—refers to a fresh salsa or relish. It is said to take its name from how it was once eaten, using the thumb and forefinger, a motion that imitates the pecking beak of a rooster.

Determining the heat of a dish can be difficult. If I call the following recipe "hot," half the people who make it will say it has the perfect amount of heat, and the other half will say it's too hot. If you're at all sensitive to chiles, use only half a jalapeño; if you love it hot, use two. And remember that the lime juice counteracts the heat. This salsa is best served freshly made; it gets hotter as it sits.

Makes 3 cups

8 to 10 Roma tomatoes, cored and coarsely chopped

1 small red onion, finely diced

1 to 2 jalapeño chiles, ribs and seeds removed and minced

¼ cup lightly packed fresh cilantro, chopped

Juice of 2 limes

3 cloves garlic, minced

1 teaspoon salt

Combine all the ingredients in a bowl.

> **TIP**
>
> We make this salsa year-round at the restaurant, so much of the time we use Roma tomatoes, but if you're making this in tomato season, definitely take advantage of other varieties that are available.

Kalamata Tapenade [v]

Tapenade, an olive paste from Provence, is traditionally made with small, black Niçoise olives. We make ours with kalamata olives because we always seem to have them on hand. Fragrant orange zest adds a memorable touch to this salty spread. Kalamata Tapenade keeps a week in your fridge, so keep a jar on hand for a last-minute appetizer to spread on crackers or slices of rustic bread, or to build a simple sandwich with sliced tomato and lettuce.

Makes about 1 cup

1 cup kalamata olives with pits (see Tip)

1 tablespoon capers, drained

2 to 3 cloves garlic

1 teaspoon grated orange zest

1 tablespoon finely chopped fresh Italian parsley

2 to 3 tablespoons olive oil

PIT THE OLIVES. Make short work of pitting olives by pressing the olives one at a time with the side of a broad knife blade to pop the pits out.

MIX THE TAPENADE. Put all the ingredients except the olive oil in a food processor. Pulse until finely chopped, about 30 seconds. Scrape down the sides of the bowl, and, with the machine running, drizzle in the olive oil until it's fully combined. Transfer the tapenade to a small serving bowl.

> **TIP**
>
> Although bulk kalamata olives are preferable, bottled olives are OK. Just make sure they're kalamata olives *with* pits and not the regular California black olives. (You know, the ones you put on the ends of your fingers as a child.) I've noticed that jars of *pitted* kalamata olives are now widely available, but these tend to have a mushy texture and are exceedingly salty. It's more work to pit the olives yourself, but definitely worth the effort.

SAUCES, PESTOS AND SPREADS

WE USE THE RECIPES IN this chapter throughout the book in pizzas, sandwiches, brunch dishes, and so on. In many cases, you can buy these sauces, pestos, and spreads ready made or bottled. But it's always good to know how to make them, to know exactly what ingredients are in them, and to have the freedom to change them to suit your taste. You can, of course, use them creatively, adapting them to dishes in your own repertoire. For example, the pestos are great tossed with pasta or spread on sandwiches.

Crème Fraîche

Crème fraîche is very easy to make and quite versatile. It makes a luscious garnish drizzled on Oaxaca Tacos (page 132), sweet or savory pancakes, and quesadillas. Unlike sour cream, crème fraîche doesn't curdle when it's cooked, so it's perfect for adding a creamy tang to soups and pasta. You can flavor it with citrus juice or zest, roasted chile purées, or toasted and ground spices like cumin or fennel. Crème fraîche will keep for several weeks in your refrigerator.

When you make crème fraîche, avoid ultrapasteurized cream and cream with stabilizers and thickeners such as carageenan and dextrose. (Read the cream cartons carefully.) If all you can find is ultrapasteurized cream, however, it could take up to twice as long to thicken into crème fraîche.

Makes 2 cups

2 cups heavy whipping cream
2 tablespoons buttermilk

Pour the cream into a jar or other container, add the buttermilk, and stir to mix them. Cover loosely. (If a jar, just rest the lid on the top of the jar; don't screw it on.) Put the container in a warm part of the kitchen, and let it sit undisturbed for 24 hours; then tightly cover the container, and refrigerate. (Even if it doesn't seem thick enough after 24 hours, which may be the case particularly for ultra-pasteurized cream, it will continue to thicken in the refrigerator.)

Lime Crème Fraîche

Makes ½ cup

½ cup crème fraîche, homemade or commercially prepared
½ teaspoon grated lime zest
2 tablespoons freshly squeezed lime juice
Pinch of salt

In a small bowl, thoroughly mix the crème fraîche, lime zest and juice, and a pinch of salt.

Lemon Oregano Yogurt Sauce

Using whole-milk yogurt results in a luxurious, rich sauce to drizzle on falafel or to top a curry burger, although you can also use low-fat or nonfat yogurt. For a flavor variation, try substituting fresh, chopped dill or mint for the oregano.

Makes 1 cup

1 cup yogurt
½ teaspoon finely chopped lemon zest
2 tablespoons freshly squeezed lemon juice
1 teaspoon finely chopped fresh oregano, or ¼ teaspoon dried oregano
2 cloves garlic, minced
Pinch of cayenne
Salt

Mix all the ingredients in a small bowl, adding salt to taste. Cover and refrigerate until ready to use.

> **TIP**
>
> If you're using nonfat yogurt, drain it beforehand to remove the whey and deepen the flavors by following the instructions in "Draining Yogurt," on page 11.

Spicy Rémoulade [V]

No matter how hard we try to get our servers to say otherwise, they always describe rémoulade as "fancy tartar sauce." Considering what normally passes for tartar sauce, that description hardly does it justice. Rémoulade should have some texture, the taste of fresh herbs, and be a little salty, a little tart, and, in my opinion, a little spicy. This will take a bit more time than adding pickle relish to mayonnaise, but it's well worth it. You can vary the herbs—tarragon or dill are good choices—but always keep the parsley.

Makes 1½ cups

1 shallot, minced

2 cloves garlic, minced

6 cornichons (French sour gherkins), minced, or 2 tablespoons minced dill pickle

1 tablespoon capers, rinsed and roughly chopped

¼ cup minced fresh parsley

1 teaspoon minced fresh thyme, or ½ teaspoon dried

1 cup Cafe Flora Vegan Mayonnaise (see next recipe), or purchased vegan mayonnaise

¼ teaspoon cayenne pepper

1 or 2 drops of Tabasco sauce

Salt and freshly ground pepper

Combine all the ingredients but the salt and pepper in a bowl, and mix until thoroughly blended. Add salt and pepper to taste.

TIP

If you use store-bought mayonnaise, vegan or otherwise, follow the recipe here, and add one tablespoon lemon juice and one teaspoon Dijon mustard. (Our vegan mayonnaise recipe is heavy on the Dijon and lemon.)

Cafe Flora Vegan Mayonnaise [V]

We make our own version of eggless mayonnaise using silken tofu, which has a custardlike texture that creates a creamy sauce when blended.

Makes 2 cups

1 (12-ounce) block silken tofu

2 tablespoons freshly squeezed lemon juice

2 teaspoons salt

3 tablespoons Dijon mustard

½ cup canola oil

Combine all the ingredients except the oil in a food processor or blender. Turn the machine on and process until well blended. With the machine running, drizzle in the canola oil slowly until it is fully combined.

Green Peppercorn Aïoli

We spread this rich, tangy sauce on our Artichoke Poorboy (see page 167), but it would be fantastic slathered on our French Dip Sandwich (see page 170) or as a dip for cooked vegetables, especially new potatoes.

Makes about ¾ cup

2 teaspoons olive oil

2 tablespoons green peppercorns, packed in brine or water, drained and crushed

2 tablespoons minced shallot (about 1 large)

1 clove garlic, minced

½ cup white wine

½ cup mayonnaise

½ teaspoon Dijon mustard

Salt

SAUTÉ THE PEPPERCORNS, SHALLOTS, AND GARLIC. In a sauté pan, heat the olive oil over medium heat.

Add the peppercorns, shallot, and garlic, and sauté until the shallot is translucent, about 10 minutes. Add the wine, and cook until most of the wine has evaporated, but the mixture is still wet.

MIX IN THE MAYONNAISE AND MUSTARD. Remove from the heat, and chill completely before mixing in the mayonnaise and mustard. Add salt to taste, and refrigerate until ready to serve.

Tahini Sauce [v]

Tahini has this weird quality of seizing up when it's blended with liquids. Also, this sauce may stiffen when refrigerated, so you may need to whisk in a little water before you use it. For a quick snack, spread this on grilled or oven-toasted pita bread, or serve it as a dip with fresh veggies.

Makes about 1 cup

½ cup tahini
1 teaspoon tamari (see page 000)
½ teaspoon sesame oil
¼ cup freshly squeezed lemon juice
2 teaspoons minced garlic
1 teaspoon rice vinegar
½ cup water

Combine all the ingredients in a blender, and blend until smooth. If it's too thick, just dribble in more water until you get the consistency you want.

Arugula Walnut Pesto [v]

It's particularly important to use young arugula in this pesto so the result isn't bitter. Look for a bunch with small leaves and skinny stems, or pick smaller leaves from a bunch of more mature arugula. This will keep up to one week in your refrigerator.

Makes about 1 cup

2 cups baby arugula leaves, stemmed and tightly packed
2 cloves garlic
½ cup canola oil
¼ cup chopped walnuts, toasted (see page 000)
Salt and freshly ground pepper

BLEND THE ARUGULA, GARLIC, AND OIL. Put the arugula in a food processor or blender with the garlic and oil. Pulse several times to get the mixture moving, and then blend until it's smooth. Turn the machine off, and scrape down the sides of the container.

ADD THE WALNUTS and process just until they're well combined, about 10 seconds. (Nuts get gummy when processed too long, and you want a little nutty texture.) Season with salt and pepper to taste.

Chervil Pesto [v]

Chervil, a member of the parsley family, is not an easy herb to find, but don't substitute dried chervil in this recipe. Your best bet is to look for it at a summertime farmer's market or, better yet, grow it in your own garden. You'll be glad you did because its elusive anise flavor makes a delicate pesto.

It would be a delicious substitute for Tarragon Parsley Pesto (below) on the Stone Fruit Pizza with Brie and Toasted Almonds (page 158). Or drizzle it on steamed vegetables, toss it with pasta, or mix some with a softened log of goat cheese as a spread for rustic bread or crackers.

Makes about ¾ cup

2 cups fresh chervil sprigs, lightly packed and roughly chopped
½ cup canola oil
Salt and freshly ground pepper

Put the chervil in a blender or food processor. Turn the machine on, and with the motor running, add the oil, and process until smooth, about 1 minute. Turn off the motor, scrape down the sides of the container, and process for 30 more seconds. Add salt and pepper to taste.

Tarragon Parsley Pesto [v]

This tasty pesto is good for more than pizza. Toss it with steamed vegetables or a pasta salad. And as always with pesto, make this only when you can get fresh tarragon. It will keep a week in the fridge.

Makes about ¾ cup

½ cup packed fresh tarragon leaves
1 cup packed fresh parsley sprigs, roughly chopped
2 cloves garlic, minced
⅓ cup olive oil
1 tablespoon freshly squeezed lemon juice
Salt and freshly ground pepper

Put the tarragon, parsley, and garlic in a blender or food processor. Turn the machine on, and with the motor running, add the oil, and process until smooth, about 1 minute. Turn off the motor, scrape down the sides of the container, and process for 30 more seconds. Add the lemon juice, and season to taste with salt and pepper.

Basil Pesto [v]

Our basil pesto is smooth so it's easy to spread on pizza dough. This is a pistou—a French version of the Italian pesto—made without cheese or nuts. When basil is in season, we make huge batches of this every couple of weeks and freeze a lot of it. If you happen to find some cheap basil in season, or you have a bountiful harvest in your garden, preserve its flavor as we do for use year-round by freezing this pesto.

Makes 1 cup

2 cups packed basil leaves
2 cloves garlic, chopped
1 pinch red pepper flakes
½ cup olive oil
Salt and freshly ground pepper

Put the basil, garlic, and red pepper flakes in a blender or food processor. Turn the machine on, and, with the motor running, add the olive oil, and process until smooth, about 1 minute. Turn off the motor, scrape down the sides of the container, and process for 30 more seconds. Add salt and pepper to taste.

ia Roasted Garlic

...e we can make for this rich and
...besides its fabulous taste, is we
...use it in dishes that are otherwise low in fat.
If you have some left over, use it as a sauce over
ravioli filled with something green but not
cheesy, or spread it on Crostini (see page 224) or
toast for a quick snack.

Makes about 1½ cups

1 large head garlic
½ cup olive oil, plus 1 tablespoon
1 cup macadamia nuts, preferably unsalted (see
Tip), toasted (page 150)
Salt

GET READY. Preheat the oven to 350 degrees.

ROAST THE GARLIC. Break up the bulb of garlic into
cloves, leaving the papery skin on each clove. Toss
the cloves with 1 tablespoon of oil to coat, and put
in a small baking dish covered with foil. Roast in
the oven until the cloves are soft, about 30 minutes.
Set aside to cool.

PURÉE THE GARLIC AND MACADAMIAS. When the
roasted cloves are cool enough to handle, squeeze
the soft garlic out of the paper skin into the bowl of
a food processor. Add the cooled macadamia nuts,
and give the mixture six or seven 1-second pulses
until it is wet and crumbly.

ADD THE OLIVE OIL. Scrape down the sides of the
bowl. Then, with the motor running, add the ½ cup
olive oil until it's completely incorporated. Add salt
to taste.

> **TIP**
>
> Unsalted macadamia nuts can be hard to find,
> although you may find them in the bulk-food
> section of your grocery or health-food store. If all
> you can find are the little jars of Mauna Loa salted
> macadamias, go ahead and use them. One 3.25-
> ounce jar is a bit less than a cup. Just make sure to
> taste the spread before you add any salt.

Fig Balsamic Reduction [v]

To make this intense syrup, you cook balsamic
vinegar just below a simmer with dried figs and
then purée it. The result gives a sweet and tart
flourish to a rich dish and makes a stunning plate
presentation.

Be very careful with the heat when reducing this
sauce; the heat must stay just below a simmer.
And allow plenty of time. If you rush it and the
heat gets too high, you will be left with bitter tar
and a tough pot-scrubbing job on your hands. (I
know, because we have ruined this many times
at Cafe Flora!)

Because we only use Fig Balsamic to finish a dish,
there will be leftovers. Good thing, because
there's lots you can do with it. Put it on a winter
squash before you roast it. For canapés, spread a
little goat cheese on a cracker or crostini, and
dribble Fig Balsamic over it.

You can keep Fig Balsamic in your refrigerator for
several weeks. To restore it to an easy-to-pour
state, warm the container in hot water or in the
microwave. For easier drizzling, store it in a plastic
squeeze bottle as we do at the restaurant, and cut
the tip a bit to accommodate the thick syrup.

Makes about 1 cup

2 cups balsamic vinegar

2 bay leaves

8 to 10 small, plump, dried figs, sliced in half, stems removed

COOK THE FIGS AND VINEGAR. Put everything in a small, heavy-bottomed saucepan over medium heat. Just before it reaches a simmer, lower the heat. With the pot uncovered, maintain the heat just below a simmer, adjusting the flame as necessary. (You may also need a heat diffuser.) Reduce the vinegar slowly until it's half its original volume and the figs are very soft, about 1 one hour. Remove the bay leaves and cool slightly.

PURÉE THE BALSAMIC. Put the cooled mixture in a blender, and purée until smooth. Strain the mixture if you want, although the tiny fig seeds are not unpleasant.

Sweet Chili Dipping Sauce [v]

This sauce is a vegetarian variation on *nuac cham*, a Vietnamese dipping sauce that typically includes fish sauce. We serve this as a dip with our lettuce-wrapped Coconut Tofu starter (see page 21). But this spicy and sweet sauce would be great with fresh spring rolls as well. This will keep two weeks in your refrigerator.

Makes 2 cups

1½ teaspoons red pepper flakes

½ cup sugar

½ cup rice vinegar

2 cups water

Combine all the ingredients in a small pan. Bring to a boil, lower the heat, and simmer for 10 minutes. Remove from the heat, and cool completely.

INGREDIENTS AND SOURCES

LISTED BELOW YOU'LL FIND THE more unusual ingredients we use more than once in this book, along with some well-researched mail-order sources for them. If a particular rare ingredient occurs only once in our recipes, you'll find this sort of information in the recipe where it's used.

Ingredients

Ancho chile See **Chiles**.

Arame is a black, dried seaweed that we've borrowed from Japanese cuisine. It looks like coarse black threads until reconstituted in water, when these threads plump up and elongate. At Cafe Flora we take advantage of arame's mild, sweet flavor to add a whiff of the sea to certain dishes. Look for it, cellophane wrapped, near other seaweed, such as nori or konbu, or next to sushi-making supplies.

Basmati rice is a long-grained, aged rice with a delicious nutty fragrance and flavor. Cultivated in the Himalayan foothills for millennia, it is typically used in Indian dishes. It cooks up dry and fluffy.

Beluga (or black) lentils See **Lentils**.

Brown mustard seeds (the seeds of mustard greens) are widely used as a seasoning in Indian food. (Another variety, black mustard seed, is difficult to grow commercially, so it's been supplanted by the brown variety.) Brown mustard seeds are highly aromatic and pungent, and when they're cooked in oil first until they pop, they add a nutty flavor to any dish.

Brown rice syrup is a honey-colored sweetener about half as sweet at sugar. We use it as a substitute for sugar or honey in vegan dishes. (Vegans won't eat honey because it's made by bees and often steer clear of sugar because some is refined using the bones of animals in one part of the process.) Look for brown rice syrup at natural-food stores near the baking ingredients and other sweeteners.

Chanterelles are a variety of wild mushroom with a trumpet-shaped cap and a pale orange or golden color from the forests of the United States and Canada, usually available in the late summer or fall. They have a mild, slightly fruity flavor reminiscent of apricot. Keep an eye out when they're in season, in specialty grocers and farmer's markets, because they go fast. Look for chanterelles that are clean and mostly dry; you can remove bits of moss and pine needles with a soft brush or towel before cooking.

Chiles You generally won't find ground dried chiles, so we toast chiles and grind them in a coffee grinder (see page 102). Look for any of these chiles at larger grocery stores and Mexican or Latino markets.

- **Ancho chile** is the dried form of the poblano chile and, like its fresh version, is mild to medium-hot with a full chile flavor that is sweet and fruity. Wrinkled and deep red to black in color, it's three to four inches long and two to three inches wide.

- **Chipotle chile** is a dried, smoked jalapeño, wrinkled and dark brown. We like it for its smoky fragrance and intense heat. If you can't find the dried version, you'll often find chipotle chiles canned and packed in adobo, a thick red sauce infused with their smoky flavor. (This sauce makes a great seasoning on its own.) Store any canned leftovers in a tightly covered container and refrigerate; they'll keep several weeks. Or freeze one or two chiles with some sauce in baggies to add to recipes as needed.

- **Poblano chile** is a fresh chile with dark green skin and a tapered, triangular shape about 4 to 6 inches long and 1½ to 2 inches wide. It has a complex peppery flavor, but it's not very hot, ranging from mild to slightly spicy. Peak season is summer to early fall, but you can often find poblano chiles year-round with jalapeños and other fresh chilies.

Chipotle chile See **Chiles.**

Egg Replacer is the brand name of a dried egg substitute that we use in place of eggs as a binder and in baking for vegan dishes. It's made of vegetable starches, gums, and leaveners and is produced by Ener-G Foods based in Seattle. You'll find it in the baking section of most natural-food stores, or you can buy it through the company's Web site: www.ener-g.com.

Fenugreek is a small, yellow, irregularly shaped seed with an unusual flavor and aroma, like a combination of celery and maple. Used extensively in Indian cooking, it's an ingredient in most curry powders. In its raw state, fenugreek has a bitter taste, so we toast it before we cook with it. In small amounts, fenugreek adds an intriguing flavor to bland vegetable dishes.

French green (or Le Puy) lentils See **Lentils.**

Lentils

- **Beluga (or black) lentils** are round lentils that look like BBs, and their name derives from their resemblance to Beluga caviar. We use them primarily because they add an interesting color to a dish and for their mild, earthy flavor, but you can always substitute French green (Le Puy) lentils in a pinch.

- **French green (or Le Puy) lentils** are dark gray-green with a peppery, earthy flavor and nutty texture when cooked. We like to use them when we want a lentil that will hold its shape and stay firm when cooked, for example, in a salad.

Millet is a round, yellow grain that has been cultivated for centuries, and it's a high-protein staple in much of Asia and Africa. Its neutral flavor absorbs and blends well with other flavors, and we cook it as we do rice, by boiling it in water.

Mirin (rice wine) is a sweet, golden wine made from glutinous rice. A staple of Japanese cooking, mirin adds subtle sweetness to Asian-influenced dishes. Look for it near the soy sauce and rice vinegar.

Miso (fermented bean paste) is a rich, salty condiment we've borrowed from Japanese cuisine and use widely in our dishes. There are many different types of miso (including versions with reduced salt), but we use two: white (*shiro* in Japanese, although it is actually pale yellow or light tan) or light miso, and red (*aka* in Japanese) or dark miso.

We use the light miso with its pale color and mellow aroma in dressings, dips, and milder dishes. We use the deeper flavor of dark miso for sauces, marinades, and soups, and where it won't overpower the other flavors in a dish. You'll most likely find miso packaged in plastic tubs or pouches in the refrigerator section of large grocery stores; if you're searching in an Asian market, look for it near the fresh tofu.

Panko are pale, flaky, Japanese-style bread crumbs sold in bags. We coat food to be fried in panko for the resulting light golden brown color and exceptionally crunchy crust.

Pickled ginger is familiar to most of us as an accompaniment to sushi. Ginger has been thinly sliced or shredded and then preserved in sweet vinegar; red or pink pickled ginger gets its color from red shiso. Look for jars in the refrigerated section of Asian markets along with other pickles.

Pimenton See **Smoked paprika.**

Poblano chile See **Chiles.**

Quinoa is a light-colored grain that was a staple in the diet of the ancient Incas. It has a higher protein content than any grain and is a complete protein, too, containing all eight essential amino acids. It's quick cooking with a light texture similar to couscous. Look for it where rice and other grains are sold.

Rice flour is the fine powder made from white rice that we use in place of wheat flour to make dishes gluten free.

Seitan is a light brown, protein-rich food made from wheat gluten (the protein of flour). It has a chewy, meatlike texture and a mild wheat flavor. It tends to soak up the flavors of whatever it is cooked with, so we usually marinate or flavor it before we cook it. It's simple to make, but time consuming, involving a long process of boiling and kneading the gluten. That's a good enough reason to buy it ready made.

You'll find it in the refrigerator section at grocers that carry vegetarian meat substitutes. Most commercial brands come in a variety of flavors and in packages of chunks or strips.

Shiitake is a dark brown cultivated mushroom with a large, spongy cap. Popular in Asian cooking, it has a silken texture and meaty flavor when cooked. Look for fresh shiitake with plump caps that are not broken or shriveled. (We never substitute dried shiitake for fresh.) We use only the cap in our dishes because the stems are tough, but save the stems to flavor soup stocks and broths—for example, in our Mushroom Essence on page 172.

Smoked paprika (also known as Pimenton de la Vera) holds a treasured space on the Cafe Flora spice rack. We add it to a variety of vegetable dishes for its rich, deep character and the roasted quality it gives to foods without the overpowering heat of chiles. Pimenton is a staple of Spanish cuisine and is an important ingredient in paella. It's made by slowly drying and smoking peppers over an oak hearth and then grinding them between stones to a silky powder. We use sweet (*dolce*) pimenton for most of our dishes, but you may also find bittersweet and hot varieties.

Seek this spice out. It will soon become a staple in your kitchen, too. Look for small square tins of Pimenton de la Vera at specialty-food stores, or order it at www.spanishtable.com.

Star anise is an 8- to 12-pointed star-shaped dark brown spice native to China. (It's an ingredient in Chinese five-spice powder.) It has a strong, sweet licorice flavor, more bitter than anise seed.

Sweet soy sauce (also called kecap manis) is made from palm sugar, soybeans, and wheat. It's a dark brown, thick syrup from Indonesia with a deep soy sauce flavor that is both salty and sweet. This makes it a great barbecue or satay sauce for grilled foods. At Cafe Flora, we use it as a condiment, for dipping, and for a dramatic and delicious flourish drizzled on dishes.

Tamari looks just like soy sauce, but it's thicker with a mellow, less salty flavor. It's made with a higher percentage of soybeans than soy sauce (which is often made with up to 60% wheat). Note that most tamari, unless labeled wheat free, also contains wheat. (At Cafe Flora we always use wheat-free tamari so even those who can't eat wheat can eat our dishes.) At the store, look for tamari and wheat-free tamari next to the soy sauce.

Tamarind concentrate or pulp is a popular flavoring in cuisines around the world including India, the Middle East, Asia, and Central America. Tamarind comes in many forms, the most convenient being concentrate or pulp. When dried, tamarind becomes very sour and is used as Western cuisine uses lemon juice. Look for plastic containers of tamarind concentrate (sometimes labeled sour soup base concentrate) at Asian grocers.

Yams If you are buying a yam in the United States., no matter the shape, size, or color, you are really buying a sweet potato. A true yam is native to tropical regions, can grow quite large, and is rarely sold in the United States and Canada. The confusion seems to stem from an effort several decades ago to differentiate newly introduced varieties of orange-fleshed sweet potatoes from the more common white- or yellow-fleshed varieties.

However, in case your produce guy knows the difference and calls sweet potatoes by their real name, look for large, roundish, red- or tan-skinned potatoes with orange flesh, such as the Garnet or Jewel "yam." "Yams" are usually available year-round.

﹏ SOURCES

Most of the foods in this section are available at larger grocery stores, natural-food stores such as Trader Joe's and Whole Foods Market, and food co-ops. You'll also find many of them in specialty-food stores that sell foods from certain countries or areas of the world such as Mexico, India, Asia, or Latin America. For spices and grains, look in the bulk-food sections of natural-food stores and grocery stores.

However, if you can't find these goods locally, here are some reliable mail-order suppliers.

Just About Any Food You Can Think Of

﹏ **Amazon.com** has a huge gourmet food department. It seems to list tens of thousands of items including most of the specialty and ethnic foods that we call for in our recipes, even fresh ingredients such as lemongrass, shiso, kaffir lime leaves, or chervil. In many cases, the suppliers have their own Web sites where you can find even more products.

How to go to Amazon.com Gourmet Food:

1. Go to www.amazon.com.

2. In the **Search** box at the left of the screen, click the tiny down arrow and click **Gourmet Food**. (You may have to hunt for it!)

3. Click **Go**.

4. In the **Search** box at the top of the Gourmet Food page, type the food you're looking for, and click **Go** again.

Fruits and Vegetables
Melissa's/World Variety Produce, Inc.

Melissa's in Los Angeles is a supplier of specialty fruits and vegetables. Asian pears, blood oranges, kumquats, and fresh chiles in season are among the hundreds of fruits and vegetables it sells.

www.melissas.com
800-588-0151

Grains, Beans, Lentils, and Flours
Bob's Red Mill Natural Foods

Order directly from their Web site, or call for a mail-order catalog.

www.bobsredmill.com
800-349-2173

Herbs
Seeds of Change

Some herbs, such as chervil and shiso, are so hard to find, you might just want to grow your own. Seeds of Change sells organic seeds and seedlings for almost every herb imaginable (vegetables and even fruit trees, as well). Request a catalog and order directly from their Web site or call to order.

www.seedsofchange.com
888-762-7333 or 888-762-4280 (toll-free)

Japanese Ingredients
Eden Foods

It is an excellent source for traditional Japanese ingredients such as arame, konbu, mirin, miso, soba, tamari, ume vinegar, umeboshi paste, and wasabi, as well as many other natural and organic, dried, canned, or bottled foods.

www.edenfoods.com
888-441-3336 or 888-424-3336 (both toll free)

Mushrooms
Prima Gourmet

This Portland, Oregon-based company sells fresh, wild mushrooms—chanterelles, hedgehogs, morels, or whatever's in season—as well as fresh shiitake. They also carry dried mushrooms and mushroom-infused oils.

www.primagourmet.com
866-499-8079 (toll free)

Spices
Penzeys Spices

Penzeys has about 20 retail stores primarily in the South and Midwest. Look for the locations at the Web site, but if there's not one nearby, you can always order the company's high-quality spices by phone or on the Web.

www.penzeys.com
800-741-7787 (toll-free)

The Spice House

This is a good mail-order source for spices, dried chiles (both whole and ground), and tamarind concentrate. They have two stores in the Chicago area, as well as the original location in Milwaukee, WI. If you want to visit, go to the Web site for addresses or phone numbers.

www.thespicehouse.com

INDEX

Warm Pear Salad, Orange Vinaigrette & Spiced Walnuts, 60–61
Pecans
    Lentil Pecan Pâté, 32–33
    Mushroom Pecan Pâté, 137–38
    Mushroom Pecan Pâté Sandwich, 172–73
    Pecan Parsley Pesto, 163–64
    Roasted Garlic Pecan Pesto, 154
    Roasted Grape Pizza, 154–155
    Roasted Mushroom Pâté, 148
    Pepitas. *See* pumpkin seeds
Pepper Jack
    Quesadillas with Tomatillo Salsa, 9–10
    Omelet-wrapped Quesadilla Stuffed with Roasted Potatoes and Corn, 198–200
Pepper Jam, Hot, 18
Peppers
    roasting, 212
    smoking, 79
    See also Ancho chiles; Bell peppers; Chipotle chiles; Poblano chiles
Perilla (shiso), 19
Persimmons Curry Spinach Salad, 58
Pestos
    Arugula Walnut Pesto, 232
    Basil Pesto, 233
    Chervil Pesto, 233
    Four-Herb Pesto, 156
    Pecan Parsley Pesto, 163–64
    Pumpkin Seed Pesto, 182
    Roasted Garlic Pecan Pesto, 154
    Sage Walnut Pesto, 150
    Tarragon Parsley Pesto, 233
Phyllo cups, 24
    Chanterelle Mushrooms in, 24–25
    Fig-and-Cabrales-Stuffed, 23–24
Pickapeppa Sauce, 173, 175
Pickled ginger, 76, 239
Pickled Red Cabbage, 77
Pico de Gallo Salsa, 226
Pimenton de la Vera (smoked paprika), 240
Pistachio
    Bulgur Wheat Salad, 169–70
    Curried Grain Salad, 83–84
    Curried Lentil Pâté, 34–35
    Pizza, 141
    Herbed Dough, 144
    using stones and peels, 142–43
    See also *table of contents* under *Pizza*
Platters
    Curried Lentil Pâté Platter, 34–35
    Lebanese Platter, 29–32
    Lentil Pecan Pâté Platter, 32–34
    Provençal Appetizer Platter, 25–27

Southern Brunch Platter, 209–13
Tuscan Appetizer Platter, 27–29
Plum (Roasted) Sandwich with Crispy Fried Onions, 164–65
Poblano chiles, 238
    Omelet-wrapped Quesadilla Stuffed with Roasted Potatoes and Corn, 198–200
    Roasted Tomatillo Sauce, 111
    Roasted Yam Enchiladas with Smoky Tomato Sauce, 111–13
    Yam Corn Chowder, 53
    See also specific chiles
Polenta
    Onion Parsley Polenta, 105
    Spicy Grilled Polenta, 101–103
    Summer Vegetable Soup with Polenta, 50–51
Pomegranate seeds
    Avocado Grapefruit Salad, 63–66
    Red Jewel Salad, 67–68
Poorboy (Artichoke) with Green Peppercorn Aïoli, 167–68
Portobello mushrooms
    Cafe Flora French Dip Sandwich, 170–71
    Portobello Wellingtons with Madeira Sauce, 135–39
    Roasted Portobellos, 138
    Salad of Grilled Portobello Carpaccio with Arugula, 74–75
    smoking, 79
Potatoes
    Dutch Potato Soup, 42
    Indian Chickpea Stew, 94–95
    Janine's Wasabi Potato Salad, 86–87
    Mushroom Madeira Stew, 44–45
    Ocean Chowder, 45
    Oaxaca Tacos, 133–34
    Omelet-Wrapped Quesadilla Stuffed with Roasted Potatoes and Corn, 198–200
    Roasted Potato and Artichoke Pizza with Kalamata Olives, 152
    Roasted Rosemary Potatoes, 213
    Roasted Vegetable Vindaloo, 106–9
    See also Sweet potato
Pressing tofu, 22
Provençal Appetizer Platter, 25–27
Provençal Fennel Sauce, 103
Provençal Tofu Scramble, 204–5
Provolone, Yam and Cheese Sandwich with Pumpkin Seed Pesto, 181–182
Puff Pastry Rolls (Spinach, Mushroom, and Gorgonzola) with Roasted Red Pepper Coulis, 123–24
Pumpkin Enchiladas with Roasted Tomatillo Sauce, 109–11
Pumpkin seeds (pepitas), 10
    Pesto, 182
    Quesadillas with Tomatillo Salsa, 9–10
    Roasted Tomatillo and Pepita Tofu Scramble, 205